PENGUIN BOOKS
BATTING FOR THE EMPIRE

Mario Rodrigues was born in Mumbai. He has been a journalist for the past two decades and writes for a host of publications on subjects as diverse as Goan music, sports, China, the church, and media.

Viceroy's XI vs Roshanara Club, Delhi, February 1932

First row (from left to right): Duleep, Thakursaheb of Limbdi, Ranji, Maharaja of Patiala, Lord and Lady Willingdon, Maharana of Porbander, Nawab of Pataudi Sr., Maharajkumar of Vizianagram (Vizzy)

Second row: Frank Tarrant, second man not known, C.K. Nayudu, Amar Singh, Anthony de Mello, Yuvraj of Patiala, Joginder Singh, Nasir Ali, P. Palia, Himmatsinhji of Jamnagar, last man not known

Last row: Jahangir Khan (*third from right*), J.G. Nawale (*last*), others not known

Batting for the Empire

A Political Biography of Ranjitsinhji

MARIO RODRIGUES

PENGUIN BOOKS

An imprint of Penguin Random House

PENGUIN BOOKS

USA | Canada | UK | Ireland | Australia
New Zealand | India | South Africa | China | Singapore

Penguin Books is part of the Penguin Random House group of companies
whose addresses can be found at global.penguinrandomhouse.com

Published by Penguin Random House India Pvt. Ltd
4th Floor, Capital Tower 1, MG Road,
Gurugram 122 002, Haryana, India

Penguin
Random House
India

First published by Penguin Books India 2003

Copyright © Mario Rodrigues 2003

Photograph copyright © Vasant Raiji 2003

ISBN 9780143029519

Typeset in Bembo by Eleven Arts, New Delhi

Printed at Repro India Limited

www.penguin.co.in

MIX
Paper from
responsible sources
FSC® C047271

For Nityanand Haldipur
Play on, pied piper

Contents

Foreword

THE world of Indian biography is governed by deference, not discrimination. Whether writing about politicians or film stars, scientists or sportsmen, authors tend to be excessively respectful of their subjects. In this context, Mario Rodrigues's book on K.S. Ranjitsinhji is a refreshing departure. 'Ranji' is justly celebrated as perhaps the first great cricketer of Indian origin, a batsman of dazzling originality and skill who made his mark on the playing fields of England. He is known for having invented the leg-glance. In fact, as a despairing Yorkshire bowler is said to have remarked, Ranji 'never made a Christian stroke in his life'. By means orthodox and unorthodox this Indian prince made a notable impact while playing for Cambridge against Oxford, for Sussex in the County Championship and, above all, for England against Australia.

Mario Rodrigues pays due respect to Ranji's cricketing achievements. But the real distinctiveness of the book lies in the careful and overdue attention it pays to his political career. For, besides his life as an English cricketer, Ranji had a second career as an Indian prince. He was the long serving Jam Saheb, or ruler, of the state of Nawanagar. Some early biographers rather uncritically presented him as a model ruler, claiming he was caring of and considerate towards his mostly illiterate subjects.

Rodrigues's work decisively and definitively lays this myth to rest. He documents in chilling detail the Jam Saheb's carelessness with both personal and public funds. More crucially, he documents his consistent and sometimes craven support to the British Empire. Early on, Ranji faced some racist insults in England; but his achievements as a cricketer were to win him recognition as a sort of honorary white. This belated acceptance, suggests Rodrigues, made him so predisposed to support and admire the British. In 1897, Ranji dedicated his *Jubilee Book of Cricket* to Queen Victoria. Later, as a ruler, he willingly became the Raj's poster-boy, what Rodrigues tellingly calls a 'role model of propriety', who set himself up as a counterpoise to popular Indian aspirations. For his years as Jam Saheb coincided with the rise of the Indian national movement. Far from identifying with the call for *swaraj*, Ranji in fact worked actively to suppress and quell the freedom struggle. Within his chiefdom of Nawanagar, he used the instruments of state power to jail or harass Gandhian protestors. Besides, as an influential member of the Chamber of Princes, he sought to make the Maharajas as a whole into a bulwark of imperial rule.

Of course, in this the Jam Saheb was no exception. The five hundred odd Maharajas and Nawabs of princely India saw in popular nationalism a threat to their own uncertainly won privileges. But even in this herd of loyalists, Ranji stood out for his fanatical devotion to the continuation of British rule in the subcontinent. He saw himself, rather fancifully, as personifying the ties of India and Indians to the Raj. The epitaph on this aspect of his career must lie in a remark quoted by Rodrigues. It relates to the visit to India in the winter of 1933–4 of the MCC cricket team led by Douglas Jardine, the side that played the first official Test matches on Indian soil. When the English cricketers came, the Jam Saheb of Nawanagar had but recently passed away. Jardine's men visited the state, where, paying their respects to the deceased ruler's memory, they said how much they missed Ranji, 'that great pillar of the Empire'.

Reading this fascinating book, I could not help but compare Ranji to two other Indians who were near contemporaries of his. The first was Palwankar Baloo, the only man who can seriously challenge him for the title of 'the first great Indian cricketer'. Baloo was born on the wrong side of the tracks, a Dalit whose struggles make Ranji's life seem almost a cakewalk by comparison. Yet he came to achieve huge renown as a spin bowler of extraordinary subtlety and skill and, beyond that, as a role model for his community. He was even an early hero of the greatest of all Dalit leaders, Dr B.R. Ambedkar.

The other figure who bears comparison with Ranji is his fellow Kathiawari, M.K. Gandhi. Rodrigues intriguingly tells us that as students Gandhi and Ranji were in London at the same time though there is no record that the two actually met. But their later careers could not have been more strikingly different. One was a pillar of the British Empire; the other the Mahatma who led his people to freedom from that very Empire. What Gandhi saw as the battle for *swaraj*, Ranji saw as sedition. Even in their personal character they were opposed, the austerity of the one contrasting with the profligacy of the other.

Mario Rodrigues's book is based on years of research, yet the learning is carried lightly. The narrative is based on a wide range of sources. Contemporary newspapers, in English as well as in Indian languages, have been skilfully mined. While the focus stays on Ranji the man and the ruler, the wider political background is deftly sketched. *Batting for the Empire* is, in the first instance, a critical biography of a fascinating and enigmatic figure. But it is also a contribution to cricket history, to the history of princely states (otherwise a sadly neglected area of research), and to the history of Indian nationalism. It satisfies the two tests to which any work of popular history should be subject: it is rich, and it is readable.

Ramachandra Guha

Acknowledgements

THIS book might never have seen the light of day had it not been for a rather fortuitous development at the office. A few years ago we started a mid-weekly sports features section and my colleague, Arunava Das, who was in charge, approached me to rustle up a few articles from Mumbai. The brief was to delve into cricket history. That is how I stumbled upon the enigmatic figure of Ranjitsinhji.

While the imperial writers had left us with their last word on Ranji as a 'pillar of Empire' and a 'loyal friend of England', there was no detailed Indian take on this great historical figure. The quest for an Indian view of Ranji took me all of four years. I immersed myself in innumerable books, newspapers, periodicals and government files and documents at the state and regional archives at Mumbai, Rajkot, Baroda; the National Archives at New Delhi and the Oriental and India Office Collections (British Library) in London. I also used the H.D. Kanga, David Sassoon, British Council and Asiatic libraries in Mumbai and the Nehru Memorial library in New Delhi.

Of all the people who helped give shape and substance to this effort, the contribution of Ramachandra Guha was exceptional. I approached him at the instance of my dear friend P. Sainath and he most willingly agreed to vet the manuscript. I am grateful for his invaluable comments and criticisms. He also graciously consented to write the foreword to this book.

There were other friends and acquaintances who played supporting roles and I'd like to acknowledge their help and encouragement. Leslie Rodricks, a perennial source of information, brought to my notice many little things which otherwise would have escaped my attention. The eminent cricket historian Vasant Raiji always made time for me and put his vast knowledge and collection of cricket literature at my disposal—I'm particularly grateful to him for the cover photograph from *Great Batsmen: Their Methods at a Glance*. Ranjana Kaul took the trouble of sending me photocopied material from her own work on her grandfather, G.R. Abhyankar. I also thank Haresh Pandya, Vinay Nayudu, Simon Alphonso, Mohandas Menon, Anandji Dossa, Marcus Couto, Rajgopal Nidamboor, Arunkumar Bhatt, Hemendra Vyas, Apoorva Bhatt, Jim Mills, Ashwin and Vivek Kotian, Maneck Daver, Hari Vaidya, Ranjit Dalvi, Atul Kamble, Errol D'Silva, Natrajan, Francis Noronha, Hemant Kenkre, Bilal Malik and Raju Mukerji.

Thanks are also due to Dinesh Raja, former editor of the *Phulchaab*, for giving me a copy of the seventy-fifth anniversary issue of the magazine; to Kundan Vyas, editor, *Janmabhoomi*, for permission to look up a few things in the staff library; to Ashok Kharade of the Maharashtra State Archives, Mr Chauhan of the Baroda Archives, Jaya Ravindran and Mr Roy of the National Archives, Parkash Wadhwaney of the Nehru Memorial Library, Mrs Garde of the David Sassoon Library and Tim Thomas of the Oriental and India Office Collections in London. I must also thank Jens Seger Andersen of Play-the-Game for providing the opportunity to visit London by inviting me to Copenhagen for a media conference.

I am grateful to all those whose previous works helped me to piece together Ranji's story. I have listed the works in the bibliography.

V.K. Karthika, Diya Kar Hazra and Devangshu Datta also played a substantial role in putting this book together.

But for the unstinting support of my wife Usha and my son Romario, who stoically put up with my preoccupation for the last few years, the finishing line would not have been reached. I thank them with all my heart.

I A Strange Light out of the East

NOBODY is so soon forgotten as a successful cricketer. Thus spake Ranji in a pensive moment. But he couldn't have been more wrong—his life itself provides a rebuttal of his own aphorism. Indeed, Colonel His Highness Shri Sir Ranjitsinhji Vibhaji, Maharaja Jam Saheb of Nawanagar, GCSI, GBE, KCIE, or Kumar Shri Ranjitsinhji, or simply, 'Ranji' as he was popularly called during his playing career and is universally known even today, will never be forgotten wherever cricket is played.

He stands paramount in the pantheon of Indian sporting gods. The ultimate accolade perhaps, is that the national cricket championship, the Ranji Trophy, was started in his name in 1934. India has produced its fair share of cricketing greats—from C.K. Nayudu to Sunil Gavaskar and from Kapil Dev[1] to Sachin Tendulkar—but in his time, Ranji (1872-1933) was not merely hailed as the 'greatest Indian cricketer' but as the 'greatest Indian of his era'.[2]

Now it is debatable whether Ranji could qualify as the 'greatest Indian of his era'. But he was certainly much more than the 'greatest Indian cricketer' of his time. He was, in fact, considered one of the half-dozen greatest players in the game's history and certainly, until the advent of the one and only Don Bradman, as one of the three greatest. What assures Ranji his place as one of the greatest wielders of the willow ever is that despite having had to ply his trade during the 'golden age of cricket' or the 'golden age of batting', he was able to equal or surpass the feats of the stalwarts of his time such as Dr William Gilbert Grace, Gilbert Jessop et al.

---

[1] *Wisden* voted Kapil Dev the Indian player of the century in 2002.
[2] Even though Ranji never played for India or much in India.

Cricket pundits like E.V. Lucas, Arthur Lilley, A.C.M. Croome, Robert Relf and Robert Thomas rated Ranji, who turned out for Cambridge, Sussex (which he also captained) and England, higher than Grace. An appraisal which the venerable doctor himself confirmed by stating, 'I assure you that you will never see a batsman to beat the Jam Saheb[3] if you live for a hundred years.' Jessop, no less a legend than Grace, acknowledged in a *Daily Mail* obituary that Ranji was 'indisputably the greatest genius who ever stepped on to a cricket field, the most brilliant figure in what, I believe, cricket's most brilliant period.'

Ranji scored runs by the thousands: 72 centuries in first-class cricket, including 14 double hundreds, an aggregate of 24,692 runs in 500 innings remaining 62 times not out at an impressive average of 56.37 scored throughout at the rate of 50 runs an hour, a Test ton on debut, a healthy Test average of 44.96 runs in 26 innings and 15 Tests (all against Australia). He set a chockful of records as well, among which were:

- an unparalleled two centuries in a match *on the same day*
- topping the English batting averages for three seasons in a row
- the first batsman to score 3,000 runs in a season (in 1899), a feat he repeated next year (his aggregates being 3,159 and 3,065 respectively in 1899 and 1900)
- five double centuries in a season when the previous record was three
- the first batsman to score 1,000 runs in a month twice in the same year (1899)
- the first man in the history of Test cricket to score a hundred runs in the same session
- the first batsman to score 11 centuries in a season (1900), the previous record being ten
- from an Indian perspective he was also the first sportsman to have

---

[3]Ranji's title after he became ruler of the princely state of Nawanagar in Kathiawar, Gujarat.

an endorsement contract, being signed up to promote Ranji matches, sandwiches, hair restorers, bats, chairs etc.

All this is heady stuff. But the greatness of Ranji did not lie in the number of runs he scored, monumental though they may have been. Rather, it lay in the way he made them. His class and character was evident even if he was there briefly at the wicket and made only a small score, say of 20, which was enough to send home the discerning spectator satiated at having watched batsmanship of the highest order. Ranji's very nickname—'Run-get-Sinhji' (*Punch's* appellation)— became 'a kind of password in cricket, a synonym for dashing, sparkling and daring batting.' Before Ranji came along, English cricket was choked by the curse of adherence to convention. He turned it into an 'Oriental poem of action' and spiced it up with saucy strokes straight from the East, giving it an international flavour.

THE legend of Ranji perhaps would have never been had it not been for the unusual circumstances associated with his childhood. Born in 1872 to Jiwasinhji, a Jadeja Rajput at Sarodar, a village some forty miles south of the Nawanagar capital of Jamnagar, Ranjitsinhji or 'the lion that conquers in battle' was shortlisted for adoption[4] by the Nawanagar ruler, Jam Vibhaji, at the tender age of six.

Vibhaji had just disinherited his wayward son Kalubha in 1877 and fearful of not siring a legitimate heir in future, had picked out Ranji, a grandson of his cousin Jhalamsinhji, an officer in his army, for adoption. The unexpected birth of Vibhaji's own son in August 1882, to a Muslim wife, Janabai, however, resulted in the script being rewritten and Ranji was knocked out from the succession sweepstakes by the late arrival.

Realizing that Ranji's prospects were bleak if he was allowed to continue living in an environment now turned hostile due to the altered circumstances, Chester Macnaghten, the magnanimous principal

---

[4]His propagandists later spun the tale that he was actually adopted and this was taken as gospel truth and repeated in subsequent literature.

of Rajkumar College, the school for royalty where Ranji was still enrolled, decided to take along the callow fifteen-year-old teenager, who must have been brooding about the 'theft of his future', to England in early 1888 to continue his education at Cambridge.

In a foreign though more congenial ambience, Ranji started limping back to normalcy. The defining incident that probably contributed to the spawning of a cricket genius was Ranji's excursion to the Kennington Oval in May in the same year to see Surrey play the Australians. The majesty of the occasion overawed the teenaged Indian who got his first taste of the magical spell that the game could cast over an English audience. The icing on the cake came during the interval when Macnaghten took Ranji to the pavilion and introduced him to some of the titans of both sides.

He was hooked, enthralled. From that moment cricket was destined to become his calling. Although he was also proficient in lawn tennis and billiards[5], that enchanting outing prompted Ranji, who had learnt the rudiments of the game at Rajkumar College under the tutorship of a Parsee coach, to work furiously at his cricket for the next few years. Many believed that Ranji was a natural born genius but nothing can be further from the truth. It was sheer practice, relentless at that, and over a sustained period of time, that endowed him with perfection. Ranji went to the extent of hiring the best professional bowlers in town to hone his expertise in the nets and even had his right foot pegged to the turf to improve his defensive technique. These hours, days and months of ceaseless endeavour developed his uncanny eyesight, the key to his batting prowess, his timing, coordination, flexibility and the lightning quickness between conception and execution of strokes that few have equalled.

The fruits of this grinding quest for perfection were being harvested soon enough as Ranji began knocking up the runs in local knockabouts for sundry teams all across the meadows, including the popular Parker's

---

[5]Ranji later went on to become a crack shot and an expert angler.

Piece. By 1892 he got into the Trinity College team, having gained admission to the institution three years earlier, but was unable to make the cut for the University side despite having some consistent performances under his belt. The Trinity and Cambridge captain, Sir F.S. Jackson, who had one day chanced upon the boy wonder farming the bowling in a local match, was far from impressed by his unorthodoxy, lack of technical rigour and 'dangerous' approach. But a tour to India with Lord Hawke's team in 1892–93 radically altered his perceptions about native aptitude for cricket. After 'Jacker', later to be appointed captain of England and Governor of Bengal, returned home, he duly gave Ranji his call-up.

Ranji's stint with Cambridge was not overtly auspicious with the bat, but he performed better in the field. A gritty 58 and 37 not out against the formidable Australian tourists gave him his coveted 'Blue'. With a modest average of 25.82, his first first-class season gave little inkling of the magnificent canvas that would unfold later, but Ranji improved those figures slightly to 32.25 the next year. Things however, changed dramatically after he signed on for Sussex in 1895.

In his debut match for Sussex against the MCC at Lord's, Ranji cracked an unbeaten 77 and a rollicking 150, besides taking 6-109 with his off-breaks and holding two catches. MCC, thanks to a fine 103 by the veteran Grace, eventually won the match by 19 runs after setting Sussex a target of 405, but Ranji walked away with the honours for his maiden first-class century, made by 'playing in a fashion which beggars description.' That productive season saw 'the Prince', as he liked to posit himself, announce his arrival on the big stage with an aggregate of 1,775 runs at an average of 49.30 with four centuries, with only Grace and Archie MacLaren forging ahead of him in the averages.

1896 was an extremely bountiful season for Ranji who by now had acquired a fan following and was being touted as one of the most exciting batsmen on the county circuit. He had also done well in side games against the Australians led by Harry Trott and was in the running for a place in the squad for the first Test coming up at Lord's. But

MCC president, Lord Harris, just returned after a posting as Governor of Bombay, left the Indian out on the justification that 'birds of passage' could not qualify for an England cap. The decision was said to be influenced more by political considerations rather than cricketing merit. In those days the right to select the Test team rested with the authorities of the staging association. But such was the outcry against the decision that the wise men of Lancashire, where the second Test was to be staged, doffed their county cap to public sentiment and gave Ranji the nod.

Ranji's dramatic Test debut at Old Trafford, another first for an Indian, is still ranked as one of the most glorious episodes in English cricket. Australia, batting first, ran up a mammoth score of 412. England collapsed for 231 of which Ranji contributed a defiant 62. Forced to follow on 181 runs behind, England were again in trouble at the close of play on the second day, 72 runs still in deficit and four wickets gone, though Ranji, who had come in at one down, was still undefeated on 41. On the third day he decided to seize the centre stage. Ernest Jones's bouncers were snorting up in all directions but Ranji was unperturbed and hooked them with disdain right off his eyebrows—the only one he missed though split his left earlobe. By the time the last England wicket fell for 305 he had tamed the rampaging Aussie attack with a barrage of incisive strokes for an unbeaten 154 in 190 minutes and studded with 23 fours. Incidentally, none of his partners could cross 19. Australia had to make 125 for victory, but they struggled to reach the target, losing seven wickets in the process. England had gone down under but Ranji, who became the first man in the history of Test cricket to score a 100 runs in the first session of play, had stolen the show. The *Manchester Guardian*, putting the feat in perspective, extolled 'our Indian ally' who 'showed us how the Australian bowling should be met'.

> No man now living has ever seen finer batting than Ranjitsinhji showed us in this match . . . when we remember that the young Indian had never seen cricket played until a few years ago, his achievement excites

not only our own strongest admiration but also astonishment. Grace has nothing to teach him as a batsman; and none of the men of renown of thirty years ago could have exhibited a more thorough mastery of every point of the game . . .

Australian cricketer George Giffen, a prodigious all-rounder, who was on the field during that knock, in a recollection for *Wisden Magazine*, was equally rapturous:

Ranji's unbeaten 154 was absolutely the finest innings I ever saw . . . Ranji is the batting wonder of the age. His play was a revelation to us, with his marvellous cutting and his extraordinary hitting to the leg. I have never seen anything to equal it.

Although he failed in the third and final Test at the Oval, just managing 8 and 11 in his two knocks, Ranji's aggregate of 235 topped the combined English and Australian batting averages for the series with 78.33. In the same season he also finished on top of the county batting averages in England with 57.91, having amassed 2,780 runs with ten centuries and having shattered Grace's record of 2,739, set way back in 1871. Of these ten tons, including a highest of 171 not out for Sussex versus Oxford University at Brighton, two (100 and 125) were against eventual champions Yorkshire at Brighton in each innings of the same match, remarkably, both scored on the same day.

In the light of this feat, the legend associated with him that he scored three centuries in a day during his early days will not be so hard to digest, improbable though it might seem. According to the legend, Ranji scored a century, got out and wandered around the University common of Parker's Piece while his side was still batting. He espied a team with a man short, went in and scored another century. When he returned to the original scene of action his first side was batting again and he went in and knocked up his third ton, to complete a good day's work!

In 1997, Ranji penned the cricket classic, *The Jubilee Book of Cricket*, and sailed off to Australia with A.E. Stoddart's team for his first and only tour Down Under where he unveiled another chapter of glorious accomplishments. A 189 in his first match against South Australia at Adelaide, followed by 13 and 64 versus Victoria and a 112 against New South Wales[6] announced his run-getting intentions. Unfortunately, his exertions took a toll on his health and he fell ill on the eve of the first Test at Sydney in December. The run-up to the Test was mired in acrimony as Ranji had expressed doubts about Ernest Jones's bowling action in his column and the hostile local press had retorted that the prince had chickened out from facing the heat by feigning illness.

In fact, Ranji would have been in no position to play, had the Test commenced on schedule, but fate intervened in the form of rain and the Test started on 13 December, three days later than its earlier scheduled date. It was with steely resolve that Ranji literally yanked himself to his feet from his sick bed where he had lain afflicted with a debilitating illness for nearly two weeks[7] and walked to the crease at No. 7. Summoning all his powers of endurance and concentration, he then produced an epic innings of 175 in three hours and 35 minutes replete with some punishing hits to the fence, 25 fours in all. He treated Jones with utter disdain and smashed him all around the park, laying to rest any speculation that he was afraid of him. It was the highest Test innings recorded for England till then and prompted the *South Australia Advertiser* to declare:

> Under any circumstances it would have been a great innings, but as it was, it was sensational . . . After this it will be difficult to assign a limit to his powers.

Ranji came back home a hero after garnering a commendable average of 50.77 for the five-Test series and an even better one of 60.89 for

---

[6]The NSW government waived a tax it used to levy on coloured persons entering the state in order to enable Ranji to play in the territory.

[7]Many of Ranji's great knocks were conceived in similar, incapacitating circumstances when he was impaired by some affliction or the other, especially asthma, which wracked him often during his career.

the entire tour. *Wisden*, which selected Ranji as one of its five 'Cricketer(s) of the Year' in 1897, noted:

> If the word genius can be employed in connection with cricket it surely applies to the young Indian batsman.

When the Australians visited England two years later, Ranji posted an unbeaten 93 against them at Trent Bridge, which he himself rated as one of his best innings, having rescued England from certain defeat after Grace, Fry, Jackson and Gunn were gone for a paltry 19 on board. Requiring 200 for victory, England ended the day with 155 for 7, saving the Test by the skin of their teeth.

As captain of Sussex, Ranji reached the peak of his powers during that summer of 1899, becoming the first batsman to top 3,000 runs in first-class cricket (3,159 runs in all with eight centuries and a top score of 197 versus Surrey at the Oval) thus setting a world record. 1900 was another lucrative year, when Ranji again bested the 3,000 mark (3,065 runs, with a best of 275 versus Leicestershire at Leicester), his average of 87.56 being his best ever.

In 1901, Ranji notched his best individual score with a 285 not out against Somerset at Taunton in five hours and 20 minutes at the crease; 200 of those runs came in boundaries which included 46 fours, 2 fives and a six. C.H.B. Pridham, who witnessed that feat, recollected,

> All day long Ranji did exactly as he pleased with the bowling and never for a moment looked like getting out. Moreover, the ball only touched his pads two or three times during that whole of his innings . . .

What is extraordinary about the effort was that Ranji had promised that he would get a triple century but rain interrupted play for about 30 minutes and he failed to live up to his prediction only because the elements intervened. And to think that he had been out fishing all of the previous night!

Expanding on Pridham's observation about the ball touching Ranji's pads once or twice, it was said that when the master batsman was in full flow, despairing bowlers considered it an achievement just rapping him on the pads. The Surrey trundler, Jephson, was constrained to declare that when he knocked Ranji on his pads he was as pleased as if he had got him out,

> Of all the men I have ever bowled at or seen bowled at, these two (Ranji and Shewsbury) made the fewest mistakes. They so rarely missed a ball they played at.

Ironically, Old Trafford, the venue of his sensational debut, would also be the scene of Ranji's humiliating fade out from Test cricket in 1902. The Aussies were yet again in town and Ranji was again summoned to the battlefront. He made 13 in the first Test, was dismissed for a duck in the only innings of the second Test and missed the third due to injury. He then scraped up single digit scores of 2 and 4 in the fourth Test, being leg before on both occasions to medium-pacer Trumble, and was not selected for the fifth. His poor aggregate of 19 from three Tests in the series—his calamitous form during this period was probably caused by the pressing attention of his creditors ensured that Ranji would never play Test cricket again, though he was only thirty.

However, the Indian was far from finished as a first-class cricketer and he garnered 1,924 runs in 1903 with five centuries, including a 204 against Surrey at the Oval. Next year he crossed the 2,000 mark (2,077) with a string of superlative performances, coasting to the top of the English averages with 74.17. A 207 not out against Lancashire at Brighton was the high point of the season, which *Wisden* hailed with fulsome praise:

> He was at his highest pitch of excellence from the first ball till the last and beyond that the art of batting cannot go.

Such superlatives were in fact quite routinely applied to the dozens of glorious knocks that Ranji conjured up during his glorious career. Most of the reports sounded strikingly similar, one speaking glowingly about the 'most brilliant and delightful pieces of batting ever seen at

Lord's' or another waxing eloquent about his 'magnificent and nearly faultless cricket' etc. Even the redoubtable Jessop went so far as to describe an innings of 146 which Ranji dished out for the MCC as 'just about as perfect a specimen of the art of batsmanship as one could desire.'

The next three seasons saw Ranji playing a different game on another pitch, the political one, in India, while trying to further his claims to the Nawanagar *gaddi*. His mission ultimately ended in success and he ascended the throne in 1907, when Vibhaji's successor, his son Jassaji, inexplicably died at the age of twenty-four. Ranji returned to England as Jam Saheb and resumed his first-class career in 1908, scoring 1,138 runs with an average of 45.52. He came back again in 1912 and compiled 1,113 runs. But by now, cricket had become secondary to his social and political pursuits.

Ranji's last fling was in 1920 at the ripe old age of forty-seven, mainly because King George V had expressed an interest in seeing him play again and partly because he wanted to prove that he could bat with one eye, having lost his right eye during a hunting accident on the Yorkshire moors in 1915, in the midst of World War I. The decision was an unmitigated disaster as, overweight and immobile, he made only 39 runs in three matches and four innings (average 9.75) with a best score of 16, evoking sympathy and ridicule in the process. In what was to be his last match against Northamptonshire at Hastings, he made just one run and in these lowly circumstances bowed out one of the greatest and most inventive batsmen to ever grace the game.

QUITE a career that was, dotted with some stupendous scores and knocks. But that apart, what exactly assures Ranji a place in cricketing history? As mentioned earlier, it was not the runs Ranji scored that made the 'Oriental conjurer' a phenomenon, though he outdid even in terms of figures what any batsman had done before. Ranji became a legend for as much as what he was as for what he did. He made waves, as cricketer-writer E.H.D. Sewell said, because he made 'runs of a quality and in a manner never seen before or since.'

Ranji's greatest contribution to the game is the 'patented stroke of his own invention' that he left behind for all posterity. If B.J.T. Bosanquet, the Oxford, Middlesex and England bowler, can be credited with the perfection of the googly, Ranji will be forever remembered as the inventor of the leg glance, an unintended fallout of his regimen of 'disciplining' his right leg. This audacious stroke, not in vogue till then, frustrated the leading bowlers of the day and amazed bowlers watched in disbelief as good length balls were dispatched, with a twist of the body and a flick of those steely wrists, his right leg rooted to the ground, to the fine leg for four. All they saw was a blur of action and all they heard was the sound of the ball hitting the fine leg fence after it had raced there like a tracer bullet.

The leg glance may have earned Ranji an infinite number of runs but hardly any admirers from among the purists. They said it was 'not cricket' and when he first exhibited this feat of legerdemain at Lord's, elderly critics shook their heads and deplored the entry of the juggler's art into a dignified game.

Ranji was also a master of the cut. His late cut was a potent weapon of destruction and so adept was he at this skill that Donald Knight, a most stylish opening batsman, observed in *Country Life* that he could have gone in with an umbrella (tightly rolled) and obtained a century against the fastest bowlers of England with strokes behind the wicket, steering the ball through the slips or gliding them to leg. In course of time, Ranji reinvented himself from an exponent of the glance and the cut to become a fluent and purposeful driver of the ball on both sides of the wicket to add to his armoury of scoring strokes.

Ranji's greatness can be further attributed to the fact that it was he who scripted the 'modern theory of batting' by making the back stroke an attacking stroke like the forward one, thus enabling every ball to be scored off. 'The idea of batting up to then,' recalled his illustrious nephew Duleepsinhji, 'was that the ball must travel back more or less in the same direction from which it came to the bat. He changed this by helping the ball in the same direction, more or less, by slightly deflecting it. This was the great difference between him and others before him. He used the forward stroke for attack and the back stroke for both attack and defence.'

Ranji's innovative flourishes at the crease also 'oriented afresh the setting of the cricket field,' the eminent historian H.S. Altham opined in *A History of Cricket*. But such was the Oriental's command over his craft that he was able to pick the gaps in the field with stunning regularity and a minimum of effort, nonchalantly setting to naught field placements that were meant to restrict his leg side play behind the wicket.

Not that Ranji did not have his own share of critics during his time. Among Ranji's early detractors was the redoubtable Sir Pelham 'Plum' Warner, who considered the Indian vulnerable on a fiery pitch. But the eminence was forced to recant after Ranji posted an 'absolutely perfect' 121 in a 'Gentleman versus Players' match at Lord's in July 1904. Perhaps Ranji's only apparent frailty was against leg spin. Sewell once observed that the leg break was the only ball against which Ranji had 'the semblance of a weakness'. These stray criticisms apart, Ranji's inventiveness and overall achievements have assured him of an unparalleled status in the history and hierarchy of the game.

To sum up, Ranji was, in essence, a complete all-round cricketer, a batsman par excellence, a change bowler who could send down some useful spells[8] and a brilliant fielder in a time when standards were abysmally low, fielding then being considered an unavoidable drudgery that did not enthuse the well-heeled 'gentlemen' who supposedly played the game for a lark.

His normal place in the field was the slip cordon where he was as quick as lightning, and was reputed, as the legend goes, to have caught a swallow in flight, an anecdote that may be difficult for most to swallow.

---

[8]Ranji took 31 wickets for Sussex at an average of 28.19 with his slow offbreaks, his 6 for 53 in 1901 for London County against Cambridge at Crystal Palace being figures which any mainline bowler would be proud of.

In another celebrated instance he was reputed to have snapped at a chance so quickly with his left hand that the wicket-keeper, thinking that the ball was proceeding to the boundary, admonished him thus: 'Don't just stand there grinning like that; go and fetch it.' Summing up his place in cricket history, biographer Alan Ross emphatically declared that 'only half a dozen in the history of the game have added something new to it and Ranji is one of them'.

Apart from his batting, it was also the 'aura' that surrounded Ranji, partly due to his claimed royal antecedents, that metamorphosed him into a 'living legend' and a 'character of epic proportions' with a 'halo of romance around him.' Just the sight of Ranji walking down the pavilion steps trailing his bat was one of the unique cricketing sights of his times and was enough to send a buzz among the spectators. 'No one has ever walked to the wicket quite as 'Ranji' did', cooed C.H. Pridham in agreement. But it must be mentioned as an aside that the much feted walk, a spectacle of inspiration to the Englishman, was plain comical to the Americans when 'the Prince from Hindoo' took a team to Philadelphia in the summer of 1899. For they described his swinging gait as 'rolling about like a barrel on pins'.

Another aspect that aroused much comment about the 'silken-shirted Hindu' was, yes, the gossamer shirt, always buttoned up to the wrists and the neck. As Leslie 'Spy' Ward observed, 'the shirt, always of silk, always fully large, was his most distinctive feature. It bellied and flapped around his body like a sail at every movement of the breeze'.

Indeed, every time 'the Prince' came out to bat with his trademark white silk shirt fluttering breezily in the wind, the finest writers of his time, Sir Neville Cardus, A.G. Gardiner et al, plunged the depths of their vocabularies for new expressions to convey the wizardry they had seen at the wicket. As 'Cricketer' reported in the *Manchester Guardian*:

> When he batted a strange light was seen for the first time on the English fields, a light out of the East, this visitation of supple dusky legerdemain. Before, the flavour of cricket everywhere was John Bull's. Then, the bowlers stood transfixed, possibly they crossed themselves.

BUT it was not roses all the way for the Indian prince. England's 'native' hero had his fair share of detractors, some going so far to suggest that superlatives were being expended merely because Ranji was a black man. R.H. Lyttelton's condescending observations in his essay on the *Giants of the Game* in 1899 on the Indian phenomenon amply bear this out:

> The English public is a curious one, and one of its peculiarities is a readiness to deify a cricketer all the more because he is not an Englishman and is of a different colour. They would have admired Ranjitsinhji as a white batsman, but they worship him because he is black. Many critics are too apt to admire the latest performer, and some have gone so far as to couple the Indian with Grace as equal in merit. The Indian has yet to show himself to be a really great bat on wickets that favour the bowler.

Racist pride also often got the better of sporting appreciation of a cricket genius and one of Ranji's avowed admirers, Sir Home Gordon, author of *Background of Cricket*, was once abused by an MCC committee member and threatened with expulsion from that august institution for having 'the disgusting degeneracy to praise a dirty black'. This was because Gordon had raved about Ranji's knock against the Aussies at Old Trafford in 1896 even as England slid to a narrow defeat.

This particular incident is perhaps symptomatic of Ranji's travails of a 'colourful' kind and the aversion that he had to put up probably went much beyond the perfunctory query, 'Does the dark fellow speak English?' That was a question asked during the Cassandra Club's tour of Yorkshire in August 1892 when the fielding side, who were told that the Indian knew only a few words of English, reputedly dished out large dollops of colourful comments when he came to the crease. When they realized he could bat (he hit 142 in that encounter), the remarks became spicier. There was considerable embarrassment all around when they heard him conversing in excellent English during the lunch break; or as another version of the anecdote goes, when he made an excellent after-dinner speech!

English writers, who couldn't put a finger to Ranji's art, tended to rationalize it as black magic or un-Christian sorcery. A 'faddling hedonist' the Indian was called, and one appalled witness confessed thus to Charles Burgess Fry, 'yes, he can play but he must have a lot of Satan in him'. Indeed, Ted Wainwright's quotable quote that 'he never made a Christian stroke in his life' aptly mirrored the confused English mindset about the gifted Oriental in their midst. But, all said and done, England sportingly rose almost to a man and adopted the 'dark-skin colonial' as one of her own, albeit in her own convoluted way.

Perhaps no treatise on Ranji's cricketing accomplishments would be complete without bringing Fry into the picture. The Indian prince and the England captain were more than just colleagues at Sussex. They were close buddies, Fry later serving as Ranji's private secretary when he became the Jam Saheb, just as another England skipper, Archie MacLaren, had done earlier. When Ranji and Fry, who was an opening bat, were at the crease, they were the scourge of bowlers, rattling up 25 century partnerships in first-class cricket, including 23 for Sussex and an unbeaten 292 at Taunton in 1901. As Neville Cardus described them, they were 'East and West, twain for hours, the occult and the rational.' Fry himself lauded Ranji as 'an artiste with an artist's eye for the game' who had 'three strokes for every ball'.

One century down the line when Ranji's sterling deeds appear distant and hazy, the cola generation, who have witnessed the exploits of a Viv Richards, Brian Lara or Sachin Tendulkar, may wonder with feigned disinterest what the fuss was all about. Well aware of this eventuality, the perceptive Cardus had posted these immortal lines for posterity:

> Modern lovers of the game, jealous of their own heroes, will no doubt tell us that Ranji, like all other masters, was a creation of our fancy in a world old-fashioned and young. We who saw him will keep silence as the sceptics commit their blasphemy. We have seen what we have seen. We can feel the spell yet. We can go back in our minds to hot days in an England of forgotten peace and plenty, days when Ranji did not

bat as enchant us, bowlers and all, in a way all his own, so that when at last he got out we were as though suddenly awakened from a dream. It was more than a cricketer and more than a game that did it for us.

'No one like him is likely to be born again. It is not in nature that there should be another Ranji,' intoned Cardus. 'He was the midsummer night's dream of cricket'.

INDEED, by all accounts, he was. But cricket comprises only half the story. Ranji's impact on history extended beyond the boundary. He was much more than a mere cricketer—and an all-time great at that.

He was also an imperial symbol and an icon of Empire, a ruler of a princely state in India whose administration, because of his cricket fame, was always in the news, and as is not so well known; not all of it was complimentary. He was a statesman who represented his country at the League of Nations. He was also Chancellor of the Chamber of Princes, a representative body of Native Princes like himself and he waged a heroic, if futile battle to secure princely interests, which were aligned with that of the British Raj even as the battle for *swaraj* (self-rule) intensified on the subcontinent.

The Empire's historians have in gratitude duly glorified the man and his mission. But look at the same person and story from a different perspective and a totally different picture emerges as will unfold in the subsequent pages.

II *Start of the Imperial Innings*

AS mentioned earlier, Ranji's achievements extended far beyond the confines of a boundary. He was also a great symbol of Empire in the days when Cricket and Empire were synonymous. Ranji was often fondly referred to as a 'pillar of Empire', 'great Imperial symbol', 'great pillar of Empire and of Empire's cricket', 'loyal friend of England' etc., a pin-up poster boy of imperialism.

In fact, when the MCC team captained by Bombay-born Douglas Jardine visited India during their historic inaugural tour of 1933–34, soon after Ranji had passed away, they could only conceive of him as an exemplar of imperial cricket. Their itinerary had included an obligatory visit to the 'shrine' at Jamnagar and while there, they told his successor, Jam Saheb Digvijaysinhji, how much they missed Ranji, 'that great pillar of the Empire, and of the Empire's cricket.'

Later, in a review of the tour, an English writer emphasized the late Jam Saheb's description of Test match-playing countries, not as being separate entities but as members of the British Empire Team. 'India, the latest member of that team to receive an Empire Cap, has thousands of players willing and eager to assist their country in its Empire career and to share in their country's well-won honour,' he asserted.

Ranji's ideological affiliations had its genesis primarily in cricket and its hoary connections to imperialism. In course of time, restive natives who appropriated the game, may have used it to undermine imperialism, as in the case of the Trinidadian writer C.L.R. James's masterly critiques. But cricket in the imperial age was the 'bond of Empire', uniting the colonies with the 'Mother Country' when playing forward with a Straight Bat was akin to 'showing the flag' and 'keeping the faith' in the colonies.

England's foremost cricket messiahs like Lord Hawke, Lord Harris and Sir Pelham Warner knew what the game was all about when they donned the white flannels in the colonies. As Hawke thundered in his introduction to *Imperial Cricket*:[1]

> The greatest game in the world is played wherever the Union Jack is unfurled, and it has no small place in cementing the ties that bond together every part of the Empire . . . On the cricket grounds of the Empire is fostered the spirit of never knowing when you are beaten, of playing for your side and not for yourself, and of never giving up a game as lost. This is as invaluable in Imperial matters as cricket . . . the future of cricket and of the Empire . . . is so inseparably connected.

But the great contribution of cricket, which its historian Benny Green described as 'a typically English compromise between a religious manifestation and an instrument of policy', to the imperial scoreboard, was not that it made the Hawkes, the Harrisses and the Warners believe they were unfurling the Union Jack every time they essayed a straight drive or executed a square cut. Cricket's trump card as imperialism's agent was because it astonishingly made the colonized peoples also think likewise, a phenomenon vividly explored by C.L.R. James in *Beyond a Boundary*, reputedly the most remarkable book about sport ever written.

Since cricket (and other team games) was offered as a paternalistic hand-me-down from the imperial overlords to the conquered peoples, it bred in the receivers a sense of gratitude and respect. Along with the technicalities came a set of values that disposed the subjects favourably towards their masters' institutions and interests.

The technicalities, like how to present a dead bat or pitch it right on line, were relevant till the end of the day's play, the values imbibed along the way remained valid till eternity. Some of these values have been deified in shibboleths like 'it's not cricket', 'play the game', 'the umpire is always right', which were applicable not merely on the field

---

[1] Edited by the great cricket ideologue, Sir Pelham 'Plum' Warner.

but on a larger canvas. Thus, eager-beaver natives became 'jolly good fellows', aping their masters in every respect and inheriting the fabled English restraint, which translated politically into the 'etiquette of polite submission'.

Sport, and especially cricket, which personified 'an unimpeachable code of cultural behaviour throughout the British Empire', was imbued with qualities and moral lessons—the phrase 'it's not cricket' paraphrased disapproval of deceptive behaviour in all walks of life—that defined modes of social interaction. The sporting virtues of team work, perseverance and respect for authority were held up as ideals and propagated by colonial administrators to ensure advancement, both spiritual and material, as well as complement the British way of life. In effect, to provide an endorsement of British rule.

In the Indian context, the role of sport and team games like cricket must be viewed in the context of a radical change of imperial tactics to hold on to the Empire after the cataclysmic upheavals of the 'first Indian war of independence' (the 'Indian Mutiny' in British parlance) of 1857. The 'Mutiny' drove home the lesson that mere guns and bayonets would be unable to keep the Empire intact. So the old imperial ideology of 'might is right' was abandoned and a 'new imperialism' walked to the crease bringing along with it concepts like the 'civilising mission' and the 'white man's burden'. Sport, with its emphasis on moral values, was very much part of this civilising mission and an important part of the cultural armoury of imperialism. It was zealously promoted by educationists, missionaries and administrators across the subcontinent.

From games like cricket could be gleaned the virtues of 'sportsmanship', which brought forth the 'new man' or the 'sporting gentleman', a product of another peculiarly British elitist tradition—the public school. While the public schools produced the men who ruled both Britain and the Empire, its playing fields provided the ethos of the ruling class. In an era where team games like cricket and religion, state, society and education were seamlessly interlinked, it was difficult to perceive where one began and the other ended.

AS a product of this system, Ranji imbibed all these qualities that sport was supposed to impart, even though the frail Indian was not the ideal representation of 'muscular Christianity', another phenomenon of imperialism that equated virtue with masculinity and athleticism. He was the perfect English 'sporting gentleman' and was no different ideologically, from his English peers like Hawke and Harris.

In an assessment of him made at the fag end of the nineteenth century when he took a crack amateur team comprising Jessop, MacLaren, Stoddart, Bosanquet, Brann, Priestley, Townsend, Robson, Robertson and others to America, at the invitation of the Associated Clubs of Philadelphia, an American lady journalist aptly commented: 'He is British to the backbone and as loyal a subject to Her Majesty as was ever born.'

'Essentially an English gentleman' in the best British public school sporting tradition, Ranji imbibed all the sporting qualities as well as wholesomely reflected the imperialist attitudes of the day. These qualities enabled him to excel in the other aspects of life as was highlighted by one of his biographers and propagandists, Naoroji Dumasia, in *Jamnagar: A Sketch of its Ruler and its Administration*:

> Some people seem to sneer at the qualification of a sportsman and think that sport is an end in itself. It is nothing of the sort. Sport in India is a great vehicle for cultivating a sound mind in a sound body; it inculcates those qualities of fairness, tolerance and discipline, of joy in seeing the best man win, which all are proud especially to associate with English character. In that sense the Jam Saheb has shown that sportsmanship is a synonym for statesmanship and good training in the atmosphere of English public life and that it connotes fairness, liberality, accessibility and camaraderie, which are still the best attributes of that life.

A number of factors transformed Ranji into an inveterate anglophile and 'pillar of Empire' whose affinity for England was matched by his corresponding antipathy to India's nationalist aspirations and disinterest in her cricketing fortunes as well. It will however be interesting to explore how, why and in what way Ranji became an icon of Empire.

The answer to the first question—how—is primarily because Ranji went to England and became a famous cricketer, thereby assimilating all the imperialist attitudes associated with the game. But it is a moot point whether Ranji took up the glorious game for its own sake or for ulterior purposes. Benny Green thought that cricket for Ranji was merely the means to an end. He claimed that our 'Prince Charming' scaled the game's pinnacle merely to pursue his obsessive political agenda and that 'the great love of his life happened to be Nawanagar and not English cricket'. Observed Green:

> A closer look at the facts of Ranji's career suggests that the prince never attached to cricket the importance which the English assumed he did, and that had he not become embroiled in certain political complications at a stage in his life when he was too callow to understand them, he might have never bothered to come to England at all; might never have taken lessons from Richardson and Lockwood; and might never have become an English hero.

Ranji had arrived in Victorian England when its 'mood was modulating from imperial pride to the stridency of jingoism . . . In a nation obsessed with its own imperial predominance and in the light of the strange ambivalent relationship which existed between England and India, Ranji was a source of fascination at the same time as exemplifying many of the curiosities of the Anglo-Indian balance,' wrote George Plumptre in *The Golden Age of Cricket*. Plumptre, an unabashed admirer of the Edwardian era, continued:

> While he did not find it in the least unusual that an Indian should play for England, neither did the majority of Englishmen. Rather the opposite: they were proud that an Indian prince should do so because it reflected well on British India and all it stood for. Ranji personified the element of the exotic which Englishmen knew was part of their empire but had not been previously found at home, and in that alone he added incalculably to the richness of cricket's flavour.

Again, had Ranji not passed himself off as a prince, with its assumptions of regal status and fabulous wealth tucked in the royal vaults back home, he may not have made the cut with the 'Gentlemen' of the English cricket establishment. Nor would the masses, living in a society that was as stratified as its cricket, have looked upon him with deference had he not come from a higher station in life. The princely prefix certainly contributed to Ranji's aura and his acceptance by high society although these doors were primarily unlocked by his flair at cricket. Ranji also spent compulsively, as befitting a prince, to retain the company he kept.

Writer-activist Reginald Reynolds made a pertinent observation in *White Sahibs in India* that the normal English middle-class girl, who looked down on natives as 'niggers' would forget her racial prejudice when confronted by the 'Public School Raja' and even consider it a privilege to be seen dancing with him. Is it any wonder that England literally danced to the prince's tune even though Ranji encountered his fair share of racist taunts both on and off the pitch?

And lastly, would Ranji ever have become an English folk hero, if, instead of being in sync with the imperialist sentiments of his time, he had struck a partnership with Dadabhai Naoroji, the 'father of Indian nationalism', who assiduously courted the cricketer to jointly take up cudgels against British misrule in India?

Apart from his cricketing feats, Ranji's sweeping social success was also partly due to the fact that he spotted the contradictions in British society and positioned himself in such a way as to reap the fullest benefits. It was a disadvantage to be a 'black man' but it was a novelty being a 'black prince'. It was a disability to belong to a subject race but being seen as a loyal subject had its own advantages. In his own enigmatic way Ranji was also undermining imperialism in the form of a native gatecrashing into the elitist, conservative and rarefied upper echelons of British society by virtue of his command over the game of Empire. But once he squeezed into the charmed circle he had to conform to the imperial code.

Ranji grasped the political equations from the very beginning and took full advantage of it to build up a political constituency and launch his assault on the Nawanagar *gaddi* and also to avoid prosecution for his financial misdemeanours, which were kept under wraps. Shockingly, the British governments of the day preferred to wink at his malfeasance in such matters even when the aggrieved persons were their own citizens.

Why did Ranji become a defender of Empire? His cricketing status established in England, Ranji's political choices were then more or less predetermined. He was already indoctrinated in the imperial mode by constantly rubbing shoulders with the likes of Hawke, Harris, Jackson and Warner.

His total assimilation into the English way of life from his impressionable teenage years, his selection for Cambridge and England, which he considered priceless honours, the adulation which the English people showered upon him for his exploits, would have been hard to forget and harder to betray.

Further, there was the need to be continually in the good books of Britain to mount his assault on the Nawanagar *gaddi*, followed by his gratitude to His Majesty's Government for allowing him to ascend the throne. And finally, the realization that the continued existence of princely privilege required the perpetuation of the British Raj and the thwarting of the nationalist advance, steeled Ranji's resolve and made him a dedicated imperialist for the rest of his life.

THE myriad ways in which Ranji personified the imperial ideal has been a subject of much consideration both during his life and after his death. Researchers Ric Sissons and Brian Stoddart (*Cricket and Empire: The 1932-33 Bodyline Tour of Australia*) singled out the Indian cricket ace as one of the lodestars of imperial politics while dissecting the issues behind the game's most searing controversy, *Bodyline*, that erupted in the early 1930s.

Spelling out his imperial attributes, the scholarly duo noted that one of the most important imperial virtues that Ranji embodied was 'cricket as a training for life', which the cricketer had himself outlined in the concluding chapter 'Cricket and the Victorian Era' of his seminal work, *The Jubilee Book of Cricket*, published on the occasion of the diamond jubilee of Queen Victoria's reign in August 1897. The monumental book, written in the winter of 1896–97, when he was confined to his bed with lung congestion for ten weeks, was an early example of Ranji emphatically making his political choices. Although it was 'a didactic work' concerned mainly with the technical aspects of the game, the prescient Ranji paid his political dues by dedicating it to Her Majesty The Great Queen-Empress and titling it appropriately in commemoration of her diamond jubilee. 'Cricket, after all,' said Ranji in 'Charm of Cricket', 'is a gem fair in itself, apart from the beauty of its setting—a gem quite worthy of a niche in Queen Victoria's crown.' He even found a connection between Cricket and the Queen:

> In this year of grace 1897 all the British Empire is joining together to congratulate her Gracious Majesty Queen Victoria upon the unparalleled duration of her reign. There is no part or condition of her loyal subjects' lives which may not be fairly be called upon to prove its right to be regarded as one of the blessings Her Majesty may associate with her happy occupation of the throne of England . . . The rise and development of athleticism until it has become a most important aspect of British life, has been one of the marked characteristics of the Victorian era . . . The names of HH Prince Albert of Schleswig-Holstein and HH Prince Christian Victor of Schleswig-Holstein are well known in the cricket field. The latter nearly secured his blue at Oxford. So it cannot be said that the Queen has no connection with cricket.

Even Ranji's official biographer, Roland Wild, had in fact earlier claimed that his subject was a fine exemplification of the truism 'cricket as a training for life'. It was Principal Chester Macnaghten who had believed that cricket was the finest education that a boy could have, and his experiment with cricket as a method of building character in Rajkumar College reached fruition in Ranji's eventual success both on and off the field, stated Wild. Remarked Sissons and Stoddart as they elaborated on this aspect:

> Most English people had never seen an Indian, and had been led to believe that their colonial subjects were weak, effete, and incapable of achievement. Yet when they flocked to the grounds, they saw one who could sustain long innings in the face of hostile bowling attacks, then go into the field to take marvellous catches. Given cricket's role as a training for life, there was little doubt about Ranji's ability to succeed there as well . . .
>
> Ranji was effectively India on trial and he demonstrated to the British public that Indians were capable of absorbing the qualities their imperial overseers thought appropriate. Moreover, it revealed the beneficial effects of cricket as an agent of imperialism's civilising mission . . . This was a powerful metaphor, cricket as imperial life and power, which Ranji would have well understood.

As an extension of this virtue, cricket not only prepared men for life, it also primed them for battle. There are a number of stirring passages in English literature about the connection between militarism and team sports. Ranji himself realized the importance of physical training provided by cricket since it prepared men for military service (a line endorsed by several other imperial writers of the day), should it be necessary, and in a pleasurable way, unlike squad drill. Because of that enjoyment, cricket encouraged men into voluntarily realizing their capabilities more easily than those trained under duress.

'Cricket had a strong tradition in the imperial military forces' and 'Ranji was just one of many to see military value in the preparation given to young men by the game,' Sissons and Stoddart remarked. The game proved its military mettle during World War I when many young cricketers, who were conscripted, willingly 'sacrificed their wickets' for the 'side'.

Another imperial quality that Ranji had grasped about cricket was its innate capacity to exercise self-control on both players and spectators as it provided the ventilator for expending emotion at the personal level and yet keeping things in check at the broader level. This, he brought home in the observation of his German friend who waxed eloquent about the game which managed 'to keep 25,000 spectators in order without external direction or suppression'.

Much was made of this tradition of 'self-discipline' at county grounds staging the 1999 World Cup Cricket matches in England where stringent security measures were not enforced despite exuberant fans, mainly of Indian sub-continental origin, invading the field once too often. The same self-discipline incidentally does not hold good for English football, or for that matter international cricket in India, where excessive security to control volatile crowds is the rule rather than the exception.

Sissons and Stoddart also said that Ranji made some valid points in the context of understanding Bodyline by arguing that cricket was synonymous with the English experience and when people played the game, be it on the rough jungle of veldt grass or the mine tailings in the outskirts of Johannesburg, 'the feel of a bat and its sound against the ball' brought back 'memories of the green turf and cool breezes of England'. Cricket therefore made colonizers and natives alike think of the 'Mother Country', since to play or watch cricket was to think (highly) of England, to behave as Englishmen and whatever else it entailed.

This assertion may sound a bit far-fetched in today's context when the flavour of cricket in the former colonies like India, Pakistan and Sri Lanka is essentially colloquial. But in the colonial era when 'native' cricket had no history of its own, the imagery of cricket could only have been English.

The proof of the pudding was provided, inadvertently, some years ago by none other than the late Australian icon, Don Bradman, the target of the English bowlers in the Bodyline series, which sent political ties between Australia and England hurtling. Bradman, despite the bitter experiences of Bodyline, revealed the depths of his attachment to the 'Mother Country' by giving a thumbs up to maintaining royalist links with Britain during the referendum on republicanism in Australia a few years ago.

Ranji had also grasped cricket's ability to unite the feuding factions of British society and noted that the game made it possible for QCs, artists, archdeacons and leader writers to rub shoulders together in the pavilion, bereft of social distinctions. 'Anything that puts many very different kinds of people on common ground must promote sympathy and kind feelings,' he perceived. The reality in England then was different though and a yawning gap divided the 'Gentleman' and the 'Players' in cricket, for instance, a gap which Ranji himself had tried to bridge.

If these then were the many imperial lessons that were to be learnt through the vehicle of cricket and sport, upwardly mobile natives were quick to seize upon it to cozy up to the colonial establishment. Cricketer, impresario, writer and imperial ideologue, J.M. Framjee Patel, who captained the Parsees against G.F. Vernon's tourists, the first English team ever to tour India in 1889-90, was acutely aware that excellence in sport could earn natives the admiration of the English— a fact borne out by Ranji's own experience in England. Observed the Parsee author in his epochal book *Stray Thoughts on Indian Cricket*:

> But there is something magical about sport, which makes the Englishman forget his racial and habitual reserve. What is more, on the cricket field, he drops all social distinctions for the time, and begins to like any man—be he an African or an Indian—who plays pluckily and well the national game he loves so dearly and devotedly. Thus, slowly, a sporting friendship grows up between them which lasts long, as one knows well from personal experience.

Implicit in this statement was the acceptance of the higher status of the ruling race as well as the fact that natives could use sporting excellence to clamber up to a level of equality. Not surprisingly, Framjee Patel saw in Kumar Shri (young prince) Ranjitsinhji the perfect embodiment of success under the imperial umbrella through the vehicle of sport who consequently bridged the gap between Britons and their Indian subjects by his splendid talents.

Surely he often makes us feel our common kinship! Men like he are likely to fertilize the Imperialistic idea—to most British subjects, who long to share in the glories, privileges and the burdens of a world-wide Empire.

A similar sentiment was expressed on the other side of the fence when a budding Ranji came up with superlative knocks of 58 and 37 not out for Cambridge against the touring Australians in June 1893. The *Cambridge Review*, apart from praising the batting of 'our dark Blue', also lauded the success of the imperial experiment:

An Indian playing against the Australians on Fenner's ground in our national game of cricket, is surely a remarkable sign of the times. Three parts of the world, each remote from one another were represented, yet each was a part of the British Empire. Peace and prosperity must likewise exist before such a thing could be.

This feat had incidentally helped Ranji bag his Cambridge Blue, an occurrence laced with much symbolism for Framjee Patel. Here was a message for young Indians that the imperial system was capable of rewarding achievement and they could 'rightly feel that the day will come when their just aspirations are bound to be realised in the land of liberty and justice, in the land of the countrymen of Bright, Gladstone and Rosebury.' When given a fair field and equal opportunities, Indians had produced a Paranjpe, a Bose[2], a Mehta and a Ranji. 'The success of a native of India in securing the 'blue ribbon of English scholarship' is a unique event, and speaks volumes for the subtle Asiatic intellect,' Framjee Patel reasoned.

Such fulsome praise of the 'subtle Asiatic intellect' on Framjee Patel's part was in tune with Neville Cardus's opinion that Ranji's feats of legerdemain on the field represented the 'genius of his race'. Ironically, whether consciously or otherwise, such arguments were not stretched

---

[2] Jagdish Chandra Bose's discoveries in science were taken as another instance of the originality and depth of the Indian mind.

to suggest that natives could perhaps also possess the genius to rule themselves. Generally speaking, at that stage of political evolution in the Empire, this was an abominable idea whose time had yet not come!

Perhaps Ranji's greatest contribution to the cause of Empire was his role as the great unifier. As mentioned earlier, he himself had noted cricket's ability to unite the various strands of British society. But cricket appropriated to itself a much larger role in the colonies, a role that has attracted much comment. There it became the bond of Empire, uniting the conquerors with the conquered, the colonies with the 'Mother Country', while also cementing the different colonial communities together in a universal brotherhood. Lord Harris, England cricket supremo, and Governor of Bombay from 1890-95, in fact regularly dilated on this quality in his speeches by claiming that the game could bring together the diverse and often mutually exclusive communities of India under one common citizenship of the Empire.

Major C.H.B. Pridham too noted in *The Charm of Cricket Past and Present* that Ranji's advent in 1893 'began to increase our interest in India, creating a common ground on which Englishmen, Hindoos and Moslems could cooperate and view one another in a more favourable light.'

Ranji himself was very conscious of this ability of cricket to unite the natives and the colonizers and from the very beginning he harped on this tune to nurse his political constituency. Opening his account for the Empire on 26 September 1893 at the annual dinner of the Old Higher Grade Cricket Club, a Cambridge club side, to celebrate the great event of his life—getting the prized Blue—Ranji showed that he had read the political 'wicket' correctly and had tempered his strokes accordingly . . .

> I do not consider myself a foreigner in Cambridge. I don't think Indians are foreigners in England (three years later Lord Harris would think otherwise and leave him out of the England team for the first Test versus Australia); that distinction has passed away long, long ago

and I think that in time we shall look upon each other as absolutely the same subjects under Her Majesty the Queen . . .

At another dinner in September 1896 hosted at the Guildhall's great banqueting room by Sussex and Cambridge to honour him for his batting feats of the just concluded season, Ranji positioned himself as a symbol of unity who could reconcile conflicting interests between the British masters and their Indian subjects:

It has always been, and will always be my endeavour in my humble way to bring about real brotherly love between the two nations . . . From the very beginning I have been connected with English people and have a great liking and admiration for their high social and intellectual qualities.

Expressing a hope that it would not be long before all Her Majesty's dominions could live together happily and trust each other in a way they had not done before, he added,

I trust the wrongs done in the past by Her Majesty's Indian subjects and the injustice, if any, which they have suffered in days gone by, will be forgotten and that England and India may in future form one united country, ready to show an united front to a common enemy, and be the admiration and envy of all other nations.

Always a firm believer in cricket's 'efficacy as an effectual agent for social relations' Ranji, during one of his visits home prior to becoming Jam Saheb, claimed that he was keen to improve the standard of Indian cricket towards this end. He elaborated on this theme in a goodwill message to Framjee Patel dated 31December 1903 in connection with the impending release of the Parsee author's aforementioned treatise on the game in India. Framjee Patel reproduced the entire missive[3]

---

[3]Surprisingly it had some good words for Lord Harris, who had prevented Ranji from playing for England.

from 'this great cricket authority—the Manu of cricket' who strongly believed in the good cricket is destined to do in India, in his book:

> Dear Mr Framji Patel
>
> Many thanks for allowing me to read your manuscript . . . . What an excellent idea it is of yours to dedicate the book to Lord Harris, who has done so much to increase the popularity of cricket and to encourage physical culture generally in his Presidency! He is a splendid sportsman, a great cricketer and the kindest of friends. I am delighted to think, therefore, that the first book on Indian cricket should be connected with so worthy and illustrious a name. I hope you will continue in your desire to ameliorate the physical condition of your people, which sadly wants regenerating.
>
> Games like cricket are a most excellent training, both to the mind and body. That paragraph of Lord Harris' speech, which you have so deftly and rightfully inserted in your book (dealing with His Lordship's desire actively to encourage cricket in India) is most pregnant with good feeling for the youth of this country. It aims not only at the welfare of the body and mind, but it must lead in the near future to the better understanding of problems, social and political, between the rulers and the ruled, by giving Englishmen and Indians an opportunity of mixing with each other without restraint and greater cordiality in out-door pastimes than is the case in the ordinary way. Our antiquated social customs are a great barrier to material and physical progress. It will be a great day for India when the precept and example of many of our rulers bring down the ancient fabric of corrupt and ill-suited customs, and make the people of India as a whole a truly fine, manly and prominent race in the great Empire of our Emperor King . . .
>
> Yours sincerely,
> Ranjitsinhji

So convinced was Framjee Patel that Ranji himself had admirably fulfilled his role of unifying Indians and Britishers that he broke into borrowed verse to convey what he felt he might have inadequately described in prose:

There's not a deed of craftsmanship
There is not a thing red-tape can do
Shall knit the Hindu with the Celt
As much as the Cambridge Blue.

Thus, from perceiving and advocating a unifying role for games like cricket, Ranji in turn would become a role model unifier himself. It was often remarked that Ranji's cricketing successes turned him into 'India's first ambassador to England' and brought the two nations closer than ever before. Lord Willingdon, Viceroy in India at the time of Ranji's death, frankly acknowledged this in a tribute, stating that 'he was an ambassador of co-operation, friendship and goodwill between the two races'.

When the political debate was heating up in the late 1920s in India following the announcement of the Indian States Inquiry Committee, this idea was expanded upon by Native States propagandists to suggest that Ranji, with his imperial qualities of sportsmanship that cricket endowed, was a splendid advertisement for the princely order in addition to being 'the finest ambassador India ever sent to England'. As Laurence Rushbrook-Williams, ex-director of the publicity department of the Government of India, foreign minister of Patiala, who later held the same post with Nawanagar, argued in this discourse:

'Ranji' was, to the best of my knowledge, the first Indian of princely blood to be taken to the heart of the British public. Before his day, the general impression which that public had formed concerning Indian princes—supposing there had been any impression at all—was that of a number of effeminate persons covered with pearls from head to foot, and spending their days reclining upon silken cushions, observing with an apathetic eye the gyrations of scantily-clad dancing girls. The better-informed classes in England, particularly those who possessed any family connection with India, did not, of course, fall into so crude an error; but even they would have been the first to admit that they could not regard the Indian Princes as being in any sense of the word comrades or co-workers in the task of upholding the Commonwealth. Now 'Ranji' altered all this; and it is an astonishing achievement for a single individual, however eminent or gifted. He worked an entire revolution in the manner in which Indian princes were regarded by Englishmen. This he did, not so much by playing cricket supremely well, as by utilising to the full the opportunities which his genius at the national game placed before him. The present ruler of Jamnagar was, it is true, marked out by fortune for athletic prowess. Some mysterious natural gift in the co-ordination of hand and eye gave him that superiority over ordinarily first-class batsmen which Mlle. Lenglen possesses over ordinarily first-class tennis players. But this of itself is insufficient to account for the place which he won, and still retains, in the hearts of the English. 'Ranji' was not merely idolised as a cricketer: he was beloved as a sportsman. The two things are quite different as anyone who considers the present generation of athletic stars will readily agree. Unaided by his miraculous cricket, 'Ranji' might never have captured the heart of the British public: but a cricketer might well be as good as 'Ranji' and still leave the heart quite untouched. It was through cricket that Prince Ranjit Sinhji found his opportunity: but opportunity is useless without the will and power to exploit it. To enquire to what extent the present Ruler of Jamnagar was animated by consciously conceived motives of high policy, or to what extent he was content to follow the natural instincts of a character of unusual force and insight, would be unnecessary. The fact remains. He taught the British public that an Indian Prince could rank supreme in a nation which prides itself on sportsmanship: which measures other nations by standards of sportsmanship: which ranks sportsmanship above all other virtues, human and divine. He could never have done this, unless his own sportsmanship had been remarkable: and sportsmanship is something quite different from supremacy in athletics. It includes a world of things which many a Champion does not possess: the faculty of playing for one's side rather than for one's self: the gift of courteous consideration for others: the power to play the game for the game's own sake, while sustaining victory with restraint and defeat with cheerfulness. In a word, a sportsman must be a 'gentleman' in the well-tried sense of the word: and it is just because 'Ranji' was so perfect a gentleman that we all loved him so much. Prince Ranjit Sinhji was the only Indian Prince we knew, and because of him, we thought better of all the Indian Princes whom we did not know . . .

But in the eyes of the British public, 'Ranji' was not only a Prince, he was also an Indian. Hence it was that from him, many Englishmen came to realise that differences in the pigmentation of the skin matter very little. Whether it was inhabited by people whose complexion was prevailingly brown, or whether, like England, a ruddy hue was more fashionable, any country which could produce a 'Ranji' must surely be 'a fairly decent sort of place'. Hundreds of thousands of Englishmen, yes, and men from the Dominions too, met India for the first time in the person of Prince Ranjit Sinhji: and because of him, came to hold a better opinion, not merely of the Indian Princes, but of India herself. In a word, if it be the function of an ambassador to encourage right understanding, and to cement cordial relations, between one country and another, 'Ranji' was the finest ambassador India ever sent to England.

It must be remembered, further, that all this was accomplished at a time when India in general and the Indian Princes in particular were far less interesting to the British public than is the case to-day. Here, as in other directions, the War has wrought a great change. India and England are to-day much more concerned with each other than they were fifteen years ago. Both the Press and the Public of England have now acquired a wholly new sense of the importance of India in the Commonwealth. To-day there are a number of Princes whose genial sportsmanship and outstanding personalities are almost as well-known in England as in India. Even the man in the street remembers their names, and recalls their war-services with gratitude. Such Princes are real links in the chain of Empire: and what the skipper of the MCC team had to say about Their Highnesses of Patiala and Jamnagar last year, found an echo in many English hearts. For the War has shown that Princes of India were not only a present help in times of trouble, but that they possessed the will, as well as the power, to play their part in the destinies of the greatest Commonwealth the world has so far seen.

Summarizing his arguments Rushbrook-Williams concluded that Ranji rendered yeoman service to the Empire in two crucial ways.

He was the first Indian Prince to open the heart of the stay-at-home Englishman to Princes of India, and to provide an opportunity of which the War allowed his brother Princes to take full advantage. The result is a solid foundation of good will, not lightly to be shattered. Again, he was the first Indian to become a popular idol in England, and thus to raise the entire reputation of his country in the eyes of a people who can be approached most readily along the avenue of sportsmanship. This was an achievement of first-class political importance: and we have yet to realise how much even politically-minded India owes thereto.

BE that as it may, that Guildhall banquet speech of September 1896 referred to earlier, heralded Ranji's entry into the political arena. The national press was completely bowled over by this off-field performance, hailing him as a true friend of the Empire. Sir Edwin Arnold, author of *The Light of Asia,* remarked in the *Daily Telegraph*: 'Last night the hearts of England and India came closer together than ever they had come before . . .' Ranji had performed 'a noble service to the two continents, by bringing them together on a field which Englishmen love and understand'. The *Star* suggested that Ranji if had any 'ambitions in the political line' he would have no difficulty in securing a nomination from some enthusiastic constituency for at this moment he is 'the most popular man in England'.

However, some dissenting voices asserted themselves amid all this brouhaha and none was more overpowering than that of the other 'black man' making waves in England at the same time, Dadabhai Naoroji. The future president of the Indian National Congress had in fact stormed to national attention a full year before Ranji made his debut for Cambridge in 1893, after Conservative prime minister, Lord Salisbury, referred to him as a 'black man' in an election speech. The uproar that this remark caused turned Naoroji into an instant celebrity. Contesting on a Liberal ticket from the Central Finsbury constituency in London in July 1892, Naoroji trounced the Conservative candidate, Captain Pentan, in the parliamentary elections that followed and entered the House of Commons in style.

It can be argued that chronologically, Naoroji was India's first superstar in Britain, not Ranji. Was the former's feat of becoming the first Indian to be elected to the British Parliament by popular mandate a lesser achievement than Ranji being selected for a University XI in cricket or earning his Cambridge 'Blue' a year later? Naoroji was never given due credit for this stupendous achievement by the imperial writers of the day. Simon Wilde has opined that Naoroji's success might have kept Ranji out of the first Test versus the Australians in the 1896 series as Lord Harris might have been instructed to oppose Ranji's selection by Salisbury's new Conservative government because of the 'international implications' of such a move. This could have set a dangerous precedent by allowing 'native' members of the British Empire to become equal to or indistinguishable from locals in Britain.

Naoroji's biographer, R.P. Masani, has recorded that when Ranji began making waves with the bat, the politician assiduously tried to woo the cricketer to the nationalist cause. While Ranji was singing the praises of Queen Victoria and the Empire during the jubilee celebrations, Naoroji used the occasion to remind the Empress of the violation of the pledges embodied in her Proclamation of 1858 and the various Acts which resulted in the impoverishment of the Indian people and the infliction of the scourges of war, pestilence and famine. The British government, trying desperately to fend off the political bouncers hurled by Naoroji in Parliament and outside, feared double trouble if the two Indian stalwarts were to strike an anti-imperial partnership. Luckily for the establishment, their political agendas were widely different.

While many held that Ranji's considerable achievements made Englishmen appreciate Indians better, Naoroji argued on the contrary that they gave his subjugated countrymen a new sense of identity vis-à-vis their white masters. Naoroji accordingly saluted the cricketer's contribution to Indian morale by quoting approvingly from an article in *The Times* for his book on *Poverty and Un-British Rule in India*:

> The service which Prince Ranjitsinhji has performed for India is not
> that he has proved one of his race to be capable of the highest

achievement in our national sport, but that he has made the fact known to the whole British people. To the masses of our country-men who pay gate-money, Prince Ranjitsinhji's performance amounts to a new discovery of India. It brings home to them the fact that among our fellow-subjects in Asia, those fellow-subjects whose very hundreds of millions turn them into numerical abstractions, there are men who can take the lead in the national sport which all Englishmen love and more or less understand. Prince Ranjitsinhji's victory has enabled the average Englishman to realise India, and has made him respect Indians to a degree that no other triumph could have secured.

Naoroji even appealed to Ranji who, Masani claims, 'was then busy arousing sympathy for the suffering people of India'[4] and advised the cricketer in the following lines:

You have to distinguish the appeal for the relief of the present calamity (the famine) from the necessity of preventing such calamities in the future, and if you can in some way impress unto your hearers their great duty to see that this is looked into, you will do a service both to England and to India. You will also be able to impress upon them that during the last fifteen years since the last great famine, this country has added to its wealth from India four or five hundred millions sterling and that from that great abundance England is bound to give in abundance. Even one per cent will mean four or five millions . . . There are people who do not, and cannot, come to relief works— women, children, old and infirm, and, more pitiful still, the respectable who would on no account seek relief and would prefer to starve and die—here private charity is most needed.

Whether Ranji responded to this appeal from India's great constitutional rights agitator nor had contacts with him is not known. Neither is it known whether he had any interaction (then or later in India) with a certain Mr M.K. Gandhi, from the neighbouring town of Porbander, who had also arrived in England

---

[4]Nobody has ever reported any such activity on Ranji's part.

in 1888, bearing a letter of introduction to the Nawanagar native.[5]

As 'England's pre-eminent example of cricket's imperial value,' Ranji's political choices were seemingly predestined. Imbibing the core values of life from cricket he translated its principles into success off the field by becoming a ruler and a statesman of sorts. The great paradox of Ranji is that while he smashed the theory of intrinsic English superiority over his own people by his astounding successes in the most English of all things, cricket, he never went on to question the political hegemony of Britain during his second innings as Jam Saheb. He also never forsook his imperial loyalties in the turbulent two-and-a-half decades of the freedom struggle that he witnessed as Jam Saheb. He stood steadfast on the side of the Raj even as the end game of Empire began to be played out in the latter stages of his reign.

---

[5]There is however one later instance when Ranji as Jam Saheb approvingly quoted the Mahatma while opposing the foundation of a Central Chief's College at Delhi at a Chamber of Princes meet in November 1921, arguing that 'educational institutions should be on the old basis, namely in the jungles'.

1907, the year that Ranji finally 'got the nod', to borrow a popular sporting analogy, was a bleak year for the British in India. It was the fiftieth anniversary of the 'Indian Mutiny' of 1857 that had rocked the very foundations of the Raj and still haunted the British like a recurring nightmare. The spirit of nationalism had since taken root in the Indian psyche giving rise to the *swadeshi* movement and the boycott of British institutions and goods. The militancy and terrorism ignited by the infamous partition of Bengal by the Viceroy, Lord Curzon, in 1905, and the seething mass of discontent in the Punjab stoked fears that another insurrection was on the cards. The repressive measures taken to quell the disturbances only aggravated the fragile situation.

A year before, in 1906, Dadabhai Naoroji, who had since returned to India, had signalled the start of the countdown for Indian independence by declaring in his presidential address at the Calcutta session of the Indian National Congress that its ultimate aim was now *swaraj*. This was the first occasion such a statement was articulated from the platform of the party founded by an activist Englishman, Allan Octavian Hume, in 1885. On the distaff side, the princes too had woken up to the possibility of a British departure and had begun to pressurize the colonial rulers for safeguards to ensure their permanence in a changed dispensation.

It was against this backdrop of political ferment that Ranji finally secured his kingdom. He had visited India on this quest on a few occasions prior to his year of reckoning. He first returned in April 1898, while the England cricketers were home bound after their disastrous tour of Australia, touching down at Madras via Colombo. Soon after he was signed on as ADC by Maharaja Rajinder Singh of Patiala, an inveterate anglophile and cricket patron. During his several homecomings in the interregnum Ranji had travelled, hunted, played a bit of cricket and lobbied for funds to fuel his extravagant lifestyle and support for his political ambitions from benefactors like Sir Pratap Singh (also spelt Partab or Pertab), the Regent of Jodhpur and later the Maharaja of Idar (a 15-gun state in Rajputana, now Rajasthan), the Maharaja of Jodhpur and the Nawab of Junagadh.

The unexpected and inexplicable death of Jassaji, Jam Vibhaji's son and successor, on August 14, 1906, at the youthful age of twenty-four, without siring or nominating a successor, resurrected Ranji's fading quest for the Nawanagar *gaddi*. Nawanagar (meaning 'new town') was a far from affluent kingdom, 3,791 square miles in area or about as large as three average English counties. It comprised 400 villages with a total population of 350,000 and a total annual revenue of Rs 21 lakhs (£140,000 at the time) and was once described in the House of Commons as 'a wild marsh inhabited by wild asses'.

No sooner did Ranji get wind of Jassaji's death, than he promptly threw his England cap into the succession ring along with other claimants from Vibhaji's extended family. He petitioned the authorities in London and India, generated favourable stories in the British media about his just claims and orchestrated declarations of support from hardline Rajput states like Jodhpur, Idar, Dhrangadhra and Kutch, whose Maharao (ruler) was the then head of the Jadeja Rajputs, the tribe from which Ranji hailed.

These rulers were rather condescending towards progeny resulting from Muslim consorts and the 'tainted' Jassaji and his Nawanagar regime were consequently not on the top of the Rajput popularity chart. By way of pressure tactics, Sir Pratap, who assumed the role of 'chief director' of Ranji's campaign, personally cautioned the Viceroy, Lord Minto, that if Ranji were declared 'out' again—his earlier petitions for the throne were all rejected—even his fabled loyalty to the Raj would weaken.

The multi-pronged campaign succeeded. After due deliberation, the British decided that Ranji was best suited to ascend the Nawanagar *gaddi*, 'consideration being had to the broad experience of life which the new Chief has enjoyed', his imperial track record and the possibility that he could embark on a political course inimical to British interests if not obliged.

Since loyalty to the British Raj was one of the important factors that determined his selection, Ranji therefore sought to secure his wicket by declaring his fidelity to Britain in advance, a solid reassurance in those troubled times. As soon as he learnt that he was the next man in, Ranji dashed off a missive requesting the Kathiawar Agent to thank the Governor and Viceroy for his selection while conveying to His Imperial Majesty the King-Emperor 'the humble assurance of his sincere loyalty and devotion to his person and throne'.

Finally, on 10 March 1907, in a ceremony marked with the full blast of tradition and religious ritual and in the presence of benefactors like Idar, Junagadh, Alwar and other rulers, Ranji ascended the Nawanagar throne. Typically, the new Jam Saheb, in his maiden speech from the Chair of State, reiterated his loyalty to the Crown and swore to execute his duties faithfully:

> . . . I can only say I shall endeavour to play the game so as not to lose whatever credit I have gained in another field . . . I hope to abide loyally by the traditions of this State, in its deep unswerving loyalty to the British throne, in which I could not have a better example to look up to than my friend the famous Maharaja General Sir Pratap Singh, Maharaja of Idar . . .

SUCH protestations of loyalty to His Majesty and the Throne consumed not only the Indian royalty but leaders of the Indian National Congress as well, which initially was more interested in securing constitutional rights under the British dispensation rather than furthering the end of the Raj itself. Congress sessions in those times began with the 'Indian National Anthem' sung to the tune of 'God Save the King' and ended with 'cheers for the King-Emperor, Lord Morley and Lord Minto'.

But the Jam Saheb's ringing words about his State's 'deep unswerving loyalty to the British throne' were deep-rooted and rock-solid. The shield of Nawanagar depicted a fish, a token of esteem when given by a friendly neighbour, a galley, denoting a seaboard state, antelopes as supporters to the shield, and a lion, denoting loyalty to the British. During the 'Indian Mutiny', Jam Vibhaji, who had ascended the throne in 1852, was the epitome of good behaviour, stout in his commitment to the Crown, even while rebellious sects had played havoc with law and order. Ranji's grandfather, Jhalamsinhji, himself commandeered the State troops to ensure that any dissidence was crushed. Vibhaji and other chiefs represented Kathiawar at the Imperial Assemblage (Durbar) on 1 January 1877, organized by the Viceroy, Lord Lytton, to proclaim Queen Victoria's assumption of the title 'Empress of India'. In 1890, like other loyal chieftains, Nawanagar too offered troops for imperial defence (the Imperial Service Troops) following an appeal by Lord Dufferin, the Viceroy. Vibhaji, whose name Ranji assumed, was among the first princes to welcome the Prince of Wales (later Edward VII) during his triumphal visit to India in 1875-76. For services rendered he was bestowed with the Order of the Knight Commander of the Star of India in 1877-78 and a personal salute of 15 guns.

Like Nawanagar, 'a small but very loyal corner of the Empire', other Kathiawar states too were locked in a comfortable relationship with the British. They had landed at nearby Surat in 1608 as traders, but had graduated to being the paramount power in the region by the early nineteenth century and the rest of the country thereafter. So secure was this bond with Britain that Ranji's chronicler Naoroji Dumasia was emboldened to declare two decades after Ranji's coronation that with his advent 'the spirit of unselfishness in which the British connection with Kathiawar commenced will permanently pervade there and will form a continued and closer unity between the Princes and the representatives of the Paramount Power to the lasting peace of the Province and mutual benefit'.

In addition to the Kathiawar kingdoms, the neighbouring princely domains of Rajputana (now Rajasthan) too were bound in eternal embrace with the British Crown. Colonel James Tod, author of *Annals and Antiquities of Rajasthan*, in his 'dedicatory epistle' to King William IV (Britain's monarch during the 1830s), had boldly proclaimed that 'your Majesty's throne may ever be surrounded by chiefs who will act up to the principles of fealty maintained at all hazards by the Rajputs', a sentiment which every Rajput Prince held dear to his heart. In exchange for the full measure of William IV's support, Tod prophesied that when the time came, the valiant Rajputs would not hesitate to make His Majesty's enemies their own by donning the 'saffron robe' emblematic of death or victory under His Majesty's banner. The subdued Rajputs had provided few occasions thereafter to negate Tod's expectations.

In 1910, the new Jam Saheb himself had occasion to invoke the spirit of Tod's covenant of fealty to the British throne (after a rosy introduction by Lord Sydenham, the former Governor of Bombay) at a Durbar of the Princes and Chiefs at Rajkot:

> . . . . I have the honour to be the present head in Kathiawar in successfully withstanding the repeated onslaughts of the invaders of our province. We as a clan feel proud of the compliment paid us, and I can assure Your Excellency that the same valour and chivalrous spirit still animate us and if ever the need arises for the display of our martial valour we would consider it a high honour and privilege to fight shoulder to shoulder with the British army in maintaining intact this great Empire and it glorious and untarnished name. The Rajputs have still the old fighting spirit burning within their breast, whether they be clad in the sombre raiments of the West or the luxurious silks of the East.

But it was the Jam Saheb's great benefactor, the short, powerfully built and moustached martial figure, Sir Pratap Singh of Idar, the very 'doyen of Rajput chivalry' and valour, who personified the race's famed loyalty to the British like no other. This terribly interesting specimen of royalty and loyalty was always seen in the company of the movers and shakers of the Raj and would have made frequent 'page three type' apparitions in the print media were he alive today.

Related to Ranji, this aristocratic-looking warrior was renowned for his fabulous feats of horsemanship and some fantastic stories were vouched for regarding his valour and 'his ever-youthful anxiety to be actively concerned in every war undertaken by the British Raj'. It was his custom to present himself fully equipped for battle to the Viceroy at the first rumour of war. On hearing of the Boxer Rebellion he appeared at Viceregal Lodge with the laconic syllables: 'Saheb, I go.' In August 1914, the aged warrior, still erect and of fierce eye, insistent on defending the Empire, was dispatched to Flanders and Egypt when the Great War broke out. But, like the Jam Saheb, he was kept at a safe distance from the hostilities due to his regal status.

Sir Pratap had attended the celebrations of Queen Victoria's diamond jubilee in 1897 and the coronation of Edward VII in 1901. As ADC to the Queen, his breast covered by ribbons, he had laid his sword at her feet, taken the hand extended for the customary kiss and put it across his eyes, signifying the surrender of the warrior's greatest treasure, his eyesight. During the formulation of the Morley–Minto reforms in 1909, Pratap had intimated to Lord Minto that India was unfit to govern herself. This statement was promptly appropriated by Minto to argue against the loosening of the imperial link by claiming that Indians didn't want it themselves, transmitting this opinion to the renowned Liberal Secretary of State, Sir John Morley, with unbounded glee.

The Rajput nobleman apparently made quite an impression on the Vicereine, Mary, Countess of Minto, who had in fact, referred to him fondly in her memoirs, *India, Minto and Morley, 1905-1901*, while relating a few incidents that confirmed his loyalty as well as his distaste for anti-British activities. While holding forth on how to combat 'sedition' in the Native States, he remarked about a man arrested for

'Not waiting to try man in Native State. Much chili, then hanging'. His loathing for the 'seditious' Bengali was such that on one occasion he is reported to have gone up to a man in a crowd and said, 'You Bengali Babu? You teaching me to make bombs? When I making bombs I not killing Englishmen I killing you.' On another occasion when troops were ordered to patrol the streets of Calcutta after disturbances had broken out there, Pratap insisted on riding out with them. He was greatly disappointed when no further disturbances occurred and he was denied the opportunity of killing a Bengali. Summing up Pratap's character, Barton wrote in a very flattering vein:

> A keen soldier, a lover of horse and hound, the intimate friend of three British sovereigns, he was a type that appealed to the Englishman.

Such was his standing among the British royalty that Pratap could even tick off the future Edward VIII who, during his visit to India in 1921, committed an elementary blunder while pig-sticking. 'I know you are the Prince of Wales and you know you are the Prince of Wales but does the pig know that you are the Prince of Wales?' Pratap had asked. But a rebuke he administered to a sibling was indicative of his slavish mindset, the episode being vividly recollected by Lady Minto. The old warrior had admonished a young relation staying with him, 'a very good-looking boy', whose 'manner was rather off-hand', with these memorable words: 'If you going Eton, although you being Prince, you staying downstairs blacking Sahib's boots; this being good teaching for you.' Rather surprising advice from a man who otherwise considered Rajputs and Englishmen as brothers!

Pratap died in 1922 and the Jam Saheb named the new magnificent eighty-room palace he built at Jamnagar after him—Pratap Vilas. But the Idar representative was also a 'man of exalted personal vanity'. True to many a princely type, Pratap could not resist the lure of intrigue. Another famous loyalist, Maharaja Bhupinder Singh of Patiala, reportedly flirted with the Nazi top brass in his time. So apparently did Pratap.

According to a report in the *Times of India*, on 2 December 1921, our 'Indian chief of no particular importance' had sailed from India to Marseilles during World War I and then taken a train to Switzerland where he appeared before the German Consul as a 'Rajah' ready to do anything against the oppressors of his country. This 'person of exalted personal vanity', doubtless harboured mental pictures of him prancing into northern India on a white horse as a conqueror which had played havoc with his imagination.

He asked for a personal audience with the Kaiser saying he wanted to organize an invasion into northern India to liberate his country. Pratap assured the Germans that the Indian princes would rise to welcome their deliverers. But Scotland Yard got wind of his mission and intercepted him at the Afghan border carrying an appeal by the Kaiser to the Indian Princes in a tube reduced by photography to almost microscopic size!

There would be no such disloyal aberrations on Ranji's part even though the newly crowned Jam Saheb would have a running battle with prickly British officialdom over administrative matters throughout his reign. Ranji remained faithful to his pledge of fidelity to the British Throne all through his reign and did everything he could to elevate the British monarchy. Whenever he visited England, he made it a point to visit the King, a major event which thrilled him and something he anticipated with pleasure and pride. Every major and minor event in the calendar of the Raj was commemorated, be it celebrating His Majesty's birthday as a state event every year or the end of World War I, with a sumptuous dinner for the poorer classes in Jamnagar. Even the Viceroy, as prime representative of His Majesty, was revered and when Lord Hardinge survived a bomb attack by some 'miscreants' at Delhi, there were 'general rejoicings' in Nawanagar state, the reaction symbolizing 'the sentiments of deep loyalty that pervaded all classes of His Highness's subjects' in the 'noblest traditions of the State and its rulers'.

HOWEVER, apart from his undoubted loyalty, another weightier consideration had a bearing on Ranji's elevation. It was purely communal and was evinced by an internal memo from the secretary of the Foreign Department, Government of India:

> One of the objects of the present selection is the rehabilitation of the Nawanagar family in the eyes of the leading Rajput houses (and) the Government of India agree that it is undesirable to sanction an arrangement (i.e., recognising any heir backed by Vibhaji's Muslim widows) which is calculated to defeat the object.

Such reasoning on officialdom's part showed that the British were not averse to playing the communal card to placate either Hindu sentiment or Muslim allegiance. Further evidence of cultural sensitivities were the hectic telegrams exchanged between officials to ensure that Ranji's installation was accomplished as fast as possible between the 'auspicious dates' of 6–10 March 1907 as dictated by the astrologers, since the next propitious period would thereafter only come in late June, and this delay could entail a dangerous invitation to political instability and princely skullduggery.

The fact that Ranji was of pure Hindu stock and immaculate pedigree was also a major propaganda point to legitimize his claims to the throne and pour scorn on those of his immediate predecessor, Jassaji. Charles A. Kincaid, a former judicial official in Kathiawar and a Ranji backer, derided Jassaji as a 'loutish bastard of a concubine' in *The Land of 'Ranji' and 'Duleep'* and called his mother a former prostitute. Roland Wild also disparagingly referred to Jassaji as the Mahomedan concubine's son and justified his derision with this explanation:

> Rajput history is coloured by many chapters of mediaeval chivalry. The pedigrees of the great clans are traced back through centuries, and the hereditary heads rule territories which were carved out by their ancestors by force of arms, and maintained stubbornly through the years against the Imperial Mahomedan invaders who controlled the destinies of the whole of India from the Court of Delhi.

Older than the children of Israel, they have ever been proud of their pure strain of their blood, and do not to this day intermarry with other races in India. So jealously did they observe their own social customs, so strenuously did they insist on the exclusion of all other influences in their blood, that it was considered a blot on the escutcheon of a Rajput Prince when he obeyed an Imperial demand from Delhi to the effect that a daughter must be given in wife to the Mohemedan Emperor.

However, in the case of the Nawanagar dynasty, argued Simon Wilde, an exacting Ranji biographer, this reputation was totally misconceived. According to him, an inquiry was started by the British government to find out if the leading Rajput states of Kathiawar objected to the idea of the Nawanagar rulers marrying Muslims or whether issues from such alliances could succeed to the throne.[1] It however established that the regime 'had never had much regard or respect for any religion but in descent and custom were in close affinity with the Muslim faith.' Wilde stated that only three Kathiawar chiefs had objected to Vibhaji's marriage to a Muslim wife, of which two were guilty of such infringements themselves.

Wilde further stated that Jam Raval, the founder of the state, had brought the Mohammadan religion with him when he had emigrated from Kutch in 1535 and had assumed the caste of a Rajput only for certain purposes. And Vibhaji's own father, Jam Ranmalji, had married a Muslim.

One has not come across any information as to why such a communal subterfuge was attempted to advance Ranji's legitimacy. It is reasonable to assume that initially this was attempted to discredit Ranji's rivals to the throne and highlight his own suitability. Later on, his positioning as a true-blue Hindu loyalist monarch, not without the active concurrence of the main protagonist himself, was probably due to sheer political

---

[1]The crisis arose when a previous son, Kalubha, was sired by a Muslim wife of Vibhaji.

expediency. It assumed critical importance from the 1920s onwards when the Indian masses rallied in overwhelming numbers against British rule and Hindu icons like the Jam Saheb were propped up by the establishment as role models of propriety as a counterpoise. It was similar to the ingratiating declamations of Sir T. Bhashyam Iyengar, a retired judge of the Madras High Court, who claimed to have discovered sanction for British rule in the Hindu *shastras* (sacred texts):

> . . . my idea of a true Hindu is that God has blessed India by relieving Indians from the most difficult and painful task of governing themselves, and God has conferred still greater blessing on India by entrusting that task to the English nation.

The Jam Saheb himself was often extolled by his chroniclers as a 'devout Hindu' and a 'Hindu Prince' well versed in the religions and psychology of the land and dutiful in the execution of its rituals and practices. They also spoke glowingly of Nawanagar as 'the premier Hindu state of Kathiawar'[2] which prided itself on its track record as a bulwark against the Moslem invaders. A prime forger of the Jam Saheb's identity as a Hindu icon was chronicler Naoroji Dumasia who deftly orchestrated this theme in his propaganda volume *Jamnagar: A Sketch of Its Ruler and Its Administration.*

Dumasia, it seems, had a one-point agenda—the preservation of the British Raj. On the one hand here he was propping up the Jam Saheb as a Hindu ideal, as evident in the aforementioned treatise. On the other hand he had also provided Muslims a loyalist role model in the Aga Khan (Sir Sultan Mahomed Shah) in order to 'give proper direction to the destinies of the Indian Moslems'. As he persuasively argued in *A Brief History of the Aga Khan*, likewise published by the *Times of India* press:

> . . . future development (of the Muslims) lies in the hands of the natural leaders of Indian Muhamadan society (and) it is of paramount

---

[2]The premier state in Kathiawar, Junagadh, was ruled by a Nawab.

importance that a few men of real eminence and enlightenment should lead, or rather compel, the public towards the ideals they have chosen.

The Jam Saheb's reputation as a Hindu icon was based on the bedrock of his lineage—stemming from none other than Krishna, the deified hero of the *Mahabharat* and ruler of nearby Dwarka over three thousand years ago. These sanctified connections were explored by Dumasia in chapters like 'Kathiawar—a Land of Legend and History' (reproduced from the *Times of India*, 21 November 1927) and 'The Story of Krishna' by Charles Kincaid in 'The Origin of the Jadejas (1000 BC)'. As Dumasia stated:

> There is a halo of religious reverence surrounding the name of the hero of the Hindu epic, a whole-hearted loyalty to the successors of that illustrious hero is an undying sentiment which the whole Hindu community hold in their hearts; respect and reverence are their natural heritage. That hereditary love of his people and 'religious reverence' for authority, the Jam Saheb has enjoyed to the full . . . He has proved that the mantle of Shree Krishna could not have fallen on worthier shoulders.

The Jam Saheb's ancestors, the Jadeja Rajputs, were linked to the Lunar dynasty, the leading representatives of the old Sind tribe of Samma Rajputs. Colonel James Tod in *The Annals and Antiquities of Rajasthan* traced the Sammas to Sambu (or Samba), son of Lord Krishna, who brought a colony of Yadavas from Dwarka, Kathiawar, to Sind.

According to one of the legends, the name 'Jadeja' originated from an early chief, Jadoji, who occupied Kutch. Another narrative said the name came from the goddess Hinglaz Mata, called 'Ashapura' ('hope fulfilled'), who gave sanctuary to one of the Jam's ancestors by concealing him in her mouth. Hence Jadeja, from Jara, the mouth. Yet another version said the Jadejas were descendants of the great Emperor Jamshed of Iran, hence the title Jam under which they ruled. 'Whatever account may be correct,' reiterated Dumasia, 'there is no doubt that the pedigree of the Jam Saheb is ancient and splendid and goes back to Krishna, the hero of the *Mahabharat*.'

Indeed, the 'successor of Shree Krishna' proved extremely worthy of his ancestry and made it a point to proclaim his religion and the sanctity it afforded his actions. Despite his veneer of Westernization and the worldliness of his lifestyle, the Jam Saheb's homegrown religiosity, his reliance on astrology, his knowledge of the Vedas and his attachment to Ganga *jal* (water) was well known. His solicitor, E.F. Hunt, in fact disclosed after his death that it was his 'regular practice' to keep himself in supply of Ganges water. The Jam Saheb's innate 'Hinduness' did not however, prohibit the Nawanagar Royal Band from striking up 'The Roast Beef of Old England' on state occasions, which E.H.D. Sewell, cricketer, raconteur and one of the Jam's regular guests, thought as being a little bit wide of the wicket for the Maharaja of a strict Hindu state.

But in retrospect, one must question the Jam's touching faith in the efficacy of astrology and the religious rituals performed at his installation in aid of his and the state's fortunes. For, immediately after, he was laid low by a near-fatal bout of typhoid. Nawanagar itself was ravaged by a severe drought in 1911, when 'the land came under the curse of God' and famine combined with pestilence in 1918, which equalled if not surpassed the horror of 1911, over 20,000 people perishing from influenza and plague.

Roland Wild however tried to rationalize Ranji's starry fixation by claiming that the Jam was different from others of his race who consulted the *joshis* before embarking on a plan whereas the Jam Saheb put the necessary machinery in motion and *then* sought to hear what the future might hold. But he did admit that the Jam Saheb secretly harboured the Western superstition about black cats, together with many of the Eastern beliefs in omens. However, let alone natives, their British masters too feared the portents, a prime example being His Majesty King George V. A painted photograph which records the Jam Saheb's visit to the Balmoral castle in the autumn of 1912 shows His Majesty sitting apart from his guests because it was suddenly discovered that they numbered thirteen. His Majesty, described by biographer Harold Nicholson as a man who possessed 'few internal resources', therefore decided to reduce the main group to a harmless number by separating himself!

That said about his mental and spiritual make-up, the Jam Saheb was a truly secular ruler. Though he aided his Hindu subjects in every way, whether by laying the Dwarka Railway extension connecting Jamnagar with the holy town of Dwarka, or restoring the 4,000-year-old historic temple of Kileshwar Mahadev, he was well liked by his Muslim subjects too. The restoration of the Kileshwar temple, said Roland Wild, was a landmark achievement under the aegis of the British Crown, which enabled a Rajput ruler to successfully restore a Shiv temple with the aid of a Vaishnavi engineer and a Mahomedan contractor. The Jam also brought several of his nieces out of *purdah*, arguing that their own conscience, and not custom, should dictate their movements.

IN addition to his claims of divine ancestry, the Jam Saheb's Hindu affiliations were further buttressed by the reputation of the Jadejas who resisted alien invaders in Sind and Kutch and the Nawanagar dynasty as a bastion of resistance against the Moghuls and other satraps. The new Jam Saheb was not averse to invoking this fabled legacy as he did on one occasion in his 'Installation Day' speech[3] of the Advisory Council of Nawanagar on 29 March 1919:

> . . . In such times of general disorder and insecurity Jam Ravalji, Jam Sattarsalji and other valiant Rulers of Halar, kept their swords unsheathed in defence of their country and religion, suffered untold hardships, marshalled their resources against religious fanaticism, fought famous battles like the Bhuchar Mori near Dhrol, sacrificed their heads and saved their country and their religion . . .

---

[3]Dumasia reproduced it as a testament on 'How they saved Kathiawar from Mahomedan Invaders and Internal Strife' and other matters.

British officials too paid regular lip service to this Nawanagar reputation, with Sir J.B. Peile, the Political Agent of Kathiawar, stating at the ceremony where the Knight Commander of the Star of India was bestowed upon Jam Vibhaji in 1877-78:

> The race of his Highness the Jam was long regarded with special veneration as the foremost Hindu dynasty of this peninsula, stout in fight with the Viceroys of Akbar . . .

But in his case especially, the leveraging of this particular aspect of his dynasty's history was laced with bitter irony, considering that he had to depend upon the Nawab of Junagadh (his biggest benefactor, according to his court historians) and Arabs guards to guarantee his safety when he came to claim his kingdom. Junagadh had taken personal responsibility for Ranji's safety and provided a posse of Arab guards and a large retinue of servants to accompany him on a special train to Jamnagar and special cooks to prepare his food, lest he be poisoned. The Arab guards were maintained well after his death.

Be that as it may, one should not be surprised if an overtly romanticized history of the Nawanagar dynasty was recorded for posterity, from which the new Jam Saheb now obviously drew political legitimacy and sustenance. The All India States' Peoples' Conference, an organization formed to fight against tyrannical Native Princes (like the Jam Saheb) and promote the interests of hapless state subjects, came to this conclusion about the Nawanagar's dynasty's exalted heritage:

> . . . It will thus be seen that the Jam has been treated all along as a dependent feudatory forced into submission with military strength and the history of treaties and engagements of the Jam Saheb clearly show that his ancestors have been some of the most recalcitrant feudatories with tendencies of a free-booter and even with the audacity to eject British Political officers. But the Jam has been latterly talking as if he were a potentate of international status and has been emphasizing and urging that the traditions of treaties should be maintained. What are these traditions? We find that the predecessors

of the present Maharaja were turbulent feudatories plundering and looting their neighbours, committing acts of piracy, making money by inflicting injury on helpless vessels touching their ports under unfavourable weather conditions and adding to the distress of the unfortunate victims. With such traditions, we wish the Jam Saheb had observed silence about his treaties and engagements. All the treaties with the Jam have been made by the Government of India through the Political Department represented by the political officers. The Jam Saheb pays tribute to the British Government, to the Gaikwad of Baroda and to the Nawab of Junagadh . . .

A critical examination of the history of the Nawanagar dynasty's valiant resistance against the Muslim invaders shows that it is true only up to a point. Several Jams indeed furiously engaged the Muslim invaders in bloody battle, but once they were subdued they paid their obeisance when the occasion demanded and sought the intercession of their Muslim overlords in succession disputes. Furthermore, the quarrelsome Jams fought not only the Muslims but against one and all, Hindus included. They took part in the factional politics of the day by siding with one Muslim overlord against another and sometimes even aligned with Muslims against their Hindu neighbours. This can be deduced from a perusal of the official gazettes and publications of the period— *Gazetteer of the Bombay Presidency, The Imperial Gazetteer of India*, Captain H. Wilberforce-Bell's *The History of Kathiawad from the Earliest Times* among others.

While there was naturally much ado made over the record of the Nawanagar dynasty in resisting 'foreign' invasion, it must be pointed out that as far as the original people of Kathiawar are concerned, the Jadeja Rajputs of Nawanagar are invaders themselves. The Jadejas are descendents of the great Jadav race, whose principal subdivisions were also the Bhatis and Chudasamas of Jaisalmer. The Chudasamas ruled at Junagadh before they were ousted by Muslims. The Jhala Rajputs[4],

---

[4]The Jhala Rajputs ruled Dhrangadhra, Limbdi, Wankaner, Wadhwan and Salya.

the Kathis and the Gohel Rajputs (Bhavnagar, Palitana, Wala and Lathi) began arriving from Sind and Kutch into Kathiawar in the eleventh and twelfth centuries. In the twelfth century, Jadeja Jan Bamanioji of Kutch captured Ghumli, the seat of the Jethwas, though according to another account, it was the Jadeja Oomur who attacked Ghumli. The Jadejas Rajputs in due course entrenched themselves at Nawanagar, Dhrol, Morbi, Rajkot and Gondal.

It was Jam Rawal, the Jadeja chieftain of Kutch, who crossed the Ravi with a numerous and well-appointed army, 'invaded' Sorath, conquered the Jodiya and Amran *paraganas* (groups of villages) from the Dedas and Chavadas, Nagnah bander from the Jethwas and the Khambhalia *paragana* from the Vadhels and founded Nawanagar in 1540. He called the district Halar, after Jam Hala. He further extended his kingdom by defeating the Jethwas and Vala Rajputs while the third Jam, Satarsal (Sataji), also absorbed many villages of Gujarati domain. Incidentally, Rawal's father, Lakhaji, had helped Bahadur Shah, Emperor of Gujarat, capture Pawansadhi, for which he got twelve villages as reward. According to Charles A. Kincaid, Jam Rawal's invasion of Kathiawar was dictated by Ashapura (Hinglaz Mata), the family goddess, whose apparition suggested it as the best course of action when confronted by the Moghul forces in the north. Apart from his undoubted bravery, Rawal's conquests were also aided by a dash of treachery, which Kincaid noted was an ordinary *ruse de guerre* in those times.

The Jadejas in fact were among the later invaders of Kathiawar that had borne the brunt of invasion since the earliest times. Scythians, Greeks, Rajputs and Mahomedans utilized this Western promontory as the doorway to India. In 155 BC, Menander, King of the Punjab and Kabul and relation of Eucradites, King of Bactria, conquered the province. In AD 126 the expansionist Saka kings of Andhra (Pradesh) usurped the territory. Between AD 470 and AD 700, during the rule of the Walabhi dynasty, Buddhism flourished in the region. 'The powers of Buddhism had grown that almost all the principal rulers were followers of that persuasion. But Brahamanism afterwards asserted itself and Buddhist converts became Kshatryas or Rajputs,' wrote Wilberforce-Bell.

The Arabs came in about AD 766 under Amru bin Jamal and the Muslim conquerors shortened the name 'Saurashtra' to 'Sorath' (later the southern-most district). The sack of Somnath in southern Kathiawar by Mahmud of Ghazni in 1026 and capture of Anhilvada in 1194 were a prelude to the Moslem invasions of Kathiawar. In 1573, Gujarat was conquered by Akbar and ruled by Viceroys from Delhi till the Marathas attacked Gujarat in 1705 and devastated the southern part. Wilberforce-Bell said that the Marathas were responsible for changing the name of the province from Saurashtra (the good country) to Kathiawar in the middle of the eighteenth century, after the Kathi tribe who offered the stiffest resistance to their plundering expeditions.

Far from resisting all Muslim overlords, the Jams actually enjoyed an intimate relationship with the Ghori rulers of Junagadh, of Afghan origin, and the independent Sultanate of Gujarat (1403–1573), ruled by the Governors of the Khalji and Tughlaq Sultans of Delhi till Muzaffar Shah I asserted his independence at Ahmedabad. In fact, Jam Sataji made common cause with the Gujarat Sultanate against the Moghul forces led by Mirza Khan, nephew of the Viceroy appointed by Akbar. But the Sultanate was apparently so unpopular that when Akbar entered Ahmedabad and dethroned Muzaffar Shah III, its populace threw open the town gates and went out *en masse* to welcome him.

Muzafar Shah III had given Sataji, the third Jam, the right of coining his own *kori* (coin), which led to the founding of the Nawanagar mint in 1570. Roland Wild may have made impassioned claims, while trying to highlight the purity of Ranji's bloodline, about hardline Rajputs refusing to give their daughters in marriage to the Muslim conquerors, but what do you make of the circumstance that the *Jamsahi kori* (coin of the Jam) enjoyed a relationship with the coin of the Sultan of Gujarat 'as one of bride and bridegroom'? According to the legend recounted by Wilberforce-Bell, on one occasion, Jam Satarsal, while paying *nazarana* (tribute) to the Sultan, produced a rupee and a coin and said by way of compliment:

Just as the dignity of the Raja is increased by the gift of their daughter
to the Sultan their overlord, so I marry my coin as a 'Kunwari' to this
rupee of yours, hoping her honour will increase.

Indeed, ever since Sataji had been defeated in the historic Battle of
Buchar Mori in 1590 by the Viceroy of Gujarat, Mirza Aziz Kokaltash,
Nawanagar was enrolled as a tributary of the Moghul empire. Sataji
sued for peace and got his kingdom back on condition that he supply
the Moghul forces with grain as long as they remained in the peninsula.
According to Kincaid, the Jadejas got back the Jamnagar throne only
because Akbar acceded to an emotional request by Vibhaji (Sataji's
grandson). Jam Jasaji (Jasoji), Sataji's successor, further provided the
Moghul Viceroy with 2,500 horses in 1609 to stave off the threat from
Malik Ambar of the Deccan. When the Emperor Jehangir visited
Gujarat in 1616, Jasaji repaired to his camp on the banks of the Mahi
and presented fifty Kutch horses as his *nazarana*. Like other vassal states,
Jasaji's quota was fixed at 2,500 horsemen for the defence of the Moghul
Empire who were posted on the southern borders of Gujarat.

Deadly intrigues in the Nawanagar court later forced an aggrieved
Rathor Rani to seek the assistance of Kutd-ud-din, *fauzdar* (viceroy)
of Sorath, in the battle for succession. Heeding her entreaties he
marched upon Nawanagar, slew Jadeja Raisinhji and renamed the state
Islamnagar. It was only in 1709, after the death of Aurangzeb weakened
central authority over the provinces, that the Jam reoccupied his capital
and restored the original name.

The gradual decline of the Moghul Empire between 1692 and 1760
paved the way for the advent of the 'maurading Marathas'. In 1722 they
moved into Saurashtra and in 1748, under Kanoji Tappar, they joined
Fakhr-ud-dowlah, Viceroy of Gujarat, in an expedition into Sorath to
collect tribute. In 1753, the Marathas took Ahmedabad from the
Moghuls. In 1794, Merman Khawas of Nawanagar offered large sums
of money to the Marathas to attack Gondal and they laid waste to the
territory.

During the latter part of the eighteenth century, the Gaikwad of Baroda, who held a contract to collect tribute for himself and his overlord, the Peshwa, enthroned at Poona, yearly sent a *mulkgiri* (revenue-collecting army) to collect contributions from the chiefs of western and northern Gujarat. The *mulkgiri* force used to appear at harvest time and in default of payment ravaged the crops and fired up the villages. Protected by the East India Company's treaties from his overlord at Poona and too weak to take part in the exciting contest for supremacy in Central India, the Gaikwad employed his army 'not in the field against a public enemy, but in the tributary provinces against those who had a right to his protection. Every year his generals took the field with what was called the *mulkgiri* army and extorted what sums they could from the cultivators or proprietors of the soil'.

Both British and Indian historians have dwelled on 'perhaps the most unfortunate period of Gujarat History' at the beginning of the eighteenth century when Gujarat was ravaged by the Maratha armies of the Peshwas and the Gaikwad. So when the British intervened in Kathiawar, they cast themselves as the liberators of the local populace, not from Moghul misrule, but from Maratha oppression. According to Wilberforce-Bell:

> They (the Kathiawar Chiefs) had reckoned not the Marathas, '*the imperial banditti*' and gauged not the measure of their power until Pilaji Gaikwad took Baroda in 1725. By 1753 they were once again laid low beneath the heel of a stranger and were enrolled as the merest vassals and tributaries of a race which by its manifold and profligate actions proved a far sterner master than the Emperors of Delhi. The Moghal from his peacock throne may have chastised them with whips; the Marathas scourged them with scorpions; but could they have known it as the long night of tribulation was far spent, the day was close at hand. In 1820 the British Government assumed the paramountcy. The ancient land of Kathiawar at length had peace and it has remained unbroken over a century, thanks to Colonel Walker's settlement which relieved the province from the exactions of the Marathas . . .

Quite coincidentally, the overreaching ambitions of Jam Jasaji II were primarily responsible for the British entry into Kathiawar, primarily his collusion with the mutinous Muslim mercenaries in the seizure of the Kandorna fort belonging to the Rana of Porbander in 1807. Jasaji's action violated the unwritten laws of conduct between chiefs at peace with each other and even the Nawab of Junagadh refused to be associated with the plot. The same Jasaji and his brother Sataji earlier unsuccessfully employed Arabs to overthrow the 'usurper', Meraman Khawas. When Jasaji took the Kandorna fort, the Rana at once appealed to the Gaikwad. Since the Jam failed to see reason despite much cajoling, Colonel Alexander Walker, the Resident, and Babaji Apaji marched on Kandorna and restored it to Rana Haolji.

When the joint British-Maratha forces entered the peninsula, the region was in a state of chronic disorder. A permanent settlement of the tribute of the Kathiawar chieftains—the first-class chiefs being designated as Junagadh, Nawanagar, Porbander, Bhavnagar, Dhrangadhra, Morvi and Gondal—was signed by all and the collection of dues undertaken by the British. The Jam too executed the engagements to pay tribute, keep order in his territory, renounce piracy and not to encroach on his neighbours' territory. Further, in 1812, the Jadeja chiefs contracted to end the 'custom' of 'the systematic murder of female children' in the tribe, ostensibly practised to avoid the difficulty and expense of providing them with husbands.

The British had one more occasion to discipline the cantankerous Jam, who refused to honour the apparently just claims of the Rao of Kutch and sheltered a Nawanagar Arab who had shot an English officer in the Morpur fort. Since the Jam refused to surrender the Arab a joint army commanded by Captain Carnac and Fatehsingh Rao Gaikwad in person marched upon Nawanagar in early 1812 and forced the Jam to eat humble pie.

The Kathiawar settlement not only terminated the Maratha threat, it also put an end to the war-like ambitions of the Jadejas and restored a semblance of order in Kathiawar. In a few years' time the British became the undisputed paramount power in the region. In 1820, Captain Barnewall was posted at Kathiawar as Political Agent and the Gaikwad agreed to make no demands on the Chiefs save through the British Government. The paramount power hitherto exercised by the Gaikwad was thus transferred to the British and Jam Sataji took their aid, along with the Gaikwad's, in his expeditions against the Maskat Arabs and Sangram Khawas. In 1865, the British started a fund to crush the rebellious Waghers and Vibhaji III was among the principal contributors. There was not much further trouble in the region thereafter.

This was the Nawanagar in pacified Kathiawar that Ranji inherited, secure in its bond with the British. As it turned out, the new Jam Saheb's reign would be a lifelong endeavour to ensure British permanence, not only in his province but also in the country.

IV Native Princes vs Native Press

THE *New Encyclopaedia Britannica* (fifteenth edition, 1993) describes Ranji as 'a progressive ruler and statesman' who 'set an example by the simplicity of his personal life'. It lists among his many achievements the introduction of telegraphs, Californian methods of farming, railway lines and the augmentation of water supply and finances of his state. For the post-colonial generation, this ready reckoner on the Jam Saheb and quick fix on history is all they will have to rest content with.

The *Britannica* is entitled to its own conclusions on Ranji, shaped as they were by the material it perused. But its claim that the Jam Saheb 'set an example by the simplicity of his personal life' is utterly fallacious and betrays either poor research on its part or is an insidious attempt to paint a sanitized picture of an imperial icon.

Even an offhand perusal of Roland Wild's authorized biography of 1934, Alan Ross' hagiography of 1983 or Simon Wilde's expose of 1990 will provide enough details of the Jam Saheb's profligate lifestyle and lavish expenditure on himself, friends and official visitors. Ross' account of the Jam Saheb's lifestyle is unambiguous on this count:

> He also had an instinctive feeling for the outward trappings of caste and position. Once installed as Jam Saheb he was able to indulge in his love of finery to his heart's content . . . His early passion for motorcars was never to leave him. The same was true of his love of clothes and jewellery, which always had to be of the best. Not only did Ranji equip himself handsomely for every conceivable social occasion in terms of suits and shoes, but he dispensed expensive watches and rings to all and sundry, as well as building up a sizeable collection of such objects for himself.

The ruler who impressed the *Britannica* by the 'simplicity of his personal life' built the magnificent new eighty-room Pratap Vilas palace[1] and considerably modernized the existing Vibha Vilas structure for his comfort. He also constructed a fancy shooting lodge, shooting camp and summer retreat (inclusive of golf course) in his territory. In England he purchased a house at Staines (later renamed Jamnagar House) for 30,000 pounds and the Ballynahinch Castle at Connemara on Ireland's west coast along with an attached estate of 30,000 acres.

He owned an impressive art collection, including works by Thorburn, Landseer, Sidney Cooper, Leighton etc. The 'Nawanagar Jewels' that he accumulated, were described by none other than Jacques Cartier, whose client he was, as a collection 'unsurpassed in the world, not perhaps in quantity but certainly in quality'. Cartier considered Ranji as 'a Prince really princely in his taste as well as by the qualities of his mind and heart'. Wild said the Jam Saheb possessed 'one of the world's greatest stores of modernized jewellery' and 'the finest collection in India'. The flawless 136.32 carat white diamond, 'Ranjitsinhji', was reputedly ranked among the most outstanding diamonds of the world. The Jam Saheb normally travelled with several suitcases full of rings, watches and ornaments and sometimes carried in his pocket jewels worth nearly 100,000 pounds.

In addition, the Jam Saheb had other expensive tastes like accumulating curios and antiques like the relics of Napoleon, importing pedigree race horses from England, breeding Kathi horses at Jamnagar, purchasing all his guns and ammunition from Purdey's, the best gunsmiths in the Empire, and blowing up pots of money on entertaining friends and officials. All of this has been faithfully recorded (though rationalized) by Wild and Ross. And yet the *Britannica* got it wrong.

However, the *Britannica* may be excused for assessing Ranji as a good man and as a progressive ruler and statesman, since it only took recourse to standard Western, Anglo-Indian and mainstream Indian

---

[1]Pratap Vilas palace was named after Sir Pratap Singh who had died in 1922.

appraisals of the Nawanagar ruler. It unwittingly fell victim to the legend of Ranji, first crafted during his glorious cricketing career and then consolidated during his second innings as ruler by imperial propagandists and gullible reviewers, which was then handed down to subsequent generations. This angelic image of Ranji generally survived right till the 1990s when British writer Simon Wilde revealed what his own countrymen had kept under wraps for decades.

The skeletons Wilde dragged out of the closet were at stark variance with the hitherto prevailing picture of Ranji as 'the noblest Roman of them all'. Ranji's on-field fame apparently bestowed him with a saintly halo off it. He was therefore consistently dubbed as the epitome of sportsmanship, grace and wit. 'Country Vicar', his contemporary at Cambridge, observed that

> Ranji was always a charming companion. He was entirely devoid of what is called 'side'. He was affable, natural, friendly, kind and courteous to everyone and his enthusiasm for cricket was a positive challenge . . . Ranji was like that—his word was his bond—in small matters as well as great.

According to A.A. Thomson 'Ranji was loved not because of his mighty scores but for something which mattered a great deal more; he was loved by many friends because he was personally charming, piquantly amusing and above all, wildly generous'. England captain A.E. Stoddart attested that 'everyone who knows Ranjitsinhji finds it hard to say whether he admires him most as a cricketer or as a man'. Ranji's cricket buddy, Charles Burgess Fry, remembered him as 'mellow and kind and single-hearted' and with 'no spark of jealousy in his composition'. An American lady journalist, who met him briefly, similarly cooed: 'One thing is certain about him. Ranji is Captain, not Prince, and there is an intemenous amount of thoroughbred sportsmanship in his make up'. Charles Kincaid, a retired civil servant and a great pal of Ranji too put down some ringing lines in a dedication to the cricketer-king which are worthy of recall:

In faith, he is a worthy gentleman,
Exceedingly well read . . . valiant as a lion,
And wondrous affable and as bountiful,
As mines of India.

Indian cricket writers too were influenced by such Western effusions. S.S. Mathur hailed Ranji as an example of probity and god-like disposition while discussing the 'game of the gods'. Respected cricket writer, Vasant Raiji, who penned the volume, *Ranji: The Legend and the Man* and edited *A Centenary Album* dedicated to Ranji, echoed comparable sentiments:

> Ranji was the most unselfish man in the world. His character was as beautiful as his batting must have been. I believe that a man's character may be seen in his batting. He radiated happiness and laughter around him.

INDEED, Ranji could surely have harboured all those virtuous traits. But fame can often be a convenient cloak for harmless idiosyncrasy at best or blatant rascality at worst. In reality, as Simon Wilde reveals in his sensational treatise, *Ranji: A Genius Rich and Strange*, 'the legend of Ranji was far removed from reality' and his 'straightforwardly attractive public persona was complemented by a less well known and altogether less acceptable side'.

This dark side pertained to Ranji's notorious unreliability in his monetary dealings and with his debts from his earliest days in England. These failings were acknowledged by original biographer Roland Wild and Alan Ross but romanticized as 'a kind of joyous fatalism', 'his superb ability to live far in excess of his income', 'a very human and almost likeable fault', 'a natural and apparently pressing need to please his friends before giving any consideration to pounds, shillings and pence' or 'the excesses of hospitality becoming of an Indian maharaja.' It was argued that Ranji became 'the victim of his own sociability.' Roland Wild even claimed that Ranji always meant to pay back his debts and eventually did—with five per cent interest—while himself sometimes becoming a victim of financial impropriety.

But Ranji's behaviour was far more deliberate, said Simon Wilde, who provided several examples of his malfeasance, detailed accounts of which can be gleaned from the 'Political and Secret' dossiers kept by the British government in his time and now stored in the vaults of the Oriental and India Office Collections at the British Library in London. As a Cambridge undergrad Ranji had perfected the art of keeping his creditors at bay. And even when he was flush with funds after he became Jam Saheb, he continued to duck his creditors with the dexterity of a master batsman evading a bouncer. He faced several court proceedings, including a bankruptcy petition. In fact, the considerable heat generated by his financial improprieties during his first visit to England as Jam Saheb in 1907-08 almost led to his ignominious retreat from the isles.

The India Office in London was saddled with a profusion of complaints against the Jam Saheb. But it did everything in its power to obstruct the due process of law, preferring to even sacrifice the rights of its own citizens in Britain in order to safeguard its political interests in India which the Native Princes were protecting. In collusion with Ranji's combative solicitors, Redfern, Hunt and Co., the India Office cunningly fostered the impression in the courts and even in the British Parliament, where questions were asked about the Jam Saheb's debts and his legal status, that as a ruling prince, he enjoyed immunity from legal action. The Nawanagar ruler construed the India Office's indolence as a signal to continue batting as he pleased. In fact, the gutsy English publication, *John Bull*, taking off from his solicitors' argument that the Jam Saheb was above the English law, rubbed in the bitter irony of the situation in its comment on 'How the Jam deals with his English debts':

> . . . In other words the Jam is above the law of the Empire of which after all, he is but a very minor 'suzerain ruler'. He may order any goods he likes, and, having got them, all he has to do is to say to the people

from whom he has purchased, 'You cannot sue me. I am a Ruler of the first class State of Nawanagar.' I will, out of the kindness of my gracious will, pay you such sum as I think fair, and when I like it, but a fig for your laws and your Courts.'

Such documented evidence on the pecuniary affairs of the Jam Saheb, in retrospect, lend credulity to a report about such alleged subterfuges by the Nawanagar chief, as reported by the *Baroda Gazette* in October 1910. It mentioned that Bai Surabja, the widowed Rani of the late Maharaja of Porbander, was assaulted by Gokulbhai Bapuji, a barrister-at-law of the Jamnagar State while staying in a place belonging to the Jam Saheb. The barrister was allegedly trying to recover from the Rani a receipt in lieu of ornaments worth Rs 75,000 and letters written by the Jam Saheb to her. Had Gokhulbhai recovered the receipt she would have been in no position to claim the ornaments back from the Jam Saheb, the report speculated. The letters written by the Jam Saheb to the Rani telling her that the Political Agent wished her to move to Modpur in his dominions, were also sought to be recovered because they might have been fabricated, it alleged. 'The belief among the Kathiawar public is that Mr Gokuldas may have done this either to serve his own purpose or under orders from his master, the Jam,' opined the paper, while calling for a full inquiry into the incident.

SO much about Ranji's character! There was equally wide divergence between the reportage on Ranji's performance as a ruler in Western and Anglo-Indian organs and the nationalist 'Native Press' of the Bombay Presidency, which included the province of Kathiawar. But while the pontifications of the former were widely disseminated and are fondly remembered even till today, the nationalist Native Press coverage has been all but forgotten and strangely never referred to, not even by Indian writers, though some post-Independence Indian historians have recorded some disparaging remarks about the Jam Saheb in volumes on the freedom movement in the Native States of Gujarat. The contrast between the Western and Native Press coverage of the Jam Saheb however can be gauged by first browsing through the reportage of British writers. J.A. Spender, who visited India in 1926 as special correspondent of the *Westminster Gazette*, posted this report on *The Changing East*:

> What to do with famous cricketers when they have made their last centuries and laid down their bats is a problem unsolved in Great Britain, and still deserving the earnest consideration of the MCC. Here in this corner of India it has found its perfect solution; for the famous cricketer, still in his prime, is devoting himself heart and soul to the welfare of the people committed to his charge and to the development of his and their estate, and bringing to his task an energetic resourceful spirit which proves that his strokes are by no means exhausted . . .
>
> Here is ample opportunity for a benevolent autocrat who takes his duties seriously. The Jam Saheb is no arbitrary despot . . . His comings and goings are not merely the gracious visitations of royalty bestowing smiles and favours; he is Prime Minister and Inspector and Chief Engineer and Court of Appeal and modern earthly Providence to all the 400,000 and wherever he goes, there is business to do, reports to be considered and action to be taken . . .
>
> I bear away from Nawanagar the impression of a very able, benevolent man doing dutifully the work which has fallen to him and combining new and old in a very interesting way . . . The thought flits through one's mind that if there were five hundred men like him in India—men trained and educated in England but knowing India only as Indians know it—and they each had half a million Indians to look after, some part of the Indian problem would be solved. There are unfortunately not five hundred Jam Sahibs in India, and though he modestly tells he is a typical case of an Indian prince, I have yet to verify that fact . . .

Or to recount another laudatory mention, H. Wilson Harris, alluding to the Jam Saheb's virtuoso performance at the League of Nations, requested his countrymen in the *Daily News* to take this 'notable man' seriously:

The impression is that India is represented by a notable cricketer. Nothing is further from the truth. The Jam Saheb is before all else a statesman—he is among the dozen most enlightened and sagacious statesmen of the Empire . . .

Alan Ross too found Ranji 'an imaginative, conscientious and progressive administrator'. The otherwise perceptive cricket historian Benny Green was also fooled and placed Ranji 'among the most dedicated and most enlightened of all the princes of the Raj' and 'perhaps the only genuinely benevolent autocrat who has ever existed'. Lt. Col. Henry W. Berthon, the Jam Saheb's right hand man and the keeper of the ruler's *abru* (prestige) whenever he went abroad, thought his employer was a 'gifted chief'. As the Jam's second innings progressed there was a concerted attempt to project a dynamic image of his rule into posterity. Pamphleteer Naoroji Dumasia therefore penned these ringing lines by way of tribute to his reign:

> As a cricketer he played many a brilliant innings; as an administrator his performance is still more dazzling and challenges comparison with the most efficient administration in the country.

Admittedly, the two Ranji hagiographies mention the fact of his being ticked off by the British for various acts of commission and omission and also the 'violent attack' by sections of the Indian and British press, 'formented by the more extreme members of the Indian National Congress.' But these were dismissed as pure overkill. The critical document about the Jam Saheb's misrule brought out by the All India States' Peoples' Conference and the excessive publicity given to it by the *Saurashtra* was likewise duly mentioned and then rubbished by Roland Wild and Alan Ross. Wild even claimed that action was taken against the newspaper by the publication of a booklet by the state in which every allegation was answered with facts and figures!

Wild and Ross have alluded that press attacks on the Jam Saheb began with the advent of the *Saurashtra* and the AISPC. But these arguments are specious. The Ranpur-based weekly was started in late

1921 and the AISPC in 1927. Native Press attacks on the Jam Saheb in reality commenced soon after Ranji ascended the *gaddi*, in 1907 itself.

In retrospect, it appears that the AISPC's conclusions in its damning document were almost like a summary of the several critiques of the Jam Saheb in the Native Press over the years. There were allegations that AISPC general-secretary Professor G.R. Abhyankar was behind the *Saurashtra* campaign against the Jam. But the publication's founder, Amritlal Dalpatbhai Sheth was, as a native of Kathiawar, in a better position to provide information on this subject than Abhyankar, who hailed from distant Sangli, at the southern tip of the Bombay Presidency. For all we know, Sheth's regular reports may have provided the ammunition for the AISPC document.

As a high-profile chief, the Jam Saheb was a prime target. But it was not the Jam Saheb alone who was under siege by the Native Press of the region. Due to the reactionary nature of their regimes and their pronounced hostility to the freedom movement and progressive trends, all the 'Rajput looters' of Gujarat and Rajputana were at the receiving end.

The regressive statements of the Maharaja of Bikaner[2], the alleged debaucheries of his brother Sir Bhairusingh, the squeeze on poor farmers by the Thakore of Morvi to recover losses in cotton speculation, the repression of Sir Pratap Singh of Idar and the *zulum* (tyranny) and maladministration of his successor, Lt. Col. Sir Dolatsinhji, all came in for censure.

The Native Press also highlighted the grievances of the Kutch subjects, the atrocities of the Gondal ruler, the depredations of the 'brute' of Alwar, the *zulum* and intrigue of the Nawab of Junagadh, the misrule at Dhrangadhra and the constant globetrotting of the Gaikwad of Baroda. The antics of rulers from outside the region like the Maharaja of Patiala (this 'much pampered pet of the Political Department of the

---

[2]The Maharaja of Bikaner once once claimed to speak for all Indians while stressing his loyalty to the Raj and running down 'agitators' in Bengal and the Punjab.

Government of India' was labelled 'a devil, murderer and assassin'), the Holkar of Indore, the Nizam of Hyderabad, the Nawab of Bhopal and the Scindia of Gwalior were also subjects of ridicule.

The Native Press also couldn't fathom why Native States scented sedition in words like 'motherland', *swadeshi* and 'Bharat' when used in dramas. The States even proscribed the sale of pictures of Lala Lajpatrai, Lokmanya Tilak, Ajitsingh and Surendranath in their territories, something not attempted in British India.

The piqued chiefs on their part were not enamoured of the fourth estate either. The Maharaja of Kashmir simply didn't let any newspapers function in his kingdom. Others like Gwalior[3], Alwar and Patiala merely banned the entry of nationalist publications into their domains, prescribing severe penalties for their possession. At one time, forty-three British Indian newspapers were banned in Patiala.

A general diatribe in the *Gujarati* regarding the 'Complaint about the tyranny exercised over their Subjects by Native Chiefs in Kathiawar' poignantly sums up the prevailing *zulum* in the region:

> A few incidents that have recently come to light go to show how the Indian Chiefs who enjoy the protection of the British Government and who have taken advantage of their non-intervention policy to pursue a tyrannical policy worse than that of the Czar, resent any awakening on the part of their subjects. *An Indian chief who poses as an enlightened ruler has prevented his subjects from taking part in the Kathiawar Political Conference by threats of confiscating their property.*[4] Another Chief who counts peers of the Realm amongst his friends has the audacity to pull down people's residences to widen streets and to refuse to pay any compensation to them. In spite of his being a Hindu he has no objections to destroy temples! A third Chief does not allow his cultivators to sell the cotton they grow. He buys the cotton himself at fixed rates and sells it in Bombay and makes a profit . . . Many petty

---

[3]The Scindia of Gwalior was the only ruler to reportedly prohibit collection of subscriptions for the Jallianwalla Bagh memorial.

[4]Emphasized by the author.

Native States in Kathiawar are guilty of such high-handedness as is seldom seen either in British India or is some of the bigger states. With rare exceptions, people in the Native States of Kathiawar are subjected to an extreme form of tyranny. If a Chief wants money he asks for it from one of his subjects who has grown rich outside his dominions and if the money is given to him he pays no interest and seldom returns the capital. If the Chief's demand is not satisfied the Chief does not hesitate to harass the relatives of the rich man. Many of the Native Chiefs indulge in luxuries and pleasures and think that they have every right over the life and property of their subjects. Such Native States should be annexed by the British Government after making due provision for the decent living of their rulers.

The fact that the excesses of these 'ruling slaves' and 'painted marionettes' in general were tolerated to this extent is a poor commentary on the rectitude of the British Raj. Of course the recalcitrant Native Princes were occasionally pulled up by 'Big Brother', but the government often gave them a long rope.

The Jam Saheb himself was rapped on his knuckles time and again for various improprieties but he continued with his wanton ways. In an early instance, in 1911, despite Nawanagar being devastated by a crippling famine, the Jam blew up pots of money in a lavish show of opulence at the Delhi Durbar held to commemorate the visit of King George V and Queen Mary to India. Incidentally, His Majesty himself (and sections of the Native Press too) had requested the rulers not to splurge on pomp and pageantry at the Royal Durbar[5] in view of the drought—advice which went unheeded by many.

The Jam took a huge loan from the government and blew it up in setting up a lavish camp at the durbar venue and was equally opulent in his banquets and gifts. With Sir Home Gordon as his ADC, he

---

[5]William Wedderburn, the English agitator for Indian aspirations and a president of the Indian National Congress, described it as 'the grandest and most bloodless revolution in history'.

drove to the actual ceremony in a silver coach—which he later desired to present to the King Emperor. It was declined as His Majesty had earlier expressed himself against the receipt of any gifts. This wanton irresponsibility on the Jam Saheb's part not only infuriated the Native Press, it also prompted the Government of India to impose an adviser, Lt. Col. Berthon, to monitor his finances. If at all Nawanagar's finances improved in the future, Berthon should get a large measure of credit for it.

IT must be stressed here at the outset that the Native Press was not initially predisposed in its hostility towards the Jam Saheb. On the contrary, it interpreted his cricketing successes in England as a political statement with a bat and envisaged him challenging British hegemony on the political pitch when he took the field as a ruler in 1907. A host of native papers like the *Gujarati, Parsee, Kathiawar News, Gujarati, Patriot, Jam-e-Jamshed,* in fact, congratulated him on his succession. The *Patriot* hoped his subjects would reap the fullest advantage of his progressive ideas and English education. The *Jam-e-Jamshed* enthused:

> Kumar Ranjitsinhji will have the congratulations of an infinitely larger circle of friends and admirers than any successor to the *gaddi* of a Native State has received as yet. And it will be the prayer of not a few that he may prove himself worthy of these felicitations. He has certainly the making in him of an enlightened and progressive ruler.

The *Indian Spectator* opined that if the new chief showed in his new role half the energy he displayed in his favourite game, he would make a more than average Kathiawar chief. The weekly however clarified that the popularity of the new Jam Saheb with his brother Rajput princes had little to do with his proficiency in cricket. 'It is as a Rajput of pure blood that he has been hailed by his Hindu brother-chiefs,' it stated. Yet, it approvingly noted (that):

> . . . he undertakes the responsibilities of government at an age when with his experience gained in other lands and his observation of the

world, he can discharge them with wisdom and devotion to the interests
of his people . . .

During his reign, the Jam occasionally elicited dollops of praise,
though these were few and far between. In an early appraisal, the
Political Bhomiya singled out his 'high and noble qualities' and the *Bombay
Samachar* eulogised him for 'striking definitely along the path of good
and beneficent government' after the Jam undertook certain works of
public utility. The Jam's revolutionary order in making secondary
education free in his state also prompted the *Mahratta* to affirm (that):

> . . . his commendable zeal in promoting the cause of education has put
> to shame many a prince and Governor in India . . . Nawanagar has
> surpassed even the most liberal Baroda and Mysore in this respect.
> Our poor British Government cannot rear its head before such heroic
> champions.

The Native Press also stood one with the Jam in his campaign
against the reimposition of the Viramgam customs line by the
Government of India in 1927. Taking up cudgels on his behalf, the
Nava Kal argued that the move exposed how the government defied
its treaties and agreements to protect British trade. It was argued that
the move was intended to artificially increase the importance of
Bombay port and curtail the initiative of Chiefs by harassing the prime
mover, the Jam himself. The *Kathiawar Samachar* spoke of the 'great
injustice' done to the Kathiawar ports and especially to the Bedi port
by the Indian Government. Highlighting the Jam's stupendous
contribution to the British cause during the Great War, it asked:

> Could Sir Ranjitsinghji have ever dreamt that he and his State would
> be completely ruined by the un-British act and conduct of the Viceroy
> of India? . . . The Viceroy has acted in the most un-British manner
> with the Jam Saheb and other rulers of Native States in Kathiawar in
> reimposing the land Customs' line at Viramgam violating the terms of
> the Agreement of 1917 and altogether disregarding the solemn promises

given by Sir Evan Maconochie for non-interference. Relying upon the agreement and the most solemn promise of Maconochie the Jam Saheb developed his Bedi port, spending more than a crore of rupees . . .

BUT such favourable coverage was the exception rather than the rule. But if blame is to be apportioned for the negative portrayal of the Jam Saheb in the Native Press, then it could be laid at the blade of the new ruler himself. The Jam Saheb attracted immediate notice over his indifference to the responsibilities of rulership by leaving on a fortnight's shooting expedition to Ratlam no sooner had he been sworn in. Further, his unfortunate incapacitation by typhoid prompted him to escape to England for recuperation—the same place incidentally where he was laid low by a plethora of illness like asthma, influenza etc. He then converted this visit into an extended holiday (from October 1907 to early 1909), disporting himself at cricket, parties and other entertainments, while his state was languishing in penury. In spite of that, after returning home, he continued with his partying in the company of guests he had brought back from England.

All this did not go unnoticed. The first press salvos were fired after Ranji failed to return within a reasonable span of time from England where he had gone to recuperate. Quick to spot this delinquency, *The Jain* hurled the first of the bouncers:

We are glad to hear that the health of His Highness the Jam of Nawanagar has been completely restored by his trip to England. We are however, concerned to learn that he does not think of returning to his capital before next winter. Of course we do not question His Highness' freedom to act as he pleases, but at the same time, we must be allowed the liberty of pointing out that as a ruler he has grave responsibilities resting on his shoulders. He is said to have made a donation of Rs 3,000 to the Sussex Cricket Club and has promised a permanent annual grant of Rs 1,500 to the same institution. That he should assist his sporting comrades in this way no doubt proves the generosity of his disposition; but he should also bear in mind that it is the people's money that he thus gives away, that he controls it as a trustee and not as an absolute master, and that he is bound to use pubic money only for the welfare of the people. At a time when the subjects of the State are in the throes of famine, plague and high prices, it is not seemly for the Jam Saheb to stay away from his capital when it is no longer necessary for him to do so. The Jamnagar State is in an indebted condition and overwhelmed by a succession of bad years. There is also ample scope for the introduction of reforms in the State. We are confident that the Jam Saheb realises the duties and responsibilities of his present position which is quite different from his former position as a great cricketer. We only wish that the Jam Saheb would take a leaf out of the book of our present Governor Sir George Clarke, who ever since his arrival in the country has devoted all his energies to stamp out the plague.

It looks like this caution did not reach the Jam Saheb's ears. Or if it did, he paid no heed to it. Even after his much delayed return from England with a posse of about twenty Englishmen[6] to fill up vacant positions on his staff[7], the Jam Saheb continued with his partying. He was promptly hauled up, among others, by the *Sanj Vartaman*:

It is said that His Highness the Jam Saheb has engaged the famous singer Gohar Jan of Calcutta at the cost of 1000 rupees per day to entertain his European guests. We strongly condemn such an action on the part of the enlightened Jam Saheb who could surely have entertained his guests in some more suitable manner. We feel sure that had the Jam Saheb given more serious thought to the expense to be undergone in this matter, he would have given up the idea altogether. The moneys that His Highness thus squanders are public moneys and should be spent on furthering the welfare of his subjects. His Highness, who has been recently installed on the *gaddi* has just arrived from

---

[6]Among these men were cricketers Harry Simms, the Australian-born Sussex fast bowler and big-hitter who replaced Archie MacLaren as private secretary, Geoffrey Foster, the Oxford University and Worcestershire batsman.

[7]An early indication of his preference for European company—he used to repeatedly flout rules requiring prior sanction and intimation of the government for appointing European officers in his state.

England, ought to have given more attention to his State affairs than to pleasures. His Highness could have better commemorated the visit of his European friends by spending the like amount on some object of public utility.

Another caution quickly followed from the *Kathiawar Times*. It heard rumours that the Jam Saheb was planning another expedition to England—no sooner had he returned home after his maiden trip as Jam Saheb. These endless sallies of Native Princes to foreign climes irked the Native Press no end and even a relatively progressive ruler like the Gaikwad was taunted for this frailty. An anonymous letter writer, protesting this uninterrupted exodus of chiefs abroad in the *Sanj Vartaman*, described this army of emigrants as the saddest and the most shame-faced lot who, out of money looted from their poor subjects, were annually going out for a joyride and picnic resulting in a drain of almost a crore on the economy. Of all the parasites they are the worst that India has ever seen, the letter writer charged.

The Jam Saheb too was in the habit of dashing off abroad at the slightest provocation, so much so that he would be eventually dubbed an 'absentee ruler' by the AISPC. In fact, a perusal of government correspondence reveals that on several issues of the day, where the views of the Nawanagar Durbar were sought, officials noted that it could not be ascertained since the ruler was not in station. Often, it was admitted in Durbar documents that 'considerations of health rendered it necessary that the Jam Saheb should undertake a journey to Europe to undergo special treatment . . .' On other occasions it was claimed that in spite of the 'great drawback of Your Highness' absence in England for the greater part of the year' the secretaries have carried on the administration very smoothly and successfully. Anyway, the *Kathiawar Times* prophetically forecast this alarming tendency on the new ruler's part so early on:

> . . . rumours are current at Rajkot that His Highness the Jam of Nawanagar, who has not been keeping good health, has been

recommended by his medical advisers to go on a voyage, and that His Highness might probably proceed to England in a short time for six months or so. If the rumours be true, it is certainly to be regretted that Indian chiefs should on some pretence or other absent themselves from their territories for weeks and months, nay even for a year or more, to the detriment of the interests of the people over whose destinies they preside. It is, for many reasons, highly objectionable that these Indian Chiefs should be allowed to leave their own territories for distant lands twice, thrice or even five times in a decade. When it is seriously alleged that European administrators lose all touch with the people whom they rule by their frequent visits to hill stations, which after all are situated in the country, what might be said of our own Indian Chiefs who consider themselves justified in leaving their States for Europe twice in three years or even shorter periods? The Government of India should put their foot down on such practices without fear or favour. The evil seems to be on the increase, and stronger measures might be adopted to put a stop to it.

It was not that the Government of India was not alive to this recurring probem. It was already seized of the issue and felt that the time had come to arrest the frequent and prolonged visits of certain Native Princes to Europe. Even though it was conceded that the habit had become so chronic as to prove incurable, the Viceroy had decided to suggest to the Princes in personal conversation that it was okay for them to leave their kingdoms once in three years for tours to Europe.

But three years down the line it was conceded that in case of 'confirmed and hopeless offenders' like the Gaikwad, Jam Saheb and the rulers of Kapurthala and Rajpipla, it would be almost cruel and in any case useless to reform their inveterate habits. In fact, a hapless Viceroy, Lord Irwin, informed Lord Peel[8] in 1929 that the Maharani of Baroda had complained bitterly about the failure of the government to discourage the European jaunts of her husband and other habitual offenders like Kapurthala, Rajpipla and Nawanagar who were described

---

[8]Lord Peel was then the Secretary of State for India.

as 'the most prominent exponents of absentee landlordism in the last ten years.' According to the statistics, the Gaikwad and Kapurthala each spent eight months in Europe per year since 1919, while Nawanagar and Rajpipla averaged between four-five months away from their states per year.

Apparently, the Jam Saheb was also in the habit of rushing to various Native States where the ruler was in trouble for some reason or the other. British officials thought that his help and advice were not being offered from disinterested motives. So they decided to caution him about it. Even Lord Birkenhead, in charge of the India Office, had a word with the Jam Saheb on the subject. But the Jam countered by saying that he could not refuse the entreaties of his brother princes if they requested his presence.

This constant travelling was but one aspect of the Jam Saheb's unconcern for his job. His apparent don't-care-a-damn-attitude to his responsibilities from so early on, the continuing state of paralysis and the emerging signs of tyranny in Nawanagar were alarming enough to provoke this stinging rebuke from the *Baroda Gazette*:

People have grave doubts about the Jamnagar Treasury being in a satisfactory state. They have reason to entertain such doubts. The general public and especially the village agriculturists are very much harassed. When the present Jam Saheb came to the *gaddi* people expected that their woes would soon end. But there has been no change in their condition and they are disappointed in their hopes. The land tax in Jamnagar is the heaviest in all the Kathiawar States. The agriculturist in that State is, besides, overburdened in other ways. When the Jam Saheb is on tour his staff have to be provided with beddings by the villagers. The beddings lent out are rarely returned. The villagers are not in a position to complain in the matter. It is sedition to lodge such complaints. The condition of the villages in the State is very poor. Any one having no means to accommodate the Jam's men is proceeded against in a law court. There is no one to espouse the cause of such people who are groaning under tyranny. If a villager with his cart is seen by a State peon the cart is taken hold of by the latter. Hire is rarely paid to the villager. The Jam has Europeanised his court and he invites friends from England whom he treats with lavish hospitality. No reform worth the name has been introduced in the State. The internal management of the States in Kathiawar gradually leads to their decline and to the impoverishment of the people. We pray the Jam Saheb to realise his duties and responsibilities as a ruler and make efforts for promoting the happiness of his people.

Some of the adverse publicity also resulted from the Jam's own lack of administrative experience. One early gaffe, meant to rectify the fall in consumption of salt, was his directive to each town and village to determine the fixed quantity of salt that each person and house shall purchase with the police being authorized to enforce it. Taking exception to this queer diktat, the *Akbhar-e-Soudagar* queried what people should do if they had no money to purchase the fixed quantity, saying it was at a loss to understand what aid the police could give in this matter. It acknowledged that a fall in consumption of salt would tell upon public health and state finances but stressed that any compulsion to consume a fixed amount was undesirable. It suggested that the best course to raise consumption is to sell salt cheaper and advised the Jam Saheb to revoke the order and take proper steps for raising consumption at an early date.

But such ill-considered *faux pas* were often compounded by deliberate excesses on the administration's part. The reporter 'Pharos' alleged in a report on the 'Evil of forced labour in Kathiawar' in the *Hindusthan*, that 'the present Jam of Jamnagar, who ought to be an enlightened ruler has had most of his private buildings in his State, built by coolies who were never remunerated'. A development confirmed (unintentionally, perhaps) by Roland Wild who observed that the Jam Saheb himself 'was spurring on gangs of workmen, under forced labour' to rebuild a guest house for the use of his first state guest, the Maharaja of Patiala in December 1913.

A conservative at heart, the Jam Saheb, like other Native Princes, was not inclined to view favourably the advance of representative institutions in the country. No wonder his regressive views on the question of self-government for Indians at the time of the formulation of the Morley-Minto Reforms of 1909 were along expected lines. The Native Press was not inclined to take kindly to such views. Incidentally, the Jam's reactionary views on the subject, like those expressed by his mentor Sir Pratap Singh, Sir T. Bhashyam Iyengar[9] and others of their ilk, pointed to a calculated orchestration of the Indian loyalist chorus by the imperial baton wielders. On his part, the Jam had told a 'celebrated German author and journalist' who visited him in 1909:

> Our ancestors were educated to be idle. Indulgence and extravagance were held up before their eyes as most sacred duties. It is only in the English schools that we were taught the lessons of *noblesse oblige*. While our forefathers were living luxuriously and at the cost of their subjects, the Indian Princes of today are working hard to advance the welfare of their people. We still want Great Britain's strong hand to lead and support us in spite of our advance in civilization. We continue to be like children. Neither at present nor at any time will the diverse elements of India be united into one single nation. Neither at present nor at any future time will India be fit for self-government; but under Britain's benevolent and powerful guidance, India will become a powerful and dominating factor in the world's arena of nations, the markets of the world . . . .

The Native Press expectedly took offence and retribution was quick to follow. *The Indu Prakash* hit back saying:

> His Highness the Jam of Jamnagar is reported to have said that the Indians are not and will never be fit for self-government . . . For aught we know there must be some misunderstanding somewhere if His Highness the Jam did express himself on the subject. If he really did so, all that can be said is that he is yet quite a novice in the branch on which he is reported to have expressed himself in this way. If there was a question of 'donning the flannels' on the part of the Indians to

---

[9]Sir T.B. Iyengar claimed that British rule was sanctioned by the *shastras*.

play the 'fools', his opinion could carry weight and authority . . .
Prince Ranji of cricket fame must be conscious of the fact that he has
just entered upon learning the ABC of the practical side of the art of
the administration and that therefore a good part of the time must
elapse before His Highness the Jam Saheb Ranjitsinghji is qualified to
throw undeserved reflections on the patriotic efforts of not only the
best of his countrymen, but even upon those of his brother rulers
who have now embarked upon a system of representative Government,
to wit, Mysore, Travancore and above all, Baroda, nearer home.

The *Bhala* too fired a broadside, claiming that the Jam Saheb was
reiterating the views of vested interests:

> We do not think his utterances would in any way damp the ardour of
> Indians for the achievement of self-government. The diversity of its
> races can never be a bar to India's reaching its goal, for it has already
> enjoyed *swarajya* (self-rule) under similar circumstances some time back.
> The tide of progress is advancing and it is futile to think of checking
> it by any earthly means.

TWO other issues on which the Jam took much stick were the
celebrated Premchand Keshavji sedition case, echoes of which reached
even the British Parliament, and the Amran Talukdar case. Premchand,
a Bombay cloth merchant and Jamnagar subject, was held on a charge
of alleged treason[10], fined one lakh rupees and sentenced to ten years'
imprisonment. A few papers defended the Jam's action, like the
Kathiawar News, which found it 'not only just but merciful' as 'for the
last few years, certain persons have been engaged in hatching treasonable
plots against the Jam'.

But many journals saw red. The *Gujarati* termed it 'the crowning
piece of maladministration in the State', wondering whether the heavy
fine of one lakh rupees was imposed with the object of making up the
loss caused to the State treasury by the Saturnalia in honour of the

---

[10]For aiding a rival's bid for the *gaddi* and opposing Ranji's candidature some ten
years before.

Jam's friends. The *Gujarati Punch* dubbed the punishment 'tyrannical and unjust' and said the people were 'horror-stricken' with the news. The *Kathiawar Times* reported that 'the scandal has been exercising the minds of the public throughout the country' and so generous and justice-loving a ruler as the Jam could not afford to take resource to such actions.

In the other controversial case concerning the Amran Talukdar, Khavas Ravaji Shamji, was allegedly kept in solitary confinement along with his Karbhari and other servants and not allowed to see each other nor any outsider; nor was he given a regular public trial. His taluka was also confiscated. The reason: his son Ratansingh, a Khavas by caste, married a Rajput girl, Surajba of Morvi, in spite of the Jam's prohibitory order at the instance of a neighbouring ruler who wanted to prevent the inter-caste marriage.

This retrogade order resulted in a severe drubbing to the progressive image of the Jam Saheb. The Jam took the position that the marriage was a presumptuous misalliance insulting and derogatory to His Highness' own Jadeja class, a defilement of the purity of Rajput blood and an offence against the Jam Saheb's pride of race. The Talukdar claimed the Jam's forbiddance was received only after the marriage ceremony was performed. He also supplied twenty-four instances of such prior marriages between his family and Rajputs, of which eleven belonged to the Jam Saheb's 'own boasted Jadeja clan'. Yet, Surabja was allegedly forced to again marry illegally a petty policeman of Morvi.

The fracas led to a series of petitions and counter-petitions to the highest authority. On one occasion, the Jam called on the Viceroy, Lord Hardinge, at Simla, the summer capital, to explain his viewpoint. The Viceroy took the opportunity to counsel him about his debts and private expenses. Later, he described the encounter in a private letter to Lord Willingdon, then Governor of Bombay and later Viceroy of India, saying he found the Jam 'delightfully pleasant and agreeable . . . and extremely plausible in all that he says' but nevertheless 'a rather slippery gentleman'.

To stem these and other criticisms the Jamnagar Durbar put out a Press Communiqué. This move was welcomed but the Durbar's arguments were flayed by the *Gujarati*, *Sanj Vartaman*, *Praja Bandhu* and others. The latter bluntly stated that as long as Premchand was denied a fair and impartial public trial and not allowed to exercise all the ordinary privileges of an accused person, there would be no cessation of comments in the press. About the Amran case, it wanted to know under what law his behaviour was an offence and reasoned that at worst an inter-caste marriage could only be construed as a 'social wrong' with which the State has no concern whatsoever.

The *Gujarati* on its part first lectured the Jam about his lackadaisical administration and reverting to the Premchand case later said the (Press) Communiqué left it 'altogether unconvinced.' There was nothing in it to show that the evidence was recorded in the accused's presence, or that he was given an opportunity to cross-examine the witnesses, the paper stated. It also delivered a stinging retort on the Amran case:

> . . . We wind up these observations by noticing one remark which we find at the end of the Communiqué. It is a pleasure to note that His Highness does not resent press criticism. Admitting that kings are not infallible the Communiqué wishes in the usual strain that newspapers should take care to be better informed before criticising. The Communiqué relates that the principle details of the Amran affair were brought to the notice of the Agency officers. Will the administration say what prevented them from keeping the public informed of these? . . .

Surprisingly, even after relenting and setting Premchand free, instead of earning plaudits, there were brickbats for the Jam, The *Jain* advised 'self-seeking' Jain leaders to refrain from presenting an address of thanks to His Highness for the release of Premji, saying that the community was reduced to secondary status under the new regime and such a gesture would be misconstrued as an endorsement of his rule.

It must be mentioned that the Anglo-Indian media was generally partial to the Jam Saheb but even it could not always ignore the rumblings in the Native Press. *The Briton*, voicing friendly concern, asked the government to institute a probe into the Jam's affairs, if only to absolve him from press criticism:

> We should like to know when the Government of India proposes to institute an enquiry into the financial affairs of His Highness the Jam of Nawanagar. The affairs of this prince have been the subject of considerable comment in Bombay during the past few weeks and certain statements made have been of such a character that they demand immediate attention. The prince, as is well known, has many interests in Europe and the West, and it certainly seems a pity that inaccurate impressions regarding his affairs and the affairs of his state, should be permitted to retain a place in the public mind. We think that, in this case in particular, the Government of India should make a definite pronouncement to the effect that the State is not involved, or order an enquiry into the allegations which are being made with much freedom.

What the *Briton* did not know was that the government was acutely concerned. As early as 1912 the Governor of Bombay found it necessary to address a 'forcible remonstration' to the Jam Saheb regarding his attitude to the reorganistion of the state finances. But after an inquiry was ordered to see if he had complied with the directives it was found that there had been a change for the better, what with Berthon, who was imposed on the administration, assisting the Jam on the financial front.

Thus, the Jam would face the music on two fronts—British officialdom and his Indian critics. He had his fair share of tangles with authority over various issues and sometimes must have deeply resented the condescending treatment he received from petty officials. He may have thought he was an equal of the Englishman by virtue of being an English cricket hero. But here, even the Bombay Gymkhana blackballed him when he applied for membership.

He was always being ticked off for some failing or the other by 'Big Brother' who was always watching over him. But being a combative person by nature, especially in the defence of his rights and interests, the Jam Saheb always fought every challenge till the last possible step.

As resentment against the Jam Saheb's perceived misrule increased and since he apparently showed no intention to reform himself, he became a perennial target of the Native Press—whether for the 'benevolent despotism' he practised, the 'unparalleled autocracy' prevalent in his kingdom or the 'various kinds of oppressive taxes' introduced in his state at the least provocation.

Any occasion, it seemed, was good enough to berate the Jam Saheb—when he delivered an innocuous speech, when he received a dignitary, when the misdeeds of other rulers were being reported, or when he was selected as India's representative for an international assignment. This last act provoked the *Saurashtra* to query about 'the depth of the hypocrisy and the intrigue underlying His Highness the Jam Saheb going to the Peace Conference as India's representative and presenting there the case of small nations of the world, in such a way as would charm, after devising a system of administration for his own State that would suck the blood of his subjects'.

The Jam was also pilloried for the vast sums of money blown up either on himself or on entertaining personal or official guests like Governors and Viceroys. The line-up of guests, both personal and official, was impressive and included Viceroys like Lords Reading and Irwin, Governors like Lords Willingdon and Sir George Lloyd and luminaries and social butterflies like General Sir Blindon Blood, Earl and Countess of Londesborough, Lady Irene Denison, French Prince Antonie D'Orleans Bragmic, the Geman Count and Countess of Koenigsmark, the Strangmans, the Pilkingtons (the Post-Master General and his wife), civil servant and writer Charles Kincaid, Sir Edwin Lutyens, Sir Lock Elliot, Major, Mrs and Miss Lang, Rabindranath Tagore, Lord and Lady Seymour, Baron and Baronness Cederstorm, Sir T. Wynne and Lady Patricia Ward among others. In addition, there were frequent visits of his brother princes but this rather elaborate guest list included hardly any political leaders of British India—unlike Bikaner and Patiala, the Jam Saheb did not believe in talking to 'the enemy', it seems.

Such extravagance on the princes' part went against the grain of the times, ordained as they were by the austere lifestyles and spirit of self-sacrifice of the leaders of India's freedom movement. But the Jam Saheb's prodigality was justified by his chroniclers as the need to maintain the *abru* (pride) of his state or because of his 'keen appreciation' of the value of display of pomp and ceremony to the Indian people. Incidentally, while himself prone to monumental opulence, the Jam had no qualms in lecturing the League of Nations on financial accountability when he was a delegate to the august body in 1920. His splendid views on financial propriety expressed at Geneva are worthy of recall:

> India has been prominent in criticism of the finances of the League. But Gentlemen, please understand that from our point of view what we most hope for is a sound system of external control over the spending department . . . First: such control is the strongest means of winning confidence in our economical working; and secondly: and above all because such control defends our Secretariat from unjust criticism . . . I have a strong and definite objection to the Secretary General or any one else being in a position of uncontrolled freedom, or if freedom is merely nominally controlled, in regard to expenditure. Such a position is not fair to him and it is nor fair to public opinion . . . After all, the money we spend is derived from all members of the League and the Assembly alone represents all members of the League . . .

At home the situation was exactly in reverse with the Jam Saheb giving free vent to his own lavish proclivities. So much so that the *Rajasthan Kesari* mourned that 'the tremendous outcries of the people against the extravagant expenditure of Ranjitsinhji of Jamnagar fall on deaf ears'. The Native Press in fact carried out a sustained campaign against the Jam's financial profligacy. Observers' 'Reflections on the purchase of an estate in Ireland by His Highness the Jam Saheb of Nawanagar' in the *Sanj Vartaman* superbly illustrates these sentiments:

> Those who have been watching 'Ranji' for some time will not be surprised at this latest prank of the Maharaja. It is now as clear as the

noon-day sun that His Highness's mind is not on his job, that is, he is not inclined to attend the affairs of his own State. He is the worst example of the absentee Maharaja and could not even bring forward the false excuse of health to cover his almost permanent absence from India. During recent years his visits to his State have been of a short duration and fewer in number. Whenever he returns to India he has a host of so-called sporting hangers-on. With them he wastes his time and money (the money of his poor subjects) and after a stay of a few months, he again runs away to Europe, to new fields and pastures of pleasure and enjoyment. The time has arrived when the Government of India must intervene to put a stop to this most scandalous of affairs . . . when one Maharaja buys a castle in Ireland, another buys a palace in Paris and a third has a palatial residence in London. I think the limit of extravagance has been reached and the time has arrived to cry 'halt'. There is not the least doubt that these princely spendthrifts create altogether a false notion that India's cry of poverty is a bogus one when they see so much money wasted—criminally wasted—by these princelings simply for their own pleasure and enjoyment. Public opinion will be solidly at the back of the Indian Government if the latter take prompt measures to put an end to this growing and scandalous evil.

There was no let up of criticism on this score and the Jam was continuously at the receiving end, as evinced from this critical summary of his administration by the *Taqat*:

. . . The reports we have of the pleasure-loving activities of His Highness are shameful to an extreme. His pleasure-seeking can be judged by the fact that neither is he aware of the administration of his State nor does he know aught of the difficulties in which the helpless inhabitants are involved. His sole and most beloved hobby is that he goes on a pilgrimage to Europe and there spends money to his heart's satisfaction. This bachelor Prince spends on himself at least 30 lakhs per annum while the State is in such an unfortunate condition that every department stands in need of reform; education is absolutely neglected and there is neither any first class college in Jamnagar nor any good high school.

We invite attention of the Maharaja to these things and request him to bring about a reform in himself, otherwise we shall fully expose him.

On the related charge of burning money on Viceregal and gubernatorial visits to the Native States, the Jam also took much stick. How much this issue rankled the Native Press can be understood from this incisive piece in the *Gujarati* on 'How wealth of Native States is wasted' during such visitations:

> . . . costly shows and displays and magnificent banquets and entertainments are a regular feature of these tours. Naturally Governors and Viceroys leave it to their princely hosts to spend or waste as much money as they wish to do. As a ruler the total outlay is a mote out of proportion to any good that might conceivably ensue from these tours which are primarily designed for the purpose of sight-seeing and indulging in mutual laudation and oft-repeated platitudes. Then, there are European guests, either official or non-official, and tourists from Europe or America who have from time to time to be hospitably entertained, if the Princes concerned are to have a pleasant and proud record in the books of the Foreign Department. During every Viceregal and gubernatorial tour Their Excellencys are of course vastly pleased with their Highnesses' splendid hospitality and magnificent displays of gorgeous splendour, or munificent donations. But none is inclined to pause for a moment, interrogate his conscience before God and man and find out how the State exchequers are filled and how far the taxes paid by the helpless subjects are utilised towards the promotion of their moral and material well-being.

The outcry in the Native Press about these spending excesses by the region's rulers and especially the staged shoots that passed off as shikar also provoked a certain M.K. Gandhi to express his own concerns on this emotive subject in *Young India* when the Governor of Bombay, Sir George Lloyd, toured Kathiawar in 1922:

> It seems that the Princes of Kathiawad have arranged *shikar* parties and other non-political but expensive amusements arranged in his honour.

Probably the Governor does not even appreciate them. Why should these functionaries always want amusements? It is not as if they are without any whilst working at headquarters. Indeed these amusements must become a task for at least some of them . . . In the circumstances it would certainly save a great deal of time and expense if these amusements were cut down and visits limited to State business only. Moreover the *shikar* parties offend vegetarian Kathiawad. The people of Kathiawad cannot but resent, even when they say nothing, the waste of animal life for no purpose whatsoever. I am told that in order to draw the beasts of prey, goats have to be sacrificed for days in advance. Such *shikar* over which so much innocent blood is split and is without any risk of life and limb on the *shikari*, is robbed of all charm and becomes a mild copy of the law that prevails between the Government and the people of India, whereby the public are always the sport of the Government which never runs any risk. It is not the mosaic law of tooth for tooth but it is the law of bullets against brickbats, life for a scratch. When the hunter runs no risk it is not good sport but downright cruelty . . .

But the legend of Nawanagar was not going to be fazed by such opinions, even assuming they were brought to his notice. An ace shot and a good shikari himself, the Jam always provided great shikar for his distinguished guests. The Jamnagar correspondent of the *Kathiawar Opinion* filed this alarming report about the groundwork being done for Lord Reading's visit in 1924:

Preparations are going on in full swing for arranging a hunting tour for His Excellency the Viceroy. Orders have been issued to bring tigers from Delhi. Men have been sent for buying tigers. Now when these tigers are brought down, they will be set free at places reserved for *shikar*. These tigers will spread terror in villages. They will injure the children and cattle of the poor farmers. Still, if anyone will molest the tigers meant for *shikar* he will be severely dealt with. He will be imprisoned, fined and punished. People cannot defend themselves in the Jamnagar State. Why should His Highness the Jam Saheb who gives long lectures in the Conference of Independent Nations of the world rob the independence of the people?

The insinuation that wild animals meant for shikar enjoyed better status than the common man in Nawanagar found its echo in an earlier report by the *Saurashtra* about the harassment of subjects by State officials for molesting hunting leopards. The paper reported that one Nagubha Kanjibha had alleged that he was fired at and his mare wounded because he was suspected of killing a hunting leopard belonging to the (Jamnagar) State. 'We are struck dumb to hear about the brutality openly exercised in the State of a Prince who proclaims loudly his views about civilization, education, independence and self-determination,' it thundered, while expressing on behalf of all readers its 'anger and contempt for the crude policy of Jamnagar'.

Be that as it may, the Jam Saheb was an undoubted master at hospitality and was said to have excelled himself, expenditure-wise, on each subsequent visit of a bigwig to his State. The entertainment expenditure of the Jam in fact became a national and international scandal of sorts. Reginald Reynolds charged in the *White Sahibs in India* that the Jam was guilty of spending fifty per cent of his state revenues on himself and the entertainment of Viceroys and lesser British officials, European and Indian royalty and cricketing cronies. Reynolds's 'scorecard' of the Jam's expenses for visits of top British officials reads as follows: 50,000 pounds on Lord Sydenham, 80,000 on Lord Willingdon, 115,000 on Sir George Lloyd and the same for Lord Reading, 200,000 on Lord Irwin.

These 'scores' even appeared in the national press in their rupee equivalent. The Delhi Hindi daily, *Arjun*, in an explosive story headlined 'Enjoyment of Indian Princes' combined a scathing attack on this wanton expenditure by the chiefs with an expose of the sexual antics of certain unnamed Princes.[11] It was also echoed by another Hindi daily, the *Dainik Bartaman* of 'Cawnpore' (Kanpur) under the headline '75 lakhs wasted'. Here is what the *Arjun* said about the Jam Saheb and other rulers:

---

[11]On this front there was apparently no whiff of scandal attached to the Jam Saheb who was said to have had a respectful attitude towards women.

Just three years past a Maharaja Bahadur gave proof of his loyalty to the Government by spending 6 lakhs on a tea party given in honour of the Viceroy. We have not forgotten that the Jam Saheb of Nawanagar spent 7 lakhs on the reception of Lord Sydenham, 10 lakhs in welcoming Lord Willingdon, 5 lakhs for gaining the goodwill of Sir George Lloyd and 5 lakhs for pleasing Lord Reading and 25 lakhs on the visit of Lord Irwin, the present Viceroy. The details of the 25 lakhs are as follows. . . . Besides this 3 lakhs were spent on items not to be disclosed. When such statements are published in English papers the British people cannot form an idea of the growing poverty of India and cannot believe the statement that the people of India are starving.

The story of the Maharja of Patiala's love of dogs is still fresh. Last time when he paid a visit to England he spent lakhs of rupees in purchasing dogs. Seeing this, the lovers of dogs in England began to wonder. We shall never forget how he was praised for his love of dogs in the English papers.

Most of the Princes are by heredity impotent but to show to the public they marry not only one or two but dozens of women, who lament over their unhappy lots and curse their parents who had given them in marriage. This woeful tale does not end here, they are forced to lead shameful and demoniacal lives. I depict a scene based on facts and it runs as follows:

The Raja Sahib and his State officials sit together and take wine until they get mad. The Raja Sahib then sends for his two or three selected Ranis and orders the officials to satisfy their sexual desire by turns. The Raja Sahib sits on a high chair and looks with lustful eyes at the satanic acts of his officials and feels a great pleasure.

Once a Rani, just as she entered the room of sin, shot dead one official who advanced to hold her in his arms and then levelled the revolver at the Prince saying: 'Is not your life at my mercy, but religion forbids me.' She shot herself and died.

Now let us turn to another Prince. His time is spent in sexual pleasure and hunting, eating and drinking are the objects of his life. A respectable missionary related to me this story witnessed by himself:

The Maharaja comes well dressed in his Dewan Khana and drinking commences. On certain occasions His Highness' friends and companions are also invited and they are maddened by drinks. Somehow or the other their wives, daughters, mothers and sisters are also called. Black bandages are bound on the eyes of both the men and women. Sometimes the daughter goes to the father, sister to her brother, son to the mother etc. When they have misbehaved under the influence of intoxication their bandages are removed and the Maharaja delights in calling them:

Wrongdoer with his daughter, Wrongdoer with his sister, Wrongdoer with his mother.

THESE constant denunciations in the Native Press obviously had the measure of the Jam. Not possessed of the inclination to reflect critically on his own lifestyle, he harboured a lasting impression of the Native Press as blackmailers, a view obviously shared by other Native Princes—and even some top government officials. One Kathiawar official even suggested that reports of injustice and maladministration in Native States were published with the sole object of extorting money from the Native Princes and hence should be ignored by government. The *Kathiawar Samachar* disagreed, arguing that such an opinion would encourage Native Princes to continue oppressing their subjects while keeping government pleased by the art of sheer flattery. The cries of the poor and helpless subjects groaning under tyranny would thus be forcibly drowned, it claimed.

The Jam's repressed emotions on this sensitive issue unfortunately got the better of him at a function in Rajkot in honour of the Governor of Bombay, Sir George Clarke, in 1910, where he made an intemperate claim that the Gujarati press was blackmailing the Native Princes. The *Rashtramat* decided to take on the Jam, but only after taking a dig at the Governor's Durbar speech lavishing praise on the valour and fighting qualities of Rajput princes . . .

There was something ludicrously pathetic about a certain remark which Prince Ranji, the Jam of Nawanagar made when proposing the health of His Excellency the Governor at the official banquet given to him.

. . . It appears from the Jam Saheb's speech that certain Gujarati journals published in British India have for long carried on a regular trade in blackmailing—the victims, being the Indian Princes . . . It is really a pity that there should be a kind of reptile press in Gujarat. But even these journalistic reptiles should not be condemned unheard . . . No Kathiawar Chief need be afraid of these journalistic leeches if, like Caesar's wife, his administration is 'above suspicion' . . . There is not a more leprous coward in the world that the professional blackmailer—nothing more heinous when he is a journalist. But we have no sympathy to spare when a sporting Rajput prince like the Jam of Nawanagar, with a rueful face, approaches the Governor of Bombay and begs to be rid of these blackmailing vermin. We are glad to see that Sir George Clarke is emphatically of the same opinion. Like a diplomat that he is, Sir George, of course, heartily sympathised with the Jam Saheb and the other Chiefs rowing in the same boat as he. But he made a present to the Chief of Nawanagar almost of a wet blanket when he said: 'I hope that the Princes and Chiefs will realise that the lucubrations of these papers can do no harm, and that no one whose opinions are of value would for a moment be influenced by anything they may publish.' Rather cold comfort this— and, perhaps, the Jam Saheb felt that silence on the point would have been more than golden. Let the princes set their own houses in order and they will be in a position to snap their fingers at all blackmailers.

Nearly two decades later the Jam Saheb would again hurl this blackmailing charge against his *bete noire*, the *Saurashtra*, with even more disastrous consequences. The fearless *Saurashtra* (the forerunner of the group that also spawned the *Phulchaab* at Rajkot and the *Janmabhoomi* in Bombay in the early thirties) became the scourge of the 222 chiefs of Kathiawar in general and the Jam Saheb in particular. Founder Amritlal Dalpatbhai Sheth was born to a Vanik teacher in Limbdi and after an uphill struggle against hostile living conditions, too became a teacher. He soon came under the influence of the radical barrister, Popatlal Chudgar, and qualified to become one himself, ultimately advancing to the post of magistrate of Limbdi.

Despite his exalted position, Sheth was moved by the harassment of common people indulging in Gandhian spinning by British officers in Dhrangadhra. Nobody was prepared to publish this news even though it was sent to the Bombay press. He also despaired of the misrule of the Dharangadhra Dewan, Mansinghji Jhala, a big oppressor, and the enslavement of the people in his own state.

So he went to Bombay and lashed out against these atrocities and the silence of the dailies at a public meeting in July 1921, regretting that the people had no organ to give vent to their true feelings. One Jagjivan Das got up from the audience and asked him why he didn't then publish the news himself. Sheth replied he would, if given Rs 25,000 to start a paper. His wish was granted. He resigned his job as judge, ignoring entreaties by the Thakore of Limbdi and renounced his possessions. On 1 September 1921, he launched his weekly, *Saurashtra*, from Ranpur in Ahmedabad district and across the border from Kathiawar, with a thundering editorial:

> . . . Wherever there is lack of freedom in the small or big states of
> Saurashtra or oppression to be overcome, we are there to give freedom
> . . . where there is expectation of freedom, we are there to bring it to
> realisation and to give strength to that realisation . . .

A champion of the struggle against misrule in the Native States and the freedom movement in Kathiawar, Sheth was associated with the formation of the Kathiawar Political Conference and the All-India States' Peoples' Conference.[12] During the Dandi *satyagraha*, Sheth and his followers 'made salt' on the shores of the Gulf of Cambay, near Dhokla, and courted mass arrest. His articles exhorting people to fight the British and the Native Princes created ripples in the region and he soon was bestowed the affectionate sobriquet 'Saurashtra Lion'. In 1927, Sheth fearlessly declared:

---

[12]More on these Conferences in subsequent chapters.

> I don't care for anybody when I'm speaking the truth. Whether Kathiawar
> is with me or not I will do what my inner voice tells me. Even if all
> forces of the Jam Saheb, all his power and wealth are against me, I will
> stand firmly by the truth and convey what my inner voice tells me to
> the world.

The weekly was outlawed in the Native States and repressed by
the British too, having to cease publication on more than one occasion.
It also faced several legal challenges from enraged Native States for its
fearsome writings. Very often, the Kathiawar Princes banned its entry
in their territories along with other crusading papers. Sheth himself
was mentioned in several secret government dispatches as a subversive
who needed to be watched carefully. But the *Saurashtra's* crusading
zeal earned the wholehearted respect of the Native Press. Commenting
on a ban placed on its entry within the limits of the Kathiawar agency
for publication of 'objectionable articles', the *Salar* screamed:

> The *Saurashtra* has been doing yeoman service in exposing the tyrannies
> of the Kathiawar Agency States. The Jam Saheb of Nawanagar is very
> much displeased with it . . . . the entire Indian press must lodge a
> written protest against it and get this order cancelled . . .

Saurashtra also faced prosecutions many times during its existence.
On one occasion it attracted government censure because it defined
the youth of the country as a 'revolter' and a revolutionary and not a
reformist. Such ideas, a government official alleged, would 'misdirect
the mental attitude of youth of the country'. But Mahatma Gandhi gave
it an unabashed thumbs up. He bestowed upon Sheth a blessing, stating
that he was greatly impressed by his fearless writings and asked him to
keep it up. The Mahatma visited the *Saurashtra* office in April 1925 and
the Sheth maxim of listening to one's inner voice that the Mahatma
spotted at the entrance moved him enough to record his approval of it:

> This is one thing which I feel like learning. Even if people who are
> considered to be meek, express their inner voice, they should be praised.

Everybody should learn from *Saurashtra* and seek the pure, total, calm, freedom . . .

Ranjitsinhji, 'the Lion that Conquers in Battle', would be unable to tame Sheth, the 'Saurashtra lion'. On the contrary, the prince would get worsted in battle. A direct confrontation arose when the Jam called Sheth a blackmailer in a speech at a banquet in early 1931 given by the Yuvrak and Yuvrani at Gondal on the occasion of the marriage of their daughter with the Maharaja of Bhavnagar. The *Times of India* gleefully reported the speech in its columns, prompting the *Saurashtra* to slap a one lakh-rupee damages suit for libel and defamation against its editor. The weekly then announced its intended course of action in an impassioned diatribe against the Jam Saheb:

. . . This poor prince could not endure the attacks commenced by the *Saurashtra* in connection with the brave people who are being ground down in the mill of oppression of the Jam Saheb. Hence he became irritated and gave vent in this way to the flames of his wrath, which has been pent up within him for such a long time. This is the long and short of the whole episode. We do not feel that by his speech he has in any way enhanced his reputation as a statesman of Kathiawar. Only one thing out of two can be true. Either the Jam Saheb is a liar or we are blackmailers. We have often stated that the Jam Saheb is a liar. But this statement of ours had not received the seal of confirmation by a court of justice up to this day. Hence we have arranged to bring this matter before the highest tribunal of justice under the British jurisdiction, viz, the Bombay High Court. The Jam Saheb lays down the principle that blackmailers are found sooner or later behind prison bars. To this we want to make the following straight addition—if such blackmailers belong to a royal family, then they have sooner or later to lose their crowns and thrones; and sometimes it becomes difficult even to save their heads. And who are the blackmailers in Kathiawar today? Who robbed the *gira* of Amran with its annual income of lakhs of rupees? Has that not been robbed unjustly? Has it not been robbed through intimidation by the rulers on the strength of his military force? Who

> plundered the *giras* of Panchdevda? Was it also not done through threats
> and intimidation? Who and in what manner, plundered money in
> various ways from many rich *soukars*? Jam Saheb, you are an unrivalled
> robber of Kathiawar as has been depicted above, and hence you are so
> well aware of the condition to which robbers are reduced.

Alarmed by this legal threat, the *Times of India* editor confidentially
wrote to the British authorities at Rajkot asking them to put him on
track of any specific instance where blackmail by the *Saurashtra* might
be provable. But despite a careful scrutiny of their files the officials
were unable to come up with any such evidence except for pointing
out Sheth's 'bad record' and his constant targeting of the Kathiawar
rulers. Even the Jam Saheb had failed to produce any real evidence in
support of his allegation, they confessed. The 'Old Lady of Boribunder'
was forced to compromise the case by shelling out a princely sum of
Rs 10,000 from which Sheth deducted Rs 2,000 for expenses on the
petition and donated Rs 7,500 to the Saurashtra Trust.

The British hated its guts but they treated the *Saurashtra* with
grudging respect. For example, when the Chief of Bajana, Malek Shri
Kamalkhan Jivankhan, complained to the Viceroy's secretary about the
'grossly false and highly malicious allegation' printed by *Saurashtra* in
a petition to the Political Agent, the Chief himself was ticked off for
his 'immorality and general behaviour which is becoming notorious'
and administered a 'very severe warning' by the authorities. So fearless
were the *Saurashtra* owners that when, at the instance of princely states
like Nawanagar, Dhrangadhra, Morvi, Gondal, the publication was
proscribed in July 1931 under the Post Office Act in the Western India
States Agency, the paper retaliated by serving a notice against the
Secretary of State challenging the legality of its decision and asking
for damages.

TO combat the scourge of unfavourable press in British India, the
Native Princes, under the aegis of the newly formed Chamber of
Princes, an organization founded to promote princely interests at the

behest of the imperial rulers in 1921, managed to persuade the Government of India to introduce a Princes' Protection Bill in lieu of the Press Act (1910) which the government had decided to repeal.

The Jam Saheb emerged as a 'strong champion' of the bill, duly enacted as the Indian States Act[13] in September 1922.[14] At the second session of the Chamber of Princes at Delhi in November 1921, the Viceroy, Lord Reading, raised the issue about the bill in his opening speech. Learning that the Viceroy was 'considering' a bill to gag the press, the *Saurashtra* sarcastically queried if the exalted official ever 'considers' the oppression of Jamnagar, Bikaner and other states:

> . . . The Princes ask for protection . . . if they get this protection, then only can Morbi freely swallow the lands of its Bhayats, then only can Jamnagar freely tyrannize, then only can the farmers of Vijolia be subjected to outrage. And is the Viceroy an outsider? Give a few parties and spend a few lakhs on the Prince of Wales, raise Imperial troops. His Excellency is a very good man, he is 'considering' the question of fettering and gagging the public. And why? Because the chiefs are asking for protection.

Despite the Viceroy and some princes being averse to the idea of such a bill, a resolution was introduced by Alwar at the session. Alwar argued that attacks against the Princes should be treated as attacks against the Crown, to whom they were bound by treaties. Pleading for its passage, he stressed that 'the Princes have never allowed their States to become breeding ground for disaffection and disloyalty to the Crown . . .' The Jam Saheb heartily seconded the resolution, stating:

> . . . The Princes by no means desire that the liberty of the Press should anymore be fettered in British India for their sakes and the sake of the British Government. There can be no possible objections on our part

---

[13]For Protection against Disaffection, Act XXIV, 1922.

[14]In 1934 it was replaced by an even more stringent bill that carried a penalty of seven years imprisonment and prescribed big fines.

to fair comments or criticisms of our public measures. What they do require, however, is adequate safeguards against gross and illegal vilification of the measures of themselves and their Governments by agitators and seditionists who may be subjects of British India, or who, for purposes mostly nefarious of their own, take shelter temporarily within British jurisdiction. How to accomplish this is a matter which it would be almost presumptuous for us even to suggest to so exalted an authority as Your Excellency. We are not much concerned with the means by which this object could be attained. But we do desire, and I believe very earnestly desire, some proper remedy to stop this evil from doing further mischief.

It may be questioned as to why the British Government should be asked to take interest of this kind in the affairs of Indian States. The answer is simple and it is two-fold. Armed invasion of our territories is not the only case which the British Government is bound by treaties to give us protection. Impalpable but insidious attacks undermining the authority of Indian Princes in their own States and resulting in the destruction of serious injury to their rights, privileges or dignities, are also instances falling within the spirit of the terms of the treaties. The Imperial Government's help should be extended in suppression of such attacks also.

But leaving aside the objection imposed by treaties, there is the further fact that the loyalty and utility of Indian States has lately—as indeed at all times—stood the crucial test of hard experience in times of difficulty and danger and as friends—and may I say—very earnestly say, the *best* friends of the Government of India and allies of the British Government, it would not be too much for the Princes to expect that the British Government should not allow seditionists and unworthy agitators against Indian States to practice their nefarious trade and practices under their protection and within their jurisdiction . . .

The Legislative Assembly rejected the bill but the Viceroy, using the special emergency powers provided by the Reforms Act of 1919, got it okayed by the Council of State, an act, which was roundly condemned by the progressive forces. Protesting the dubious passage of the bill, the Bombay Progressive Association noted (that):

. . . those who are familiar with the autocratic methods of Indian States will admit that the right of protest within the State itself is as good as non-existent. There are no representative institutions in all but a few of them, there is no press worth the name in most of the Indian States . . . It is hardly correct to say that the Imperial Government has permanently guaranteed to the Indian Princes the right of unfettered autocracy or of misgovernance against which every freedom-loving subject has the inherent right to protest, and it cannot be contended that such a guarantee was ever contemplated by the authorities that signed and authorized the treaties and agreements of which so much is made in this controversy . . .

The bill notwithstanding, the Native Press kept up their unflinching tirade against princely misrule. So much so that in the early thirties a frustrated Jam Saheb tried to rally the princes of Kathiawar against the menace of 'scurrilous literature and seditious movements' in a letter addressed to them. But his initiative only drew a withering response from the *Roznama-e-Khilafat*:

We have no sympathy with those newspapers which carry on propaganda against the States and thereby mislead the people, but in spite of this we consider the proposals made by the Maharaja of Nawanagar are quite contrary to the principles of democracy and they constitute a deadly blow to the freedom of the Indian Press. The position of the Princes cannot be protected by such measures. The rulers of the States should keep their accounts clear and then they need not entertain any fear as regards auditing. The despotism displayed by certain rulers of the States could have been tolerated ten years ago but now in the present days of freedom and democracy, when even the British Government has to bow its head before public opinion, the despotic view of the Jam Saheb of Nawanagar cannot gain any acceptance.

The princely battle against the Native Press took an interesting turn in the late twenties. In their bid to rein in criticism, some princes hit upon a novel ruse—if you can't beat 'em, own 'em. By this brilliant stratagem they would not only eliminate criticism against their own regimes but also be able to project themselves in favourable light and lobby support for their political aspirations.

Loyalists and collaborators like Rai Sufi Lachman Parshad, a landlord from Lahore, had in fact already sounded out the government about publishing a newspaper to serve the interests of the Indian States. Parshad had offered his services to start a 'powerful organ' in defence of the States and peaceful British Indian citizens in order to promote the cause of imperial solidarity and to protect the Native Princes from the 'extortion' rackets of papers posing as 'nationalists'.

In 1927, Chimanlal Setalvad and Lalji Naranji, two well-known moderate politicians of Bombay, requested the Jam Saheb to bail out the radical *Bombay Chronicle* so that it could be turned into a moderate organ. The Jam Saheb in turn asked his good friends Patiala and Bhopal to also help out. Patiala eventually came in control of debentures worth Rs 1 lakh and shares worth Rs 50,000, making him a virtual owner of the publication while Mr Naranji held shares worth Rs 50,000 on behalf of the Jam Saheb. There was also a proposal that the Jam Saheb and other princes pick up a stake in the *Indian Daily Mail* which the sole Parsee owner was trying to pop off. One paper also reported that the *Chronicle* was to be sold to the Jam Saheb who was also taking over the *Bombay Samachar*.

Other Native Princes like Bikaner began eyeing the *Pioneer* while Bhopal cast his covetous glances elsewhere. The acquisitive trend among the princes however sent alarm bells ringing through government corridors and a top official warned that 'we are likely to see in the future Ruling Princes having a very considerable share of the control of British Indian newspapers'.

In early 1932, the Chamber of Princes decided to bid for a controlling stake in the *Pioneer* to support their proposed Centre Party which they had conceived as a moderate forum to take forward the reforms proposals and Federation. Nawanagar himself agreed to contribute Rs 5,000 to the cause but later on, when he came under the spell of the 'diehards' acting through advisers like Laurence Rushbrook-Williams, he distanced himself from the Centre Party and the acquisition of the paper.

Ultimately, the Native Princes were made to divest their holdings in the *Bombay Chronicle*. The campaign launched by the publication against the Simon Commission unnerved the British. It was not countenanced how papers financially supported by princely allies could continually disparage government policies. Concern in particular was expressed by British officials about the 'financial relations' between the Jam Saheb and the 'extremist newspaper' and it was thought that they would be better advised to use their money to support respectable newspapers, which can then stand up to extremist organs and minimise the harm they do.

Subtle pressures were brought to bear on the concerned rulers through intermediaries like Naoroji Dumasia and Lord Irwin himself asked Nawanagar, Patiala and Bhopal to divest their stake in the offending publication. Dumasia took up this 'delicate matter' with the Jam Saheb by pointing out that 'the *Bombay Chronicle* is doing irreparable harm to the country and to the cause of the Princes by carrying out propaganda against the Government at a time where it is our duty to stand by Government'. Ultimately, the pressure succeeded and the princes agreed to sever their connections with the radical paper.

V *Invading Affections and Conquering Hearts*

AS far as the Native Princes were concerned, there was no greater object of veneration than the British Crown. Native Princes were wont to swear their loyalty to the inmate of Buckingham Palace on every conceivable occasion. This phenomenon was dictated by their abject subjugation to a foreign overlord, but it also conveniently reinforced the principle of kingship among their own subjects. The Jam Saheb was no different from his fellow rulers. As Roland Wild and others have affirmed, it was part of his 'religion to reverence his Emperor, and loyalty was deep in his heart'.

No wonder, when His Majesty, King George V, decided to send down his own son, the Prince of Wales[1] to redeem the restive tribes of the India in 1921-22, the Native Princes, the Jam Saheb included, rallied to the occasion.

The visit of the Prince of Wales was one of the defining moments of the Indian freedom movement. It polarized Indian society down the line between those supporting and opposing the visit. On the loyalist side were ranged the British colonial establishment and its Indian minions, the Anglo-Indians[2], the traditionally loyal Parsees, Christians and Jews barring a few exceptions. Loyalist Hindus and Muslims and of course, the Native Princes, also bent over backwards to welcome the Prince.

For example, one sect, the Lingayats of Bijapur, under the presidentship of His Holiness Shri Kantha Shivayogi Swami of Sampgaon, strongly protested against the 'insidious movement set by some political agitators to boycott the Prince of Wales' and assured the British

---

[1] The future king, Edward VIII.
[2] Britons resident in India.

Government of 'our steadfast loyalty and staunch determination to stand by our benevolent sovereign'.

Moderate sections of Indian opinion, which wanted *swaraj* but disagreed on the means to achieve it, also supported the visit. Against this motley crew of collaborators were massed the Indian people united under the banner of the Indian National Congress under the leadership of the Mahatma.

The role of the Jam Saheb as an important functionary of the Princely Order which backed the visit all the way, must therefore be seen in the context of this polarization of Indian society and the fierce opposition to it by the nationalist forces. How the Jam Saheb rallied to the call of the Raj in its hour of peril, when it faced one of its most concerted challenges from the Indian freedom movement, reinforced his standing as a veritable pillar of Empire. For this show of loyalty, the Jam Saheb, like other Native Princes, duly received a letter of appreciation from the government for ensuring the success of the royal visit. But it was only natural that he would have done his duty.

The mood in India at the time of the royal visit was one of defiance and despair. Despite India's splendid contribution to the Great War, 'she got, not peace but a sword'. After the flush of the war victory wore off, India was rewarded with higher levels of repression. Forced by the unwillingness of the government of India to take meaningful action against the perpetrators of the Jallianwalla Bagh massacre of April 1919[3] and determined to wrest *swaraj*, the All India Congress Committee had launched the (non-violent) non-cooperation movement (1920–24) calling for a boycott of all government institutions and foreign goods. By linking the non-cooperation agitation with the Khilafat movement[4], the Muslim masses too were roped into the struggle, thus posing the stiffest challenge to the Raj since the Mutiny of 1857.

---

[3] The Native Princes in general maintained a discreet silence on this atrocity though rulers like Alwar justified it.

[4] For the restoration of the rights of the Turkish Caliphate, severely curtailed by the British after World War I.

Believing the visit was conceived by the much-reviled bureaucracy to trump the freedom movement with this royal ace, the Indian National Congress decided to boycott the prince and hold black flag demonstrations against him wherever he went. The AICC also took an unanimous decision to resume the civil disobedience campaign during this period. Gandhiji, who by now had emerged as the uncrowned king of the freedom forces, convincingly articulated the national sentiment for the boycott in *Young India*:

> We must isolate the Prince from the Person! We have no ill-will against the Prince as man. He probably knows nothing of the feeling in India, he probably knows nothing about the repression. Equally probably he is ignorant of the fact that the Punjab wound is still bleeding, that the treachery towards India in the matter of the Khilafat is still rankling in every Indian breast . . .

The period preceding the Prince's arrival saw the contending forces unleash a heated media campaign espousing the justness of their respective cause. Pro-establishment organs like the Anglo-Indian *Times of India* and conservative and moderate native journals like the *Jam-e-Jamshed*, *Akhbar-e-Islam*, *Gujarat Vartaman*, *Bombay Samachar* and others, held forth on the 'duty of Indians to welcome him as a guest who has come into their house' and not to mix politics with the visit. But nationalist periodicals like the English language daily, *Bombay Chronicle*, founded by Sir Pherozeshah Mehta in 1913, which was at the vanguard of the boycott campaign in Bombay, took a radically different stand:

> Despite protestations to the contrary, the visit is meant to create the illusion in the mind of people outside India and especially the British people that all's well with India, that her people are satisfied with the present policy of the Government of India and the British Government. The Indian people regard it as a duty they owe to their country to protest against the propaganda of deception.

Many papers alleged that the Prince was coming here as the guest of the bureaucracy and the *Mahratta* declared (that):

India never sent its invitation—and that bureaucracy has been a party to the oppression and humiliation of India in the matter of the Punjab and the Khilafat. We have been insulted beyond measure, we have been subjected to inhuman repression. We are therefore in mourning. It would be cowardly, servile, sinful hypocrisy for us to wear gala dresses and go out as merry-makers and decorate and illuminate our houses . . .

Threatened with an avalanche of patriotic rejection the government resorted to every trick in the book to ensure the success of the royal visit. Since sports events promised an ideal platform for public relations, they were generously fitted into the prince's itinerary. The Bombay establishment, after much deliberation, decided that the Prince would patronize the Quadrangular cricket tournament featuring the Parsee, European, Hindu and Muslim teams. Although usually held in the first week of December, the Quadrangular was brought forward to mid-November to coincide with the visit. A trip to the Willingdon Gymkhana in south central Bombay to play polo and preside over the final of the Commemoration Polo Cup was also scheduled.

A rousing media debate however ensued among the people over the desirability of participating in this politically-motivated Quadrangular. Hindu Gymkhana members were asked to donate their ticket monies to the Congress-sponsored Malabar relief fund and Muslims and Parsees too were asked to shun the event. But ultimately, the Indian clubs preferred cricket to country and pitched in for participating in the tournament.

Concerted attempts were also made to muster conformity from the 'majority' community which posed the greatest obstacle to the government's plans. In Bombay, the royal route was decorated with pictures of Hindu gods and goddesses, despite objections from several quarters. In Poona, the Prince of Wales laid the foundation stone of the Chhattrapati Shivaji war memorial, an act intended to appease the Marathas at the cost of the restive Brahmins. In the Central Provinces, leaflets in the vernacular language were distributed by the local administration to schools advising that 'according to the Hindu Scriptures, the King's Son was a part of God, therefore all Hindu boys should fulfil their religion by assembling to cheer the Prince of Wales'.

But the critical support for the visit came from the Native Princes. The Viceroy, Lord Reading, brought the Native Princes into battle formation by formally asking for their support in his opening speech at the second session of the newly formed Chamber of Princes held at Delhi from 7 November 1921. Describing the Prince of Wales as the 'first ambassador of the Empire', he expressed the hope that his visit would bind the Princes of India still more closely to the throne.

The Maharaja of Gwalior then moved a resolution of welcome for the Prince of Wales. 'The heart of India is sound at the core and indeed this characteristic loyalty is as traditional and inbred as it is abiding and unshakeable and His Royal Highness may count upon being welcomed with open arms,' the Scindia declared. The Jam Saheb, on behalf of the Chiefs of Kathiawar and Gujarat, supported the resolution wholeheartedly:

> His Royal Highness' visit at this time is indeed an epoch-making event, and I trust that the hope cherished by his visit will be realised in full by British India and the Indian States, who will both give, in spite of any doubt, a whole-hearted, a warm-hearted, a cordial and loyal welcome to His Royal Highness.

The Viceroy's exhortation to the Native Princes to shoulder the welcome to the Prince of Wales drew a sharp riposte from the *Bombay Chronicle*:

> . . . the Viceroy knows that the people of India have solemnly resolved to boycott the visit of the Prince of Wales, because the Prince is made to support a tottering and discredited system—without bearing the least ill-will personally to the Prince—are the remarks of His Excellency to the Princes to be taken as a challenge to the people that the 600 odd Princes at least will participate in the visit, even though the three hundred million may refrain from it, that they will consider it of grave

political significance, even though the people are assured that the visit is strictly non-political?

With both sides not relenting, the stage was set for a massive showdown. The days preceding the arrival of the Prince of Wales saw big advertisements being released by the Indian National Congress in the *Bombay Chronicle* and other nationalist papers asking people to observe a complete *hartal* on the day the Prince was due to dock at Bombay habour.

The Prince duly arrived on the morning of 17 November on the *HMS Renown*. The entire establishment comprising the Viceroy, Governor of Bombay Presidency and other top officials were on hand to receive him. Prominent among them was the delegation of the Native Princes under the able stewardship of the Aga Khan.[5]

The Jam Saheb was in the thick of action at the time of touchdown and played a prominent role at the reception ceremony. The *Times of India* observed that after he came ashore, 'the Prince had more than a formal word with at least one of those who were introduced to him, notably the Maharaja of Nawanagar, an old friend, who, as 'Ranji', must have been the subject of the Prince's boyish admiration'. According to Naoroji Dumasia, who as special secretary of the Subscriptions Committee and School Children's Entertainment Committee, donated Rs 25,000 towards the visit, the Jam was privileged to take a 'prominent part in organizing the reception of the Prince of Wales at the unanimous desire of the Ruling Princes present in Bombay on his historic visit to the Indian Empire'. The Jam's private secretary, Charles Burgess Fry, who claimed that he saw the celebrations of welcome under the Jam's shadow not only in Bombay but also in Delhi and several Indian States, stated (that):

---

[5]His Highness Sir Sultan Muhammad Shah, the Aga Khan III, later commissioned a bronze portrait of the Prince of Wales in his naval uniform which was unveiled in December 1927 by Sir Leslie Wilson, Governor of Bombay. Wilson extolled the Aga Khan as a 'First Citizen of the World' and 'the Ambassador of Empire' whose 'loyalty to the Crown is the cement of the Empire'.

When the Prince of Wales visited India in the cold weather of 1922,
I myself saw Ranjitsinhji exercise his influence effectively in dissuading
the leaders of the Congress Party from the projected demonstration
in the shape of a *hartal*, or public strike, in Bombay . . .

On the second morning, the Jam Saheb had a private interview
with the Prince of Wales at the Government House along with middling
rulers of Kolhapur, Khairpur, Idar, Junagadh, Rajpipla, Bhavnagar and
others, while in the afternoon a delegation of lesser princes got their
turn.

In the five days he spent in Bombay the Prince of Wales was felicitated
at numerous gatherings. But his appearance on the opening day of the
Quadrangular final between the Parsees and the Bombay Presidency
(Europeans) at the Bombay Gymkhana on 21 November was, by many
accounts, a grand success. By the time the Prince arrived in the afternoon
there were close to 10,000 people present. He was welcomed by the
Governor and the president of the Bombay Gymkhana. He watched
the match for some time and during the tea break met the four
participating teams and the top officials of the four gymkhanas.[6]

During a pause in the play he visited all the stands and mixed with
the spectators and then crossed to the wicket and shook hand with
Colonel K.M. Mistry, the Parsee skipper, and also conversed with the
players. George Hirst and Wilfred Rhodes were batting at that time,
the former offered the Prince the bat and the Prince then faced a
couple of deliveries from the Parsee bowler, J.S. Warden. He missed the
first but the second he neatly put past cover point to the delight of the
spectators. Charles Kincaid, who was present on the occasion, however,
disapprovingly noted later, 'I am afraid the Prince's style of play was
not that as favoured in our large public schools'. But the prince left the
gymkhana to 'tumultuous cheers' after watching the cricket for an hour.
Fry himself came in at No. 6 and made a lively 44, before being stumped

---

[6]The Parsee, Hindu, Islam and Bombay Gym.

by Dolly Kapadia off D.D. Driver. The Presidency team, which ultimately won the match, reached 248 for 5 that day and declared next day at 482 with Wilfred Rhodes scoring a swashbuckling 183.

But the flashpoint of the royal visit was reached on the streets of Bombay soon after the Prince's arrival. To coincide with that moment, Gandhiji himself presided over a massive meeting near the Elphinstone Mills in south-central Bombay which culminated in the lighting of a huge bonfire of foreign cloth as a mark of protest. As the crowds dispersed they embarked 'upon the work of destruction', pelting stones at Europeans, burning liquor shops (mainly owned by Parsees) and tram cars and molesting Parsee women returning from the welcome meeting, inviting severe police reprisals in retaliation. The situation soon degenerated into 'an unprecedented outbreak of racial and political violence' as agitating Hindus and Muslims clashed with gangs of Parsees, Anglo-Indians and Jews, leading to the loss of much property and a few lives.

The carnage caused immense damage to Gandhiji's intentions to keep the non-cooperation movement non-violent. Even though the nationalists claimed that the violence was triggered by 'hooligans who had disguised themselves by wearing white caps and dressing in khadi' and actively abetted by the authorities, a stunned Gandhiji apologized to the traumatized communities and called off the agitation.

The acute polarization between the 'nationalists' and 'loyalists' was also reflected in the widely contrasting reportage of the visit and the violent outbreaks in Bombay that followed. The nationalist media saw the prince's coming as an unmitigated flop, a view incidentally shared by the *New Republic* of New York. The *Bombay Chronicle* dubbed the official welcome to the Prince as 'A Poor Show' while highlighting the 'Gloomy Appearance' during the Prince of Wales's arrival:

Practically all the roads and localities were deserted and gave a gloomy holiday appearance instead of the glee of a gala day which one expected on an auspicious occasion like this. The only people taking notice, one accosted were a few Parsee ladies and gentlemen, some Anglo-Indians and Europeans and local Christians and their families, otherwise some were struggling here and there were scattered about . . .

Nationalist papers were quite emphatic about the success of the boycott. The *Hindusthan* asserted that the Elphinstone Road 'demonstration has proved that if any proof were needed that the people of India have now learnt to place their national honour and self-respect above their proverbial hospitality and traditional loyalty' and the citizens of Bombay 'have demonstrated in unmistakable terms the attitude of the people of India towards this visit and thus discharged their debt to the country's honour'.

But the view from the other side of the fence was totally contradictory. The establishment mouthpiece, the *Times of India*, in a triumphal tone, blared with screaming headlines like 'Bombay Greets the Prince' and 'Vast crowds on shore' (that):

> . . . from the earliest dawn, despite the thousands of placards displayed in every nook and corner of the city appealing in the name of Mr Gandhi for a boycott of the Prince's visit, people of every class and community began to flock towards their chosen points of vantage along the route fixed for the Royal procession.

Loyalist papers like the *Jam-e-Jamshed*, *Kaiser-i-Hind*, *Bharat Seva* and the *Praja Mitra and Parsee* believed that the 'hearty reception' accorded to the Prince was 'positive proof that Bombay is loyal at heart'. The *Gujarat Vartaman* echoed in similar vein:

> His Royal Highness the Prince of Wales, our future sovereign to reign over the destinies of India, has arrived and he was met with a right royal welcome though a certain section of people have left no stone unturned to boycott the visit . . . we as Indians are bound to pay him our traditional respect and homage, for his presence amongst us is a precursor of a permanent bond of closer ties of love and friendship of this great and glorious land, with the British Empire.

The Jam Saheb and his cohorts obviously subscribed to the establishment version of history. Appraising the event in *Jamnagar: A Sketch of Its Ruler and Administration*, Naoroji Dumasia not only asserted that the Prince enjoyed 'an unexpectedly enthusiastic welcome' but also argued that the successful completion of his tour was actually a major setback for the leaders of the non-cooperation movement:

> Considering that before the Prince came to India the non co-operators had decided to boycott him and all the ceremonies and functions held in his honour on the plea that the Prince was the guest of the bureaucracy only and was used by them in an attempt to bolster up a tottering regime—a nonsensical idea—and considering the situation of the country the Prince had a remarkable and an unexpectedly enthusiastic welcome in which loyal Princes of India played an important part . . .
>
> Upon the non-co-operation movement itself, the visit of His Royal Highness has not been without effect. Before His Royal Highness left India there was a general feeling among the substantial classes of the population that the outrageous conduct of the no-co-operators had disgraced India's fair name. The fact that His Royal Highness's programme was carried out in detail despite the loudly proclaimed efforts of the non-co-operation leaders, has not failed to prove a severe set-back to their claims, on the whole it may be said that His Royal Highness's visit to India has been an inspiring example to every subject of His Majesty the King-Emperor, and for this reason alone, has proved of notable service to the Empire.

Private secretary Fry, who was also the Jam Saheb's speechwriter, had some interesting insights to offer in his autobiography published nearly two decades after the event. He arrived in Bombay to take up his assignment with the Jam Saheb about ten days before the Prince of Wales did. He was present at the many public functions of the Prince in Bombay along with the Jam Saheb and affirmed that he was therefore 'well informed of everything that happened.' Fry claimed that the enormous crowds lining the Prince's route 'welcomed him with every sign of respect, which in India does not consist of making a noise.[7] Indeed, when there is a public procession in a city of India, great or small, on a public occasion in honour of a personage, the most respectful and reverential treatment that the Indian crowd can accord is silence. So that if you read that His Royal Highness was received by the huge concourse in complete silence by European standards this would appear to present an exhibition of unpopularity or disapproval, whereas in India it would be evidence of exactly the contrary.'[8]

Though Fry admitted that the Heir-Apparent's visit was ill-timed, he nevertheless claimed he never heard of a single instance of discourtesy or discontent directed against the royal visitor:

> . . . the unsettled state of India at the time threw a heavy responsibility upon the Government of India in conducting a tour for the Prince of Wales. Not that there was any feeling at all in India, even among the bitterest agitators, against the King-Emperor and the Royal Family; in fact, a peculiar feature of the Indian world was an intensely loyal and affectionate feeling towards the King-Emperor, combined with a poignant dissatisfaction with the Government of India. Edward, Prince of Wales, was sure to be personally welcomed everywhere, but it was impossible to expect that the occasion of his visit would not afford a ready opportunity to the militant agitators for what they were bound to regard as effective demonstrations. A few sporadic demonstrations were there in the big towns, but the reports circulated in England representing these as directed against the Heir-Apparent were entirely misleading.

According to Fry, the one 'considerable riot'[9] in the bazaar quarters of Bombay, was started by 'a band of hooligans imported for that

---

[7]Even the *Bombay Samachar* reported that the crowds lining the royal route were silent.

[8]Strange behaviour indeed by an Indian crowd expressing their appreciation, considering that occidental cricketers often complain that they are intimidated by the din of subcontinental crowds when they play in this part of the world!

[9]On another occasion Fry dismissed it as a 'small irrelevant disturbance'.

purpose' which ended in 'a lively clash' between Mohemmedans and Hindus. It had nothing whatever to do with the arrival of His Royal Highness except as an occasion, he contended. Even the Allahabad incident, which Fry stated was 'the only serious demonstration', had nothing to do with the royal visit except in so far as the agitators took advantage of the occasion for publicity. But Fry regretted that newspapers at home falsely represented the Bombay riot as an outrageous exhibition of disloyalty and the fact that the political discontent in India had expressed itself loudly against the Royal Family.

Even though the Prince did not stop over at Kathiawar but journeyed past the region en route from Baroda to Rajputana[10], the Jam Saheb contributed one of the defining moments of the royal tour. The Jam Saheb apparently lobbied hard for a stopover at Jamnagar—he had even made lavish preparations in anticipation of securing one—but the Prince gave it the royal miss. While this may have had to do with the relative unimportance of Nawanagar and Kathiawar in the imperial pecking order, the government also might have not wanted to put a strain on Nawanagar's meagre resources or it may have wanted to punish the Jam's indolence by denying him a royal stopover.

Despite being turned down the Jam Saheb would eventually seize the occasion provided by the visit to show his imperial colours. The Jam's moment of glory came at the Imperial Durbar hosted in the Prince's honour by the Native Princes of India at the famous *Diwan-i-Am* in Delhi on 16 February 1922. Since the Government of India did not issue formal invitations to the Durbar, many Princes refused to attend. Not the Jam Saheb. He, in fact, played a most loyal and active part in organising the reception, said Dumasia. What is more, he was one of the four members of the Princely Order who was assigned the honour of addressing words of welcome to His Royal Highness at the gathering.

In a speech resounding with glorious incantations to the Raj and

---

[10]He visited Ajmer, Bikaner, Jodhpur, Jaipur and Bharatpur among other places.

the 'first family', the Jam Saheb began by humbly stating that he was
unequal to the task of matching the oratory of the earlier speakers
(Gwalior, Bikaner and Patiala) or even attempting a tribute worthy of
the distinguished guest. But in due course he proceeded to produce yet
another scintillating knock extolling the royal guest and the Empire:

> . . . Your Royal Highness, the Ruling Princes and Chiefs of India
> united here, offer you, above all, a welcome of unity—the unity of our
> Order in deep and enduring loyalty towards His Imperial Majesty the
> King-Emperor, towards the glorious House of Windsor and towards
> Your Royal Highness, his beloved and so distinguished heir; nay further,
> the unity of our Order with the rest of India in the mighty fabric of the
> British Empire as a true member of that great body politic. With unity
> as the keynote of our welcome we salute Your Royal Highness as a
> most happy and most successful instrument of unity and of amity. Your
> Royal Highness unites in your single person many attributes that
> merit the deep warmth of our welcome.
>
> Your Royal Highness is welcome to us as a living and shining
> symbol of the splendid function which the Crown exercises as binding
> and holding together, an attachment and loyalty, the various and diverse
> parts of the Great Empire, to which we are so proud to belong.
>
> A critic might say that we live in troublous times and that your visit
> has found India in heavy waters; but may it not be that the unpropitious
> elements now visible are but the froth and foam which ever appear on
> the surface when progress rides the waves. May we not conceive that
> the present troubles are but healthy signs of a great forward movement,
> of a great striving after better things? And surely the history of the
> world teaches us that we progress only by striving and there is no
> striving without strife. However this may be, I believe that the deepest
> student of Indian history will find nothing in our age-long past that
> can compare with the progressive vitality of social and political life
> which has blossomed in India under the aegis and sceptre of three
> Imperial Sovereigns, of the last of whom you are the beloved heir . . .
>
> Truly Your Royal Highness's visit is in the nature of a conquest
> but one vastly different from those which India has so often suffered

in the past. We have been invaded by the sword; we have been invaded by the pen; we have been invaded even by the tongue. Your Royal Highness in contrast has invaded our affections and has conquered our hearts, garnering a swift and enduring success, the fruits of which will hereafter ensure happiness to millions in this immense land.

When Your Royal Highness returns to tell His Imperial Majesty of your visit to us, you, Sir, will be able to use the words of another great conqueror but with a new meaning and respectfully present to His Imperial Majesty another triple plume—the triple plume of your own Indian tour—Veni, Vedi, Vici.

Amazing rhetoric and laced with bitter irony indeed. Imagine a ruler who took pride in the record of his dynasty as valiant resistors of the Moslem invaders of yore, now welcoming an 'invasion' by the Prince of Wales of his countrymen's affections and the 'conquest' of their hearts—which incidentally a few hundred million Indians had stoutly resisted with all their moral might!

VI *The Princes and the Reforms*

WHATEVER delusions of grandeur the Native Princes may have entertained about themselves, their patronising British overlords had a far from flattering opinion of the tribe. No matter the accolades heaped upon them in public. Lord Macaulay's vivid portraits of 'nominal sovereigns sunk in indolence and debauchery . . . chewing *bang*, fondling concubines and listening to buffoons' set the general tone of British perceptions.

But, from the earliest times, the utility of these degenerate regimes to imperial rule did not escape attention. Mighty statesman and Governor of Bombay, Lord Mountstuart Elphinstone, beheld the princes not only as buffers but also as cess-pits of the Raj into which the accumulating miseries of the rest of India could seep, and like warring germs, prey on each other. His brutal assessment was that 'we must have some sink to receive all the corrupt matter that abounds in India, unless we are willing to taint our own system by stopping the discharge of it'.

It took the 'sepoy mutiny' of 1857, which rocked the very foundations of the Raj, to comprehensively alter British perceptions of the Native Princes. But for the staunch support of princely states like Patiala, Jind, Hyderabad, Gwalior, Indore, Baroda, Travancore, Mysore and of Rajputana, besides the Punjabi Muslims and the Gurkhas, the fires of rebellion would have otherwise consumed the Raj. The Viceroy, Earl 'Clemency' Canning, frankly acknowledged this debt when he described the Native States as 'breakwaters in the storm which would have swept over us in one great wave'. Summing up this chapter in imperial history, Sir Richard Temple observed,

> They rendered a priceless service to the British cause at the moment of its extreme depression. They deserved then, as they will never deserve

to be esteemed as bulwarks of imperial stability and as conservative elements in a country where subversive and explosive forces may at times burst forth.

The cathartic experience, however, proved priceless for the British. It identified the chieftains as potential allies in the task of holding on to 'the jewel in the Crown'. Thus began a process of roping in the princes as props of the Raj and as a 'counterpoise' to the nationalist forces. This policy was refined and furthered by a succession of Viceroys like Lytton, Dufferin, Lansdowne, Curzon and Minto right up to Willingdon and Linlithgow in the 1930s.

Canning himself had inaugurated this policy of 'conciliating the princely, aristocratic and otherwise influential classes of India and strengthening them as a buttress to British rule'.

The imperious Lord Curzon tried his best to cement this relationship. He decreed that no longer would the Princes be beheld as 'detached appendages of Empire but its participants and instruments' who 'have ceased to be the architectural adornments of the Imperial edifice and have become the pillars that help to sustain the main roof'.

Curzon's successor, Lord Minto, sought the association of the Indian States in the governing of the Empire by seeking their views on how to combat 'sedition' in British India so that the princes might become helpers and colleagues in the great task of imperial rule. He perceptively declared, 'The foundation of the whole system is the recognition of identity of interests between the Imperial Government and the Durbars'.

Many of the 565-odd Native States of 'Indian India', comprising two-fifths of the area and one-fifth of the population of India, were 'sinks of reaction and incompetence and unrestrained autocratic power sometimes exercised by vicious and deranged individuals'. But the growing entente between imperialism and the princes nevertheless bound them in 'in perpetual alliance and friendship' with Britain.

Thanks to this policy of appeasement, the princes were given a long rope and their many excesses tolerated, barring a few exceptions. They were also honoured with durbars, honours, titles and appointments to imperial and provincial councils. They were assured of protection and security by the paramount power. But in return the defanged princes had to accept 'the corresponding obligation to act in all things with loyalty to the Sovereign Power and to abstain from all acts injurious to the Government'.

The bedrock of this grand alliance between the Princes and imperialism was the famous proclamation of Queen Victoria in 1858 when the governance of India was transferred from the East India Company to the Crown. Offering the hand of friendship and protection to the Native States, Her Majesty reiterated the sanctity of their treaties with Britain and swore, 'We shall respect the rights, dignity and honour of the Native Princes as our own'. The Princes would desperately cling on to this promise in the turbulent times of the next century.

Time and again, British officials from the Viceroy downwards, harked back to this assurance and promised that Britain would stand by the Princes, come hell or high water. But in the end game of Empire the Princes would be ditched by their paladins due to the compulsions of realpolitik.

The concordat between the Princes and the Raj assumed vital import in the first decade of the twentieth century itself when 'sedition' reared its ugly head over the subcontinent. In the immediate period after the Great War, there was a mass upsurge due to the failure of the Montagu-Chelmsford Reforms[1] to address the demand for self-determination. This saw the Raj rattled by *satyagraha*, *swadeshi*, boycott, the non-cooperation movement and civil disobedience as the nationalist forces upped the ante.

This outburst in turn was met by repressive legislation like the Rowlatt Act leading to the Jallianwala Bagh massacre and the imposition of martial law in the Punjab and countrywide strife. Mahatma Gandhiji in turn threatened at the Nagpur session of the Indian National Congress

---

[1]More on the Reforms in subsequent chapters.

in December 1920 that 'if they do not want to do justice it will be the bounden duty of every Indian to destroy the Empire'. An ominous INC resolution also called for 'the attainment of *swaraj* by all legitimate and peaceful means'.

IN such a volatile period of political ferment, the imperatives of mutual self-preservation helped cement the bond that had been forged between the Native Princes and the Raj during the Great War like never before. Even though all of India gave generously of its resources to help Britain fight a war that she had no connection with, the Princes outdid British India in their enthusiasm. Their unstinting support of the war effort earned them the deepest gratitude of Britain.

The Great War saw the Jam Saheb script his greatest service to the Empire. It was a glorious chapter in his life and 'one of the brightest episodes in the history of the country'. The hostilities provided the Jam Saheb an unexpected opportunity to redeem his 1910 pledge before Lord Sydenham that the Rajputs would fight shoulder to shoulder with Britain if the Empire came under threat.

Although the overall contribution of the Princes to the war effort was substantial, in proportion to its size and resources, the munificence of Nawanagar was simply phenomenal. The Jam put his person[2] in addition to his purse (his people's, in reality) at the disposal of the Empire. He mobilized all the resources of his state, scanty as they were, stopped every development scheme, levied a multitude of new taxes and pledged the Viceroy *carte blanche* every horse and motor-car in his state for the war effort.

> I have asked the Government to call upon my State for all its war resources. I fear the trouble is going to be very serious and therefore every unit of the Empire should contribute its mite towards its strength, consolidation and preservation.

---

[2]The Jam was posted on the French front but as a 'tin soldier' did not see any action.

In Britain the Jam Saheb partnered Dr W.G. Grace in recruiting campaigns for military service. The old doctor called upon cricketers to 'sacrifice their wickets' for the cause. 'I should like to see all first-class cricketers of suitable age set a good example, and come to the help of their country without delay in its hour of need,' Grace implored. Not to be outdone, at Eastbourne, the Jam too made a personal appeal to Britons 'to join the Army and to fight, and to die if need be', for to do so 'is to live in history for ever, to the lasting honour not only of yourself but of the Empire'.

At home too the Jam Saheb continued the propaganda blitz and was heartened when people responded positively. He believed that the overwhelming response towards the defence of the Empire was 'a sure test of the deep and genuine loyalty cherished by one and all, rich and poor, towards British rule'. At a War Conference convened by Lord Willingdon, Governor of Bombay, in June 1918, to encourage India to redouble the war effort, the Jam Saheb came up with one of his finest knocks for the Empire:

> Brethren, what can be more pleasing to your sense of patriotism and nationality than the fact that the Empire stands before you and asks your assistance? . . . Shall we stand at the door haggling over the price of our assistance as some sort of exchange for what we give—when the Empire is shaking convulsively with the heroic effort that it is making to crush inhuman despotism? Shall we be asking for a barter and naming a return for our services at the present moment? It is my firm, nay, reasoned conviction, gentlemen, that this is not the right moment for pressing forward political claims in any way that would embarrass the action or disturb or divert the energies of any single one of us, no less that those of Government or cause but one slight deflection from the supreme end we all have in view, viz, the prosecution of war to the bitterest end—and end that spells a victorious end. Let us remember that loyalty and service to the Empire are our noblest traditions; . . . Gentlemen, let us not forget that loyalty is our tradition and freedom is our birth-right, and that neither can be bought nor sold. You have already before you a sacred pledge given by the National Cabinet of

the Empire, backed by British democracy. India is promised full responsible government and I cannot conceive that such a solemn pledge can be or will be broken by the British Cabinet or by that great people who control our destinies . . . Shall we stand haggling for obtaining to-day what is yours to-morrow, where the shores of noble Britain are in peril, gallant France is bleeding, Belgium is ravished, Serbia remains destroyed, and great Russia is dismembered and disfigured out of all recognition of her past greatness and entity, not to speak of unlucky Rumania bled white from forced concessions? I beseech, earnestly beseech, all leaders of public opinion, whom His Excellency has convened to-day representing as they do, various shades and schools of thought, to be statesmen and to look ahead, well ahead. Let us not be petty men, brooding over disappointments, great and small. The instance of Russia should be a sufficient warning to us to arrest all political discord and disunion; we should and must close the ranks at the present time when the most gigantic war known to history is being waged to a finish . . . .

Years later, the Viceroy, Lord Reading, laid the foundation of a 'Victory Memorial' at Jamnagar in 1924 in commemoration of 'the sacrifices made in the great war by this State, its subjects and its ruler'. The Jam Saheb could then justly claim:

We did our humble share in the stupendous effort the Empire put forth under His Imperial Majesty's banner. It was in proportion to our modest resources but I may be permitted to say so, we were second to none either in the output of our contribution in men, money and materials or in the spirit and zeal which inspired and animated our cooperation.

WORLD War I had a cataclysmic effect on imperial fortunes as the liberation forces in several colonies escaped to freedom in its aftermath. The war greatly weakened Britain's hold over its colonies and nowhere was the need to stem the rot more acutely felt than in India itself. During the war years, Edwin S. Montagu, a man considered favourably disposed towards the Princes, visited India to realize Britain's intentions of increasing the association of Indians in the administration and aiding the gradual development of self-governing institutions. This was with a view to encouraging the realization of responsible government in (British) India as an integral part of the Empire.

The proposals, which the new secretary of state for India finally submitted in collaboration with the Viceroy, Lord Chelmsford, was known as the Montagu-Chelmsford Report.[3] They were incorporated in the Government of India Act of 1919 as a follow-up to the inaugural Morley-Minto Reforms of 1909. But the report failed to satisfy Indian aspirations, imbued as it was more by 'the need for securing Imperial responsibilities' rather than making self-determination a reality.

The Native Princes played a vital role in the formulation of the Montford report. The Jam Saheb, according to Lord Willingdon, comprised 'the intellect and the leadership of the Rajput Princes' along with Bikaner and Alwar. Naturally, he was one of the four royals picked by the newly formed Conference of Princes and Chiefs in November 1917 to provide inputs to Montagu during his visit.

The Jam Saheb in particular emphasized in his interactions with Montagu the rights of the Princes and demanded non-interference in their internal affairs. Nawanagar was also in the delegation of ten princes that met the Viceroy and secretary of state in February 1918 and presented him a draft of the final scheme. Some points from the draft were later incorporated by Montagu in the final report.

One fallout of these reforms, which introduced the concept of dyarchy (dual rule) in British India, required the introduction of a degree of popular opinion in the governance of the Native States. Perhaps, this move was designed to dilute the autocratic image of Native States for public consumption. The Jam Saheb had to fall in line even though he was reputedly 'no compromising democrat, but a full-blooded autocrat, believing in the ancient exercise of kingship, in its fullest meaning, for an Eastern people'. For had not the Vedas themselves

---

[3]Montford Report for short.

decreed that 'the Princes are the representatives of God on earth?'

The reluctant reformer nevertheless inaugurated an Advisory Council of Nawanagar State composed of representatives of agriculturalists, mercantilists and professionals on 29 March 1919. But the Jam's 'installation day' speech clearly indicated that his hand had been forced:

. . . My leanings are towards introducing changes and reforms after consulting the feelings of the people and giving effect to them as far as possible . . . But it is to be remembered that we carry heavy responsibilities. We live in the British Empire and that Empire recognises and acknowledges hereditary kingship. We are bound by certain treaties and engagements with the Imperial Crown. In these circumstances it is beyond my powers to transform Jamnagar into a republic. I will even go further, I conscientiously believe in hereditary kingship; from the beginning that principle has been running in our blood for untold generations and as I said above I have firm faith in the creed. For these reasons also, I cannot act against my conviction and promote methods of undiluted democracy. If I am not much mistaken, a large majority of you, gentlemen, believe in the time-honoured cult of hereditary rulership . . . But what is really essential is this: we must know the needs of the people, and in all measures that we adopt for their protection and betterment, we should secure their concurrence and goodwill . . . I also honour the sacred injunction of our *Shastras*, which asks men not to inhabit a place which possesses no ruler . . .

Let me inform you candidly that I do not desire to announce paper constitutions carrying high-sounding denominations like the 'Representative Assembly'; that would be misleading the public and a dishonest endeavour to carry popular favour. I dislike any such sham. Our people are still backward in education . . . we have before us members showing a wide divergence of ability and calibre. We cannot expect a uniform level of capacity here as elsewhere. For these reasons, I think it is convenient to invite advice and opinion on public matters from councillors, carefully selected and nominated . . .

But critics were not convinced that monarchist leopards like the Jam Saheb had changed their autocratic spots. The *Kathiawar Samachar* dismissed such reforms as 'merely a show for being trumpeted abroad, while in reality the Native Chiefs enjoy autocratic power and use them in a manner that is prejudiced to the interests of the people . . .' Neither did the Jam's flowery rhetoric convince the *Servant of India* which slammed him in no uncertain terms:

> . . . And what laudations were heaped upon the Jam Saheb for introducing this modicum of reform! The Jam Saheb is honorary secretary to the Chiefs' Conference and has herein given a fair specimen of the reform that may be expected of the chiefs in general. The only councils they can be persuaded to constitute are, to use the language of Sir William Lee Warner 'sham representative councils intended to quieten the British conscience and to mislead the press. They may avert the evil eye of foreign opinion while they retard real reform.' Let the ruling princes understand that if they are not prepared to temper their personal rule by the advice of popular representatives and gradually part with power to them, these mock councils will deceive no one these days.

Inasmuch as they were reluctant reformers in their own territories some princes however cautiously welcomed the advance of democracy in British India. There was a rider attached though—provided it did not threaten their relationship with the Empire or destablize their regimes. But they also realized that the growing democratic aspirations of British India, which were now sought to be (partly) fulfilled by the reforms, could constitute a grave threat to the princely order in the long run.

As a good reader of the political wicket, the prescient Jam Saheb could intuitively see the bunkers ahead. He rightly deduced that the princes' well-being lay in the perpetuation of the Raj and vice versa. He believed 'the unity of Empire depended to a great extent upon the appreciation of the Princes' importance by the paramount power and there was no man so ready to prove that the strength of the British connection was bound up with the continuance of the dignity and integrity of the Princes . . .'

Not only was the Jam apprehensive about the approaching tides of democracy at home; like other conservatives, he was also in dread of the revolutionary rumblings in distant lands. At Geneva, as one of the three Indian representatives at the First Assembly of the League of Nations in 1922, the Jam Saheb flayed revolution with some fiery strokes: 'The very essence of Bolshevist attack on the existing order is an attack on intellect; its special instrument of death, its very symbol, is a hammer that beats out the brain . . .' His phobia of revolution was shared by conservative cricketing comrades like Lord Harris who in his dotage ranted that the menace had targeted the holy game itself. 'Bolshevism is rampant, and seeks to abolish all laws and rules, and this year cricket has not escaped its attack,' Harris claimed.

The Jam Saheb did his best to unite the Princes against the impending threat of democracy and traversed the length and breadth of the country to counsel them. In the process he earned the affectionate sobriquet of 'grandmother' from them. He repeatedly warned his colleagues that they were in danger of losing the positions that their ancestors had carved out for them by the sword. As biographer Roland Wild queried:

> Was he perhaps looking down the years and seeing the time when the issue would lie between home-ruling British India and the States? Did he envisage the time when the armies of Rajputana and Gujerat and the Southern lands would appear once more in all their ancient panoply of warfare, banners flying, to defend their privileges against heterogeneous peoples whose head had been turned by politics?

The Jam Saheb however adroitly played the democratic tune when the situation demanded. He stated he was 'in full sympathy with new aspirations and ideas, and optimistic as to the future of this great country'. He felt that the churning was a healthy sign and that a 'clash of opinions and views inevitably occurs when a new order is being evolved':

> We must not forget that we are living in extraordinary times, when an epoch is being linked to an epoch. We all know that science is achieving miracles and that the future of humanity is pregnant with immediate

and untold possibilities. Humanity is taking a step forward and the 'travail' is bound to be enormous.

That said, the Jam Saheb did not want the princes to be bypassed when crucial decisions concerning the devolution of powers to the Indian people would be taken in future. Great expectations were already being generated about his forthcoming role in the reforms process. At a birthday banquet in Jamnagar in 1917, E. Maconochie, Agent to the Governor, Kathiawar, touched on this aspect while lauding the Jam as 'an Imperial asset and a pillar of the Empire'. Maconochie hoped the Jam's 'loyal and patriotic services and influence would be particularly useful in the coming anxious times of the remodelling of the Empire'.

In fact, cricketer-writer E.H.D. Sewell would lament after the Jam Saheb's death that the British Government did not take him more into their confidence. Otherwise, he could have done much to help solve its political difficulties in India, given his great influence in Bombay 'even with the "difficult and unnecessarily obstructionist white-capped Gandhiites".'

Fully aware that the very existence of his order was at stake, the Jam Saheb sportingly assumed the 'major task' of 'awakening the Princes of India to the need for safeguarding their rights'. And not only against attack from nationalist politicians but also from encroachments by the British government itself. He therefore worked hard to bring them on a common platform. But this, as mentioned earlier, was a part of the grand imperial design as well.

The combined orchestrations of the Native Princes and the Government of India bore fruition in the formation of the Chamber of Princes. This historic denouement was a 'recognition of the rights of the Princes to be consulted in framing the policy of the Government relating to the States and to have a voice in the Councils of the Empire'. The Jam Saheb would in turn serve as standing committee member, secretary, pro-Chancellor and finally Chancellor of this high-profile organization.

Recounting the Jam Saheb's work for this cause, Roland Wild noted, 'It will never be known how much time and labour he devoted to the Chamber of Princes, incurring enormous expenses in the process. Many visits to Delhi, England and most of the States of India, meant not only large sums in travelling expenses, but increased social obligations. Hospitality had to be repaid, but he never grudged a rupee of that expenditure'. C.B. Fry, who as personal secretary also aided the Jam Saheb in his Chamber-related work, claimed that his boss was 'one of its most able and energetic members'.

The Jam's critical role in its formation was heartily commended no less than by the departing Lord Chelmsford. The Viceroy acknowledged that he was 'much indebted to Your Highness for your admirable work in the Committee of Princes and your assistance in bringing to a successful fruition the scheme for the establishment of a Chamber of Princes'.

Another offshoot of the Montford Reforms, this 'Princes' Trade Union' of sorts was the imperial googly by which the colonial rulers hoped to stump the nationalist advance. The British well realized that many of the by now Westernized princes could prove valuable allies in the future since their interests too were imperial and they were 'likely to be a useful check on the ultra-democratic tendency throughout the rest of India'. But not always did the Chamber of Princes act as Britain's handmaiden. Its actions were often dictated by the personal predilections and bloated egos of its ruling caucus and the intense rivalry between the contending blocks of princely interests.

The idea of bringing the princes on a common platform had actually taken root several decades before. Lord Lytton, Viceroy from 1876–80, first harboured the notion of an Indian Privy Council. Baron Curzon of Kedleston, although unpopular with both the princes and the nationalists, also vigourously toyed with this concept 'as a device for countering the Congress'. The Earl of Minto, whose laissez faire approach towards the princes marked the high point of imperial indulgence, actually recommended the creation of an imperial council composed solely of Ruling Chiefs appointed by the Viceroy. But the idea failed to take off. Baron Hardinge of Penshurst, the next Viceroy, got the princely consultation process off the ground, holding the first such conference in March 1913. After much confabulations he was emboldened to declare in February 1916:

> We have made it our aim to cultivate close and friendly relations with the ruling Princes, to show by every means that we trust them and look on them as helpers and colleagues in the great task of imperial rule . . .

Lord Chelmsford, who convened the first regular conference of princes in October 1916, provided an inkling of what was expected of the princely order in the post-war scenario at a meeting of the 'Princes' Conference' in November 1919:

> There is a new spirit abroad in the world, impatient of restraint, prone to look upon order as tyranny, prosperity as profiteering and expensiveness of living as the result of maladministration. This spirit, embittered by high prices due partly to the failure of the last monsoon and partly to the diversion of the world's energies from production to destruction, excited by the downfall of great powers, and encouraged by the secret and subtle propaganda, to think that anarchy mean happiness and prosperity for all—this spirit is the most subtle and the greatest danger that has ever come upon mankind. The Indian States, perhaps also India as a whole, are less likely than Europe to be primarily assailed but sooner or later we may all be forced to repel the attack, whether it comes from without or within the body politic . . . Your Highness can, however, lend invaluable assistance by ensuring that your States are places in which the lawless and malicious spirit is not tolerated, where lying stories find no favour, where the motives of the British Government are not misrepresented and where British rule is not held up to obloquy . . .

A Royal Proclamation of 8 February 1921 finally brought the Chamber of Princes into being. His Majesty, King George V, sent his uncle, Prince Arthur, the Duke of Connaught, to inaugurate the Chamber and the Indian Legislative Assembly and Council of State created under the 1919 Act. But this visit, like that of the Prince of Wales a few months later, was stoutly opposed by the nationalist forces and marked by *hartals* and *bandhs*.

Also called the Narendra Mandal, meaning 'Rulers of Men' or 'Rulers of Kings', the 120-member assembly[4] contained representatives from the formidable 21-gun salute states to nine gun entities and less. However, rulers of 'middling' states like Nawanagar[5], Patiala and Bikaner (17 guns each) and Bhopal (19 guns) monopolized the action while the 'big guns' like Hyderabad, Indore, Baroda and Kashmir generally remained aloof.

The Chamber was launched with regal pomp at the Dewan-i-am of the Moghul Red Fort in Delhi at which the Jam Saheb was present. The Royal pledges about the sanctity of the treaties with the States were emphatically reaffirmed by Connaught. He also assured the gathering that the British would stand by its promises to the princes and appealed to them in return to stand by the Empire:

> . . . Loyalty is a tradition with the Indian States. His Majesty knows well that, in good times or evil, he can always count upon the fidelity and unswerving support of the Indian Princes . . . I am confident that the same spirit of loyalty and co-operation that your Highness displayed during the war will continue to animate you in the years to come.

Though wracked by heavy politicking, the Chamber of Princes authored several initiatives, though many of these were flayed by British India representatives. A major issue it facilitated was the proposed transfer of political relations of certain states from the presidencies to the central government. This was one of the overriding concerns of

---

[4]Attendance at its meetings, however, rarely touched the halfway mark on the best of occasions.

[5]Nawanagar was a 13-gun state while the Jam was personally worth 15 guns.

the Jam Saheb who was keen to rid himself of the yoke of the Bombay government. Besides, it whetted his *abru* to have direct dealings with the central authority rather than having to go through lesser state officials. Another reason why the Jam Saheb wholeheartedly backed this move was because he was peeved at the neglect of the Kathiawar princes in terms of receipt of honours and titles as compared to the bounty showered on the Rajputana rulers due to their direct association with the centre.

The Jam Saheb had raised this issue with Montagu during his visit to India. He also used every forum to drum up support for it. He made representations, signed petitions and even lobbied the Viceroy along with a delegation of nineteen princes of the Bombay Presidency led by the Maharana of Kutch. Finally, in 1924, the Kathiawar states were placed in direct relationship with the Government of India and the Western India States Agency came into being.

Ironically in the 1920s, during a period of great peril to the Raj from the nationalist forces, the relationship between the princes and the Government of India deteriorated to a point of uncertainty despite the general convergence of interests. The point of divergence was the prickly issue of paramountcy. This was re-emphasized by the new Viceroy, Lord Reading, in a reprimand to the upstart Nizam over his claims on the Berar province. It stressed the absolute paramountcy of the Government of India over princely states in any matter involving imperial interests. Naturally, this development dampened princely ardour towards the Raj.

The Chamber of Princes, eager for a decisive statement on the vital issue, as well as on the fragile relationship with British India, prevailed upon the next Viceroy, Lord Irwin, to appoint a commission to go into these contentious subjects. Accordingly, a three-man Indian States Inquiry Committee headed by Sir Harcourt Butler[6] was appointed in December 1927 to probe the relationship between the Native States and the Government of India on matters concerning paramountcy,

---

[6]The recently retired governor of the United Provinces.

internal sovereignty, financial relations between British India and the Native States.

Correspondingly, the Sir John Simon Commission was set up to look into the problems of British India. But while the princes cooperated with the Butler committee the nationalists boycotted the Simon Commission, principally because no natives were part of it. Instead, the Pandit Motilal Nehru Committee report of 1928 formulated alternative proposals for the future Constitution of India.

The Jam Saheb reacted with alacrity to the appointment of the Indian States Inquiry Committee. All along he had been keenly monitoring political developments which would affect Native States. In 1924 itself he had summoned the chiefs of Kathiawar, Kutch and Gujarat to his capital to discuss issues of vital import. Keen to influence the trends of this political discourse in favour of the princely order, the Nawanagar durbar fired a preemptive propaganda rocket into the political stratosphere.

This was in the form of the book, *Jamnagar: A Sketch of its Ruler and its Administration*, authored by Naoroji Dumasia and published by the *Times of India* Press. It was intended as a 'guide to those who are considering the future of the Indian States in relation to British India already started on the adventurous road to responsible government'. With a preface by Laurence Rushbrook-Williams, ex-director of the publicity department of the Government of India, member of the Standing Committee of the Chamber of Princes and foreign minister of Patiala and later of Nawanagar, and a lavish spread of pictures of the luminaries of the Raj and the princely order, the tome made no bones about its overtly monarchist and imperial agenda.

Quite simply put, *Jamnagar: A Sketch of its Ruler and its Administration* was a powerful plea to the British 'to keep faith with the Indian States at any sacrifice' and to secure their interests in the uncertain future. The book highlighted the virtues of kingship in general and the track record of its main protagonist, the Jam Saheb, in particular, a man well-known, among other things 'in the larger field of service to the Empire.'

It highlighted his long-standing connections with the 'Mother Country' due to his cricketing career, his qualities of sportsmanship, his splendid contribution during the Great War and the inseparable bond between him and the Empire forged from this ordeal, his unstinting support during the controversial visit of the Prince of Wales etc. It argued that in view of these reasons and the conjugation of imperial interests, the sanctity of Britain's treaties with the Native States should be maintained at all costs when the next batch of reforms came into effect. The counsel of the Jam Saheb and other capable princes should also be availed for the purpose. The book also abounded with invectives against the nationalists who were vilified as 'hot-headed politicians' and 'seditionists' threatening the stability of the Empire and the British connection.

Obviously, the Jam Saheb was cast as the undoubted hero of the exercise. He was variously described as an 'enlightened administrator', 'a man of many and varied accomplishments' and 'the father of his people' who has 'has reduced statecraft to a fine art' and 'brought Jamnagar to the front rank of civilised States'. 'Those who know His Highness recognize in him not only a Prince Charming who compels their admiration but a man of frank and simple character which requires no elaborate explanation in order that it may be fully understood,' Dumasia stated.

A few partisans are also summoned to confirm this appraisal like noted essayist A.G. Gardiner, whose admirable volume, *The Pillars of Society*, contained this interesting dissertation on the cricketer-turned-king:

There is not a greater friend of the people of British India than the Jam Saheb. A great lover of liberty, imbued with a real patriotic desire, he has on occasions espoused the cause of Indians for a larger share in the government of the country: and in his own State he has introduced reforms in advance of the times. In his own person he has furnished a shining example of the capacity of an Indian for progress and constructive genius. He understands Englishmen and the latter understand and respect him. His name lives in the hearts of hundreds of thousands of British people and his influence will be far more productive of good to India than the agitation of the politicians in broad-basing the Government on the people's will. But the Jam Saheb is the butt of the extremists and they are never tired of dubbing him as a reactionary Prince and an enemy of progress! It is said that he is an Imperialist at heart; but if that be so, it is an article of faith with him that true 'Imperialism is a spiritual sympathy more than a material bondage.' Having spent his early life in England, the nursery of free institutions, he is naturally inclined to the orderly growth and development of free institutions suited to the times and environment, but he is an enemy of revolutionary ideas and has set a stern face against disloyal Indians bent on wrecking the Empire. India's safety lies in the Empire's strength.

The Jam Saheb is one of those who believe in sound and well-thought out political advance, suited to the spirit of the age . . . The Jam Saheb's devotion to the person and throne of His Majesty the King-Emperor is founded on his deep sense of loyal duty, and he is a great pillar of the Empire . . .'

The main thrust of the book was however the preservation of the monarchist tradition of the Indian states and the need for Britain to ensure their survival in the insecure future. Towards this end Dumasia mustered a variety of arguments to make the same points: that the 'aggressive nationalism' in British India had made the states nervous; that monarchy, with or without modifications, can equally provide for the well-being of subjects as compared to Western democracy; that the peculiar Indian mind was unsuitable for the rough and tumble of democratic institutions and that India understood one kind of rule only: the rule of the person rather than the rule of the machine (bureaucracy) as prevalent in British India.

Dumasia cautioned that the new ideals spawned after the Great War had created great unrest in British India. Therefore, the government would have to rely more and more upon the Indian Princes for preserving the stability of the Empire. This made it imperative for the maintenance of good relations between the two. What would the powers and prerogatives of the ancient states be, if and when the fate of India passes into the hands of lawyers, schoolmasters and professional politicians, he wondered.

Dumasia also railed against the introduction of democracy in the States. The states' subjects, he claimed, were more conservative than their rulers, remained unmoved and unaffected by the changes in British India. They were contented and did not understand the meaning of statecraft which they were inclined to leave to their hereditary rulers. Neither was there any demand nor any capacity for self-government which was quite foreign to their nature and traditions. 'Paternal rule is, with but one or two exceptions, the only government to which they are accustomed and they are content to continue it,' he stressed.

He also ridiculed fears that at the first symptoms of an outbreak in British India, the subjects of Indian states would join the revolutionaries there and make short shrift of the princes. He argued that rulers, like Mewar, enjoyed the deepest veneration because of their descent. Moreover, representative institutions in the states were nowhere entrusted even with that imperfect control over the executive which they possessed in British India. There is no press in the states and public opinion is far weaker than in British India. There is neither any demand nor any capacity for self-government which is quite foreign to their nature and traditions, he stated. Expressing concern about the threat to the states due to the ambition and sinister motives of the extremists, he asked:

Would they ever consent to be controlled and swayed by a popular assembly deriving its powers from an ignorant electorate in British India? Indian politicians do not possess the tradition of rule and . . . from the standpoint of an Indian aristocrat, this particular class has no place in the scheme of Government. How can they be expected to rule successfully? Have they any real stake in the country? . . . Can they command the unquestioning allegiance of fighting men, prepared to die in their service? Have they any traditions of knightly honour and the pride of breeding which can alone enable power to be exercised wisely and firmly? The Indian Princes see that the personnel of the

Government of India is being increasingly indianised. They apprehend that a day may come when a Prince may perhaps find himself under the political control of his own native born subjects.

To ensure the continuance of British supremacy in India, Dumasia suggested mutual cooperation and strengthening of those Indian States that have been keeping the mighty Empire afloat. He bemoaned that seditionists and extremists were calling the shots and putting the very existence of British rule in peril. He also rued that 'hair-brained agitators in British India' were making vain attempts to destroy that still extant loyalty to the throne so that the fate of India may pass in their hands!

> It is obvious that all the demands put forward by hot-headed politicians claiming to speak on behalf of united India when unity is non-existent cannot be satisfied for a long time to come. If they were to be satisfied, British authority would be reduced to a pale shadow and that such a thing may be allowed to happen is inconceivable so long as Great Britain is responsible for the good governance of India. But that is not all. A new cult has sprung up—non-violent non-co-operation which aims at revolution and destruction of British power and British authority. If that were unexpectedly realised it would mean the ruin of the ancient country, and would usher in the unspeakable horrors of anarchy. But, fortunately, for India, the bulk of the people never looks for wisdom in that quarter and moreover that cult has almost died of its own inanity.

Highlighting the prevalence of communal harmony and mutual tolerance in Native States, Dumasia suggested that the princes could play an effective part in maintaining communal amity. He further observed that communal trouble in India had increased since Mr Gandhi appeared on the scene as a peace-maker.

A quote by the Aga Khan from his 'India in Transition' neatly summed up the case: that 'the Indian Princes are the real bulwarks of the Imperial connection and an insuperable barrier to the success of the ambition of those who are determined to wreck the British power in India'.

'Will British statesmen realise the necessity of upholding the prestige and dignity of the States, which have proved themselves the staunchest allies of the British Government and which have considered no sacrifice too great for cementing their ties with the Empire?' Dumasia asked.

SO much for Nawanagar's timely initiative. At the collective level the princes too started gearing up for the arrival of the Indian States Inquiry Committee during the winter of 1927-28. The Chamber of Princes, under the chancellorship of the Maharaja of Patiala, set up a high flying 'Special Organization' headed by Kailash Haskar, Dewan of Gwalior, and Rushbrook-Williams, to present their case to the committee.

The leading princes were asked to fund the unit and Nawanagar himself pledged Rs 1 lakh for the purpose. The Special Organization in turn hired the pricey Conservative barrister, Sir Leslie Scott, KC, to prepare its brief for a juicy fee, despite opposition from states like Mysore, Baroda and Hyderabad. Consequently, some states refused to pay up their pledged amounts and the Jam Saheb, who would become terribly enamoured of the English lawyer, sanctioned a loan to meet the shortfall.

The Jam Saheb, in fact, appealed to the rulers of the more important states of Kathiawar like Morvi, Wankaner, Wadhwan and Palitana, to send in their contribution to this cause. He made it known to them that the failure to raise the amount would constitute a grave slight to the Chamber of Princes.

Scott's appointment and the public relations campaign that the Special Organization orchestrated on behalf of the Native Princes impressed few at home. The *Indian National Herald* criticized the princes for 'wasting the money filched out of the poorest peasantry in the world in enjoying the best available and costliest legal talent in England, at fabulous fees, and creating a spurious sympathy for them in the English Press through ways which cannot by any means be called very desirable'.

For all the fat fee that he commanded, the conservative Scott would badly let the princes down. Propelled by his own imperial logic, he prepared an unrealistic brief on the paramountcy question, heavily tilted in favour of the states. This was akin to waving the red flag before the all-paramount British bull. Scott's hardline manifesto—the creation of an executive 'States Council' comprising three princes nominated by the Chamber of Princes, two English politicians nominated by the Crown and the political secretary to deliberate on the vexatious subjects—alarmed not only the moderate princes but also nationalist opinion. Scott's proposals, outlined in his speech at a grand celebration in Jamnagar to mark the anniversary of the installation of the Jam Saheb on the *gaddi*, set off alarm bells in the *Rajasthan Kesari*:

> That speech is very terrible for the subjects of the Native States. And the subjects of Indian India should take a warning from it and it is necessary that they should even from now raise their strong protest against it. Looking at the terrible words uttered by Sir Leslie Scott at Jamnagar, we feel that a terrible plot is being hatched against the people of the Native States. And the Native Princes are themselves forming a scheme for the purpose . . .

Ironically, when the Butler committee arrived in India to commence its inquiry, the Native Princes were not quite ready to present their case. They had to send a delegation to London later for the purpose, inviting further ridicule. Nevertheless, the committee did its rounds of the Native States gathering evidence. It however refused to entertain representations from Native States' subjects. The committee also visited Jamnagar to meet the regional princes. The highlight of the visit was a lovely banquet which concluded with Dame Clara Butt, a guest of the Jam Saheb, singing 'God Save the King' to rapturous applause.

The Jam Saheb made a hard-hitting speech on the occasion. He did not mince his words and flatly accused the government of failing to observe its treaties:

> We credit the government with a sincere desire to respect our treaties in letter and in spirit, but in practice results have not kept pace with intentions . . . Thus in spite of an identity of interests and the best of intentions on both sides, harmonious working is not achieved, and

the Princes and Chiefs have felt that treaties are not faithfully achieved in spite of repeated pledges and assurances in the past.

But the *Jam-e-Jamshed* thought that the whole *tamasha* was a washout:

It is not very frequently we hear of the activities of the Indian States Inquiry Committee and if their activities have been, even since their appointment, what an account of their visit to Jamnagar would lead us to think, we are afraid nothing substantial is likely to be achieved by the British trio . . . If the speech delivered by the Jam Saheb is to any extent an index to the mentality of the Ruling Princes of Kathiawar, one may well predict that so far as the people of the States are concerned, they will hardly mind a place in the deliberations of these big folks . . . . The Princes have so far only been too conscious of their own rights and privileges which they are out to safeguard against any undue and uncalled for aggression on the part of the Government of India . . .

The Chamber of Princes was further embarrassed by a leak of an alleged 'confidential memorandum' prepared by the Special Organization for the perusal of the committee. It was believed that this missive was penned by either the Jam Saheb or the Maharaja of Bikaner, a surmise quite in keeping with the opinion held of the Nawanagar leader by the nationalist press. It was alleged that the Native Princes had suggested in the memorandum that the Political Department should be entirely manned by Britishers on the specious reason that it was 'derogatory to our dignity' to obey the orders of Indians in the Department, more so if they were subjects of Native States. Commenting on the alleged proposal, the *Indian National Herald* asked:

Can degeneration and mental perversity go any further? Is it not humiliating to these worthies to be dictated to by the foreigners? It is, we suppose, a high honour. But the moment one from their own race is brought in, their dignity is insulted. Moreover, they want foreigners 'in view of the special relations existing between the States and the Paramount Power' and because 'the rulers of Indian States are Indians themselves . . . Why it is derogatory to obey the orders of Indians is not stated. But we need not expect logic or reason from such quarters. They are entirely guided by their prejudices and false sense of dignity and the Paramount Power has taken mighty care to see that those prejudices are anti-Indian and that their sense of dignity should revolt against their countrymen.

The report was however contradicted by Colonel Haskar. He stated that neither Nawanagar nor Bikaner was the author of the note and that the question of the appointment of Indians in the Political Department formed no part of the case presented on behalf of the states to the Butler committee.

IN the end, all the exertions of the Jam Saheb and the Native Princes went in vain. The *Report of the Indian States Committee 1928–29* released in March 1929, refused to humour princely aspirations on paramountcy, which it decreed rested firmly in the hands of the Paramount Power. 'Not a single of the Princes' political or economic aspirations have been fulfilled but on the contrary,' the *Bombay Samachar* noted, 'the unmitigated supremacy of the Paramount Power has been thrust upon them'.

The denouement may have come as a rude shock to the Princes but could anything else have been expected? For example, in the nineteenth century itself, Sir Bartle Frere, the Governor of Bombay, touching on this issue in his minute of 21 March 1863 addressed to the Secretary of State, had declared:

It seems to me that the Kathiawar chiefs have always enjoyed independent jurisdiction within their own possessions but I think there is a wide difference between this and independent sovereignty. I hardly think that any tributary chief can be considered practically independent.

If the British Crown is not sovereign and does not claim the allegiance of the inhabitants of Kathiawar as its subjects, who is sovereign, and to whom is allegiance due? Clearly not to the Gaikwad, for he has transferred his rights to us; clearly not to any one of the chiefs for as among themselves they admit no superior. The sovereign power of making war and peace must reside somewhere; if not in the British Crown, where does it reside?

And even if the Jam Saheb was as disappointed as the rest of his princely colleagues, he should have known better. He himself conceded the paramountcy of the Government of India during one of his early skirmishes with the bureaucracy, when he wrote to a British official on 13 August 1913:

> . . . if however the Government of India are still determined to interfere with the internal affairs of my State I can only reply that Government is paramount and can do so as it may please . . .

The princes rushed to London to salvage the situation. They earned brownie points by shouting from the rooftops that they were loyal only to the Crown and would refuse to ally with a *swaraj* government. But it was of no use. The Jam Saheb tried to repair the damage by a series of speeches to important audiences. Addressing the National Liberal Club under the presidency of Lord Beauchamp, he called for fair treatment from the British government and for the exclusion of party politics from Indian affairs. The rights of the States had been overlooked, he alleged, and pressures had been brought on them to conclude agreements entirely for the benefit of British India:

> . . . The Princes want justice to be done . . . The 108 Princes who are members of the Council of Princes are quite reasonable men, and it is as human beings that they wish to be approached. The Indian Princes ask the British public to help them by getting their many questions into a right focus with a view to action thereupon. I know enough of Englishmen to cherish the conviction that nothing but justice will be done. To that end I ask you to exert yourselves to see that the word of Great Britain, which was pledged to the Princes, is not broken; that just as we have played the game and will continue to play the game by Great Britain, with unswerving loyalty and attachment to the Crown, so Britain will play the game by us in the spirit of true sportsmanship . . .

AS their ill luck would have had it, the Native Princes suffered a double blow on account of the formation of Indian States Inquiry Committee. Not only were they let down by it on the vital issue of paramountcy but its appointment inadvertently resulted in the opening of another front against the princes. In as much as the princes geared up to present their case to the committee it also propelled Native States subjects to unite at the national level to articulate their grievances against the 'unparalleled autocracy' of the states. The Jam Saheb, in particular, became a prime casualty in these developments.

The process of ferment in the region against princely misrule had begun a long time ago. In December 1917 Kutch-Kathiawadis residing in Bombay decided to unite for carrying out agitations to secure the rights of their brethren back home. The non-cooperation movement in British India after World War I provided the push for Native States subjects to join the freedom struggle. They began picketing shops selling liquor and foreign cloth in Kathiawar.

Since the Congress anyway was outlawed in most Kathiawar states[7], citizens of the patriotic states began to form their own pro-Congress organizations, *praja mandals* (people's organizations) and *parishads* (conferences). Their aims were two-fold: to promote the rule of law in the states and self-rule for the country.

Angered by princely excesses and frustrated by their own individual impotence, Mansukhlal Rajivbhai Mehta, a jeweller and Gandhian activist, founded the Kathiawar Rajkiya Parishad (Kathiawar Political Conference) after a series of discussions with activists like Amritlal Sheth on the possibilities of forming 'an institution to represent the needs of the people'. An offshoot of the 'comparatively moderate body' the Kathiawar Hitvardhak Sabha (Kathiawar Welfare Promotion Group), the KPC's first conference was held in Rajkot in 1921, albeit with the permission of the local ruler.

---

[7]Nawanagar, Junagadh and Gondal refused to even allow public meetings or distribution of nationalist literature.

The Native States rulers obviously did not take kindly to these popular movements and either banned them or kept their citizens on a tight leash. The *Sanj Vartaman* singled out the Chiefs of Jamnagar, Porbander and Rajkot as those who had adopted a repressive policy towards popular movements. The *Gujarati* claimed that 'an Indian chief who poses as an enlightened ruler has prevented his subjects from taking part in the KPC by threats of confiscating their property'. The Jamnagar police had made their intentions clear during the non-cooperation movement itself by clamping down immediately on a group of agitators who were ordered to leave the city at once. They were also prevented from making any speech on the Khilafat issue.

One particular incident which created a furore in early 1921 was the dispersal with a baton charge by the Jamnagar police of a public meeting to highlight grievances of Native States subjects. It was to be addressed by Manilal Kothari, the KPC honorary secretary. A meeting to be addressed by Mr Shukla to protest against the police action was also banned in Rajkot, a civil station. Howled the *Bombay Chronicle* in disgust:

> Jamnagar has lately demonstrated its concern for the greater happiness and progress of its 'subjects'. Our readers may have read how the State Police, on the advice, no doubt, of those who are running the State in the absence of the Ruler on a more 'momentous' mission abroad, dispersed with a baton charge a peaceful meeting of the inhabitants of the city who had assembled to hear an address from the honorary secretary of the KPC on 'Native States' . . .

Commenting on the same incident, 'Pharos' said in the *Hindusthan*:

> Indian States are difficult to improve. Some of them are so disgustingly antediluvian that no modern light can ever penetrate there. It appears that Mr Kothari went to lecture about Indian States to Jamnagar. Any number of citizens had collected to hear him but before he could speak, the police came and dispersed the audience by force. Mr Kothari then went to somewhere near the railway station. The audience followed

him there and the lecture was delivered. These facts prove that there are many people in the Indian States who want to have their States reformed. But their rulers are perverse brutes. The Jam of Jamnagar is not enlightened although he has received his education in England. He is most unjust and autocratic. The Chamber of Princes will help him but not his people! A tragical institution indeed!

In December 1927 Native States subjects finally decided to bite the bullet by forming an all-India organization, the All India States' Peoples' Conference, in Bombay. They demanded the rule of law in their territories, the right to have a say in their governance and the speedy attainment of *swarajya* for India. If the princes could have their own chamber to partake in the administration of India, why should not Indian States subjects have a voice in their own administration, they asked.

The AISPC rendered yeoman service in creating a nationwide awareness of princely misrule. Radicals however dismissed it as an emasculated body and a front for entrepreneurs wanting to enlarge their business in the Native States. There may have been an inkling of truth to this charge, considering that the likes of entrepreneur Jamnalal Bajaj were among its core members.

The *Saurashtra* office functioned as the AISPC's regional headquarters in Kathiawar. Many of the AISPC's founder-members like Manilal Kothari, Balwantrai Mehta, Ganesh Raghunath Abhyankar and Amritlal Sheth were Congressmen or connected with the party or freedom struggle in some way. The organization, in fact, was considered as 'Indian India's' equivalent of the Congress. The Indian National Congress however followed a policy of non-intervention in the affairs of the Native States, even though its Calcutta session of 1928 assured the states' peoples of its sympathy and support in their legitimate struggle for responsible government.

Gandhiji had praised the sacrifices of Kothari and Mansukhlal in *Young India* in early 1922 and Sardar Vallabhbhai Patel declared in his presidential address to the KPC at Morvi that the people have the right to dethrone an oppressive ruler. Yet the Congress kept a hands-off policy towards the Native States which disappointed many, including the indefatigable Sheth. His differences with the two titans of the freedom struggle on their approach to the liberation of the states' peoples were obvious.

Gandhiji, who hailed from the princely state of Porbander where his father was Dewan to the ruler, naively visualized the Indian prince as a 'trustee' of the people and custodian of Indian culture. He believed the princes would make common cause with the Indian people and join the freedom struggle. Hence his ambivalence about supporting the struggles in the states. This was amply reflected in his mild speeches at a KPC rally in June 1925, which came as a big disappointment to states' subjects.

Ultimately however, the Mahatma veered around to the view that 'the princes are puppets, created or tolerated for the upkeep and prestige of British power'. At the Haripura session in 1938, Congressmen finally decided to participate in agitations in the states. A year later Jawaharlal Nehru was made president of the AISPC at Ludhiana and the organization formally became an extension of the Congress.

Men like the AISPC's scholarly general secretary Professor Abhyankar[8] and its future president C.Y. Chintamani were at best moderates. The *Bombay Samachar* hailed Abhyankar as a 'scholar' and Chintamani as a 'patriot' and noted that these gentlemen had not resorted to outlawry against the Native States nor had they any personal grievances against the princes. However, Alan Ross has alleged that Abhyankar nursed a personal grudge against the Jam Saheb and hence carried out an unrelenting campaign against the latter.

According to Ross, in 1919, when the Jam Saheb was general secretary of the Princes' Conference, Abhyankar was found present in the Conference Hall at Delhi holding a false ticket and the Jam had the responsibility of evicting him. From that day the 'pamphleteer'

[8]The father of the states' peoples' movement.

began waging an 'unremitting campaign' against the Jam Saheb, whose motivation appeared to be no more than resentment against the humiliation of that incident, charged Ross.

However, a different rendition of that incident is offered by Abhyankar's biographer and granddaughter, Ranjana Kaul. Abhyankar had begun delving into the problems of Native States subjects from an early age, she informed. In November 1917, following the announcement of the Montford Reforms, he published a booklet entitled 'Native States and Post War Reforms'. This, along with his press articles, brought him national recognition.

In January 1919 Abhyankar attended the second Princes Conference session in Delhi with Shahu Chattrapati, Maharaja of Kolhapur. Kaul revealed that although Kolhapur was given his tickets and entry permits to the visitors' gallery for his retinue, bigger princes immediately complained about this to the officer in charge of arrangements, Major O'Brien. And although Kolhapur backed him, Abhyankar was not allowed to attend the session.

The Sangli lawyer himself later explained in the *Indian States Journal* why he was expelled. Abhyankar believed that finding themselves unable to oust Kolhapur, the princes decided to make him the scapegoat and also punish him for the views he had expressed in his book. However, the dissenting note Kolhapur presented at the session made Lord Chelmsford recommend the inclusion of other lesser states in the organization to enable them to have a voice in matters affecting their interest. In February 1921 Kolhapur once again took Abhyankar as one of his advisers to the inauguration of the Chamber of Princes. He then asked in advance if there were any objections to the latter attending. There were none and Abhyankar duly attended the opening ceremony.

In due course Abhyankar plunged full time into the struggle of the Native States' subjects. A persuasive journalist, he wrote convincingly about the massacre of about 600 poor 'ryots' of Nemuchana village in Alwar in May 1925 and the 'Malabar Hill Tragedy' of January 1925 which resulted in the abdication of Tukojirao Holkar of Indore.[9] Abhyankar also started the publication *Sansthani Swarajya* with the active support of his friend Amritlal Sheth.

The AISPC did not enjoy any official leverage with either the Native Princes or the British government. Lord Irwin even refused to let them present their case at the ISIC sittings. The AISPC president, Dewan Bahadur Ramachandra Rao, Abhyankar and the famous activist-lawyer, Popatlal Chudgar, had followed the Butler committee to London. But they were rebuffed. So were their attempts to get representation at the Round Table Conference later.

The trio however managed to present a memorandum to the ISIC dated 19 November 1928 detailing the excesses in the Native States. Speaking about the 'Absence of Rule of Law' in Nawanagar, the AISPC quoted an order in the *State Gazette of Nawanagar* which read as follows:

> All are hereby informed that no person, association or gathering should address a public meeting in political matters, without the permission of the Political Secretary, which should be secured in advance. Further, no political meeting of any kind should be held. Those who act otherwise would be legally proceeded against.

In 1929 the AISPC launched a sustained propaganda blitz against tyrannical regimes. At its second session in Bombay (25-26 May), accounts of the repression in the states were tabled. In his principal speech, Abhyankar railed against conditions prevailing in most States and claimed that there was no responsible government nor rule of law there. Neither were the rulers responsible to their subjects nor had the latter any voice in taxation, legislation or administration. Except in three states, namely Mysore, Travancore and Cochin, absolute autocracy and despotism prevailed in most others. There was no security of personal property, no freedom of conscience, no liberty of speech and discussion, no association of the people in the government, no control

---

[9]*See*, Notes, pages 156–58.

over finances, and lastly, no provision against arbitrary acts of officials.

Later that year, the release of Popatlal Chudgar's *Indian Princes Under British Protection: A Study of their Personal Rule, their Constitutional Position and their Future* came as another body blow to princely prestige. The stated aim of the exposé was to emancipate the millions of the Indian States citizens groaning under the autocratic rule of the princes. Chudgar stated that he had drawn upon his considerable experience as a first-class magistrate in his own state, as a legal practitioner in the Western India States Agency for over fourteen years, as an activist of the AISPC and upon records such as the administrative reports of states and such other authorized publications in compiling his case.

Chudgar dissected various aspects of princely rule like slavery and forced labour, taxation, land tenure, legislation, public services, judiciary and the police, education, public health and illustrations of arbitrary rule in various Native States to highlight the 'enormity off the suffering and misery under which such a large portion of humanity is groaning'. Not surprisingly, affairs at Nawanagar came in for more than a passing mention.

The 'unbearably heavy' taxation prevailing in Nawanagar—an extensive list of taxes was provided—was offered as a fairly accurate idea of taxes common to all states. 'The people's "capacity to pay" may be exploited almost to starvation point, for the Prince's power to enforce his demand is absolutely unlimited,' he noted. Apart from direct taxes, he also drew reference to many means of indirect taxation, including the issuing of licences for selling commodities such as tobacco, drugs and intoxicating liquors, and the granting of monopolies in respect of particular trade and industries.

'In the particular list under consideration, it will be seen that His Highness the Maharaj Ranjitsinhji of Jamnagar, known as "Prince Ranji" of cricket fame, has granted monopolies for selling goods such as matches and cigarettes, petrol and kerosene oil. In each case the monopoly has been granted in consideration of a sum of from 5,000 to about 10,000 pounds,' Chudgar said.

Providing 'Illustrations of Arbitrary Rule' of the Jam Saheb, Chudgar highlighted the arrests of Mansinh Jhala of Bodi, Mulji Naagji of Lalpur, the fifty servants of the Amran Jagirdar and Mr Lavanprasad. The last named was summarily arrested in July 1929 and kept in prison without charge or trial for submitting a petition to His Highness protesting against the tyranny of monopolies for the sale of articles of daily necessities (as mentioned earlier). He was released after forty-five days' confinement, His Highness declaring that that this was done 'in exercise of our Royal clemency'.

'His offence was never alluded to, and he was never convicted. Yet, in the opinion of His Highness, to submit a petition was a serious offence meriting summary imprisonment for an indefinite period, and to release the culprit was an act of "Royal clemency",' Chudgar commented. 'The Stuart Kings of England used to talk in this strain. Evidently, His Highness the Maharaja still lives in those days'.

On the count of security of property Chudgar pointed out to the notorious examples of the seizures of the properties of the Amran Jagir and Jagir of Panchdeva. In the latter case the grounds for this seizure were that the then occupant was a spurious child of the last holder. Sir Thomas J. Stragman, ex-advocate general of Bombay, whose opinion was sought, said:

> The chain of events is really remarkable. First it is discovered 37 years after the event that his father committed a fraud, and Panch Devda should really be a 'jiwai' (a grant for maintenance). Next he is fined Rs 5,000 (400 pounds) and all his villages are attached, for what, assuming everything against him, was a mere misunderstanding. Lastly it is discovered 39 years after the event that he is illegitimate (the discovery being one which would lead to a loss of all his villages) . . . It is clear from the bare recital of facts as above that the querist can look for no justice in Nawanagar . . . If a judge could grant a drastic order depriving the querist of his villages, although no prima facie case has been made and then say it did not harm the querist so to be deprived, there is no particular reason why on no evidence whatever

he should not hold that the querist's father was guilty of fraud, that
the querist is liable for mesne profits, and that the querist is illegitimate.

The Jam Saheb's 'sham' advisory council too came in for flak.
Chudgar said it had died the day it was born and had thence showed
no signs of resurrection. He quoted the Butler committee report (para
15) which stated that 'of the 108 Princes in Class I, 30 have established
legislative councils, most of which are at present of a consultative nature
only'. And indeed, among the thirty are included deliberative bodies,
of the kind described in the State of Jamnagar. That is to say, many of
these 'Assemblies' exist only on paper!

He also dissected the administrative reports of Nawanagar state in
order to arrive at the personal expenditure of its flamboyant ruler.
According to his reading of the 1926-27 budget, the Jam Saheb included
palace expenditure, Public Works Department[10], repairs and building
of new palaces, guest departments, minor departments and unforseen
expenses in his personal expenses[11] which amounted to £700,000
out of a total revenue of £1,000,000. According to an analysis of the
budgets of various princely states, Nawanagar's taxation per head and
percentage of personal and palace expenses was found to be the highest
whereas the expenditure per head on education, public health etc.,
was among the lowest.[12]

---

[10]For motor roads used exclusively by himself and his guests.

[11]This practice by rulers in general to pass off such expenses under the head of
'public works' has been noted even by other observers.

[12]A cursory scrutiny of some earlier Nawanagar State administration reports offers
some similar interesting insights. For example, of the list of 'original works' undertaken
by the administration in 1907-08, the first year of the Jam Saheb's reign, Rs 2.55 lakhs out
of the total expenditure of Rs 2.71 lakhs was spent on items like additions and alterations
to the palaces, badminton court, duck house, cricket pavilion, roads to palace and guest
house etc. The sale of opium during the year also increased as against the previous year,
'chiefly due to the increase in the number of state guests'. In the year 1922-23, for
example, the total expenditure on education borne by the state was Rs 150,308 while
the cost of education of seven Rajkumars at Rajkumar College was Rs 45,935 during
the year, not counting those studying in England.

Summing up his testimony against the Nawanagar ruler, Chudgar declared:

> This Maharaja is a great pet of the British people, probably on account of his fame as a sportsman, a fact that enables him to defy, with impunity and even contempt, the public opinion of India . . . These are the rulers who get certificates of enlightened and progressive rule from men like Sir Walter Lawrence, Sir Sydney Low and from the British Press generally. The British Empire would be poor indeed if supported by pillars such as these.

Chudgar's charges against Nawanagar did not go uncontested. The Durbar prepared charts showing the progress made by the state during the last twenty-four years and the Jam Saheb personally informed the secretary of the Viceroy from Aden about their postage to him. He specifically mentioned that they were a reply to Chudgar's book of charges 'levelled against us in several directions'. But from the seeming lack of enthusiasm about the receipt of the rejoinder, it appears that British officials did not pay much heed to these protestations.

To add to the discomfiture of the Jam Saheb, the AISPC themselves orchestrated a campaign against tyrannical regimes through an Indian States Series of booklets that were lapped up by the public. The most sensational of these was the 'Indictment of Patiala' (1930). It presented a hair-raising account of the alleged misdeeds (which included murder, abduction, torture, rape and burning alive of women etc.) of the Punjab ruler. The *Hindustan Times* described it as 'one of the most terrible indictments of modern times'. Lord Irwin tried to get the matter investigated but it turned out to be a half-baked inquiry by the Agent to Governor-General FitzPatrick.

The Jam Saheb was also an initial target. A booklet by Abhyankar entitled 'Indian Princes as their People see them—an Inside View of the Administration of the State of Nawanagar of "Prince Ranji"' indicted the Nawanagar administration for its curtailment of freedom of speech, absence of freedom of the press, legislation and representative institutions, tyranny of monopolies and taxation, compulsory labour, poverty of education, unparalleled huge expenses on the person of His Highness and mad waste of public money over friends and entertainment. Incidentally, these very charges had been aired in various fora against the Jam Saheb from time to time.

The Durbar hit back with Naoroji Dumasia's *Nawanagar and Its Critics*, a 'critical examination and review' of these charges wherein the twenty-one main criticisms made by the AISPC were printed on the left-hand page and the Durbar's detailed replies on the right. In Britain, Charles Kincaid's hagiography, *The Land of Ranji and Duleep*, was also released to assuage public feelings over the unrelenting criticism of the Jam Saheb. But the damage had been done.

Alan Ross, an unabashed admirer of Ranji, seems to have been taken in by the Durbar's explanations, for he has commented in hindsight: 'In isolation, many of the (AISPC) criticisms seem to contain elements of truth, but when examined in context their formulation appears specious. The Durbar's refutations were supported by meticulously presented facts and figures, the authority of which was independently vouched for'.

However, some Indian historians have preferred to go along with the AISPC brief. What is more, internal correspondence of the time has revealed that British officials were not dismissive of them either.

Among Indian historians, S.B. Rajyogar, chief editor of the District Gazetteer from 1973-78, has provided a critical account of Nawanagar affairs in his *History of Gujarat*. Rajyogar recounts that in Jamnagar State under Ranjitsinghji, the doyen of cricket and Chancellor of the Chamber of Princes, people were groaning under heavy taxes. The freedom of exporting and importing commodities was so restricted as to turn it into a state monopoly. The Nawanagar people were also heavily taxed. But such taxes, he said, were common in many states. There were special taxes when the ruler wanted to build a palace or buy a motor car or when there was a marriage ceremony of his

sons and daughters. When the rulers visited the villages under their
jurisdiction, the whole village had to bear the burden of entertaining
the chief:

> In Jamnagar a number of oppressive laws restricting people's liberty
> and creating monopolies were enacted. All protests and petitions had
> failed. So the States People's Conference took up the cause of the
> people of Jamnagar. They organised protest meetings and started a
> campaign against the state administration in the press. *Saurashtra* was
> the weekly which exposed the hollowness of Jam Ranajit's so called
> progressive administration. A prominent worker of the state presented
> a petition to the Jam Saheb. Instead of hearing him, the worker was
> slapped on the face and imprisoned. After much public pressure, the
> men were released but the Jam Saheb denied any oppression and
> system of monopoly. So a committee was appointed for investigation.
> There was a ban on the entry of the committee but the committee
> had investigated and published a report in 1928 indicting the Jam
> Saheb. There was a black flag demonstration when the Jam Saheb
> returned from England. The state had resorted to terrorising activities
> to suppress the agitation.

Nawanagar's repression and the oppressive system of monopolies
had indeed triggered off protests in the territory. The Jamnagar Praja
Parishad decided to institute an inquiry under the leadership of Jamnadas
Mehta into the monopolies issue. The Jam Saheb banned the entry of
Mehta and members of JPP into the state. Its three prominent leaders
were jailed and the AISPC agitation slowly fizzled out.

Saurashtra brought out a special supplement on 17 August 1929, in
connection with the agitation against heavy taxation and monopolies
in Nawanagar. It reported that the Nawanagar police had been posted
at all entrances and at all important places in the state to prevent the
members of the JPP inquiry committee into the alleged monopolies
from entering Jamnagar limits. The Jamnagar police detectives have
gone as far afield as the Rajkot, Wankaner and Wadhwan stations, it
said, to provide warnings of the approach of the committee. It reported

that Manilal Kothari (described by the British as a 'notorious agitator') was at Rajkot watching developments, and that a cable had been sent to the Jam Saheb who is in England. The paper reported that the Jamnagar public were anxiously awaiting the arrival of the committee and exhorted its members to proceed to the capital at all costs.

The unrest in Nawanagar was obviously being carefully monitored by the British too. An official from Camp Dhrangadhra, reporting on 'Jamnagar affairs' to Sir Charles Watson, Political Secretary, Government of India, commented that the *Saurashtra* supplement was written in the usual florid style of the editor, Amritlal Sheth, and that the facts were probably greatly exaggerated. But it was true, he said, that a posse of Jamnagar police were for a short time posted at Jamnagar railway station; and that civilian informers in *mufti* frequented the Rajkot station at the times of departure of trains for Jamnagar.

Nawanagar's repressive tactics generated such indignation that they invited censure at a Kathiawar Yuvak Parishad conference held at Rajkot in August 1929. According to a British government intelligence report, 3,000 persons attended the function at Nutan Theatre, including twenty-five ladies and some Mahommedans. National songs were sung and messages of sympathy received from Gandhi, Vallabhbhai Patel and Jinnah among others. Secret agents of Jamnagar and Gondal were present among the audience.

On the second day of the conference, seventeen resolutions were brought forward, including one condemning the prohibitory order issued by the Jamnagar State in forbidding its youth to attend the conference. Another resolution congratulated Mr Lavanprasad, 'who gladly accepted with public spirit and courage all these atrocities perpetrated on him by Jamshahi for his petition to the latter against the *ijaras* (monopolies) in the state'. Yet another resolution asked for the restoration of rights of independence of speech and right of public meeting which has been taken away in certain states, Jamnagar included.

The British may have winked at the repressive nature of the Nawanagar administration. But they were seemingly more concerned about the Jam Saheb's financial and administrative affairs. A Palitan official's complaint in July 1929 to the Simla-based Watson on the 'Unsatisfactory position of Nawanagar finances and alleged grant of monopolies by the State' could be taken as an indirect endorsement of his critics' charges:

> Evidence as to the Jam Saheb's financial straits is accumulating. I have only just ascertained the facts about the unpleasantness in Bombay at the time of his departure for England. The Nawanagar Durbar recently sold the five-year monopoly for the sale of kerosene oil and petrol for a sum of Rs 1,01,000. This caused some agitation in Jamnagar, in the course of which one Lavanprasad was arrested on the ground that his applications to the Jam Saheb contained seditious matter. This led to further agitation in Bombay . . . The Jamnagar Praja Mandal sent a delegation to wait on the Jam Saheb in Bombay and asked for an interview . . . He refused at first, later granted one at the Taj Mahal Hotel to Jamandas Mehta, president of the JPM. He denied monopolies, except for salt. Agreed to set up independent committee. I haven't heard of the results of this committee's deliberations but the Jam Saheb's denial of monopolies can hardly be true, and I believe that other monopolies exist in Nawanagar, on matches for instance. I hear that he has cut down expenses in Jamnagar in every way. The Military Advisers visiting Jamnagar now have to sign for drinks and say that the food at the Rest House is worse than that usually obtainable at a dak bungalow.

But the Jam Saheb's newfound scruples on the entertainment front at home were apparently not matched by any restraint abroad, judging from a pithy notation by another official on the same file: 'His Highness' financial position is not likely to improve by his mode of life in England'.

Notes

1. On 15 May 1925 a massacre of poor ryots took place at Nemuchana village in Alwar. The massacre came to light when a survivor who

escaped to Kanpur revealed the story to the *Pratap*. According to him, about 600 people were killed, hundreds of cattle destroyed and the entire village was set ablaze by hoodlums allegedly owing allegiance to the Maharaja. The story was picked up by the entire Hindi and nationalist press and the Delhi Congress Committee and the Rajasthan Seva Sangh demanded an inquiry. The Maharaja issued a belated and vague press note explaining the incident but Abhyankar's impassioned denunciations of the martial law imposed by the state to quell the agitation of the ryots generated enormous public pressure for an inquiry by the government into the internal affairs of the state. Ultimately, the tyrannical Alwar was deposed in 1933 when an uprising of his Meo subjects resulted in a conflagration that required emphatic British intervention.

2. The 'Malabar Hill Tragedy' of January 1925 was more in the nature of a sensational and squeamish potboiler and Abhyankar's sustained campaign ultimately resulted in the abdication of the chief villain, Tukojirao Holkar, the Maharaja of Indore. On 12 Jan 1925, around midnight, a businessman Abdul Kader Bawla and his mistress Mumtaz Begum were driving along Walkeshwar Road on Malabar Hill when they were waylaid by men travelling in a red Maxwell bearing an Indore State number plate. The men began firing at Mr Bawla and his companions and in the scuffle that ensued, Bawla was shot (he died later in hospital), Mumtaz was grievously stabbed and another person sustained a bullet injury. Two army officers who were passing by and came to the help of the victims were also attacked. In the investigations and trial that followed it was found that the assailants were connected to the Indore Durbar and that other Durbar personnel and infrastructure were involved or used in the conspiracy. It further transpired that Mumtaz Begum was a former mistress of the Indore Maharaja but had escaped his clutches to secure her freedom. The incensed Maharaja had therefore apparently hatched a conspiracy to kidnap her and take her back. While the assailants were tried and several of them

found guilty and sentenced, Abhyankar relentlessly campaigned that the 'ultimate source or sources which inspired and bribed the condemned wretched to undertake the sinister crime' be also brought to book. Ultimately, pressure was built up to such an extent that a year later the Maharaja abdicated the throne in favour of his son rather than face a government Commission of Inquiry to investigate his alleged connection to the crime.

VII *Federation Exalted, Federation Betrayed*

WHEN the Native Princes were clean bowled by the Butler Committee on the vexatious issue of paramountcy, they never imagined that they would get another chance to bat again. The unexpected second innings came in the form of the Irwin Declaration of 1 November 1929, inviting all Indian political leaders to a Round Table Conference on constitutional reforms leading ultimately towards 'Dominion Status' to take place in London in late 1930.

By virtue of being imperial allies, the Native Princes could not say no. But the Indian National Congress at its Lahore session in December 1929 rejected the RTC bait. Instead, it passed a resolution demanding *purna swaraj* (complete self-rule). It followed this up with an 'Independence Day' celebration on 26 January 1930. Two months later Gandhiji signalled the start of the Civil Disobedience Movement with his Dandi march-for-salt, *satyagraha*. Had the Native Princes not played ball with the Government of India, albeit to further their own agenda, the political process and the RTC would have been derailed.

There would be three editions of the RTC in London, the first from 12 November 1930 to 19 January 1931, the second from 7 September to 1 December 1931 and the third and final one from 17 November to 24 December 1932. The INC boycotted the first and the third RTCs[1] while Gandhiji attended the second as its sole representative after brokering a truce with Lord Irwin.

The idea of an all-India Federation had been around since 1918. Under this constitutional arrangement the Native States, the provinces of British India and other sectional interests such as the minorities

---

[1] These were not attended even by the Labour Party.

and depressed classes were to be brought together under one governing roof.

Liberal representatives of the princely order like Kailash Haskar and K.M. Pannikar sold this concept to the princes as an ideal opportunity to free themselves from the shackles of paramountcy. Hence the enthusiastic participation of most of them in the process, at least in the beginning. Nevertheless, Federation took five years in the making, the embryo being delivered as the Government of India Act of 1935, two years after the Jam Saheb's death.

The 1935 Act envisaged a conservative lobby of princes in the Upper House to check popular decisions taken in the Lower House. The British hoped that this conservative bloc, by holding together, would prevent any legislation that diluted their interests. British officials, like the new conservative Viceroy, the Marquess of Linlithgow, saw Federation as the perfect vehicle for propelling India towards self-government without endangering imperial interests.

However, nobody else was fooled. Independent historians like R.J. Moore have opined that the underlying motives of the RTCs (meant to usher in Federation) were 'not to fix any date for independence, chiefly to put this off to the kalends'. Moore described the 1935 Act as a dubious stratagem meant to condemn India to 'a constitutional dead end,' inspired as it was by the 'hardly concealed desire to evade tranference of power'.

Indian nationalist opinion was equally scathing and labelled the Act as a 'slave constitution' and 'a new charter of bondage'. Pandit Jawaharlal Nehru said that 'a more incompatible and absurd Union . . . is difficult to imagine between the autocracy of the states and the democracy of the rest of India'. But the Congress decided to take part in the provincial elections proposed later under the Act, if only to undermine it.

Linlithgow moved heaven and earth to get the princes to assent to the terms of the 1935 Act. But one by one they fell out. The government's offer was finally rejected by the Chamber of Princes at Bombay in 1939. The sudden outbreak of World War II was the last straw that broke Federation's back. Linlithgow himself believed that if the war had not intervened, Federation would have come by 1941.

When the war ended, India's inexorable march towards independence had entered the slog overs. There was no way that Federation could have been revived. Ultimately, the princes were asked by the last Viceroy, Lord Mountbatten, to join one or the other Dominions (India or Pakistan). And almost all did so by Independence, some voluntarily, others by persuasion.

In a way Federation was doomed from the very beginning because the impossibility of forging a working alliance between the contending forces of democrats and feudalists made it a non-starter. All in all, Federation met an inglorious end due to its own complexities and contradictions and the broad range of forces opposing it, including those from the princely cabal and the British government itself.

BUT Federation's dismal end was in start contrast to the rosy optimism that greeted its inception and that of the reforms process. And no man was keener to see India advance along the long and winding road to self-government, which the reforms promised, than the Jam Saheb himself.

As Chancellor of the Chamber of Princes, the Jam Saheb had devoted '700 hours' to bring forth the 'Federated India of the future'. But he eventually grew disillusioned with Federation. His travails over it, coupled with the setbacks he faced due to the reimposition of the Viramgam Customs Line by the Government of India in 1927, took a heavy toll on his health, leading to his premature death in April 1933.

But it was a gung-ho Jam Saheb who marked out his guard when the whole process began, waxing positive about the need for political advance for the people of (British) India. At a glittering state banquet for Lord Irwin at the Badminton Hall of the Pratap Vilas Palace in Jamnagar on 18 November 1927, the Jam Saheb outlined his thoughts on this subject, albeit after articulating the standard pledges of 'individual and collective loyalty to his Imperial Majesty and the Empire' and 'as faithful allies of the British Crown, under all conditions'.

> . . . Our position in the new India that is being evolved needs to be thoroughly safeguarded . . . The Princes are, I hope, credited with the full significance of the changing times: and this I can assert, with knowledge, that they have full sympathy with the aspirations of their countrymen beyond their frontiers. Such a feeling can—and in fact does—co-exist with the natural instinct of self-preservation: we have no desire to interfere in the affairs of British India and do not wish that there should be outside interference in our domestic affairs; but there exists a common platform for co-operation in matters of imperial and mutual concern . . .

The Jam Saheb's sporting intentions were warmly applauded on the other side of the fence. Dewan Bahadur Ramchandra Rao, in his presidential speech to the newly sired AISPC, praised the Jam Saheb and the new attitude of the princes in support of the legitimate aspirations of the Indian people. The *Bombay Chronicle* too gave the Jam Saheb full marks in an editorial comment:

> Recent utterances of several Princes, the latest of them being His Highness the Jam Saheb of Nawanagar, to which the President of the All India States' Peoples' Conference rightly drew particular attention, clearly shows that the Princes as a class are as anxious as the people of India to see the country free. Left to themselves, the Princes, we are confident, will soon adjust their policy in relation to their own people as well as the people of India to see the country free . . .

Indeed, the Jam Saheb's positive outlook on the contemplated reforms were even noted by British officialdom. Australian historian Professor Ian Copland, an expert on South Asian affairs, and author of the authoritative book, *The Princes of India in the Endgame of Empire: 1917–1947*, has stated that the Jam Saheb, like several other princes at that time, was willing to countenance an alliance with nationalist politicians of moderate hue. Labour secretary of state, Wedgewood-Benn, meeting the Jam Saheb for the first time in October 1929, gathered (that):

> . . . the Jam Saheb and most of those with whom he is associated have a good deal of sympathy with the Moderate Politicians in British India; and he committed himself to the view that a clear definition by the Governor-General as to the goal of British policy . . . would greatly help in clearing away the suspicion that the British are not entirely sincere in their professions of a desire for India's political advancement.

But the princes gradually began frittering away the goodwill they had generated in British India by their faux pas. The Chamber of Princes, under Patiala's chancellorship, passed a resolution on 1 March 1930 declaring its emphatic disapproval of the independence movement and the Congress' intentions to separate from the British Empire. British India was naturally aghast. After the start of the CDM, the hostility towards the government and its collaborators escalated. Like at the time of the non-cooperation movement the country was once again polarized. The RTC delegates were dubbed as 'traitors' by protestors and they were greeted by black flags as they embarked on the sea voyage to England. Some protestors even wished that the *Viceroy of India*, which ferried some of the delegates, would prove unworthy during the voyage!

The Jam Saheb had reached England much earlier in June 1930. Naturally, all of England was worried whether the reforms would lead to India snapping links with the Empire. The Jam Saheb therefore took it upon himself to assure all and sundry that the princes would never let the Empire down whatever the outcome of the reforms. As a cricketing great, an avowed loyalist and a ruling prince, the Jam Saheb enjoyed his fair share of public speaking engagements. He made full use of such opportunities to inject his own political concerns couched in cricketing terminology in his speeches to captive audiences.

One such occasion was a farewell dinner hosted by the President of Marylebone Cricket Club, Sir Kynaston Studd, to the Australian visiting team captained by W.M. Woodful in September 1930. The Jam Saheb recreated 'a striking analogy between the British Empire and cricket' while replying to the toast of 'Cricket':

> I very much doubt whether there is any country in the world to-day, except Britain, in which a man not belonging to the country would have been selected to reply to the toast of the most characteristic national game.
>
> The countries which together compose the British Empire constitute the greatest cricket team which the world has ever seen. Just as the members of a cricket team differ from each other in stature, in personal characteristics, in ability of one kind or the other, so the various components of the British Empire differ widely among themselves. But, in one case and in the other, it is not with a series of individual units which we are concerned, but with a great team working for the common good by bringing out the best from each component member. It is this spirit, I think, which has brought the British Empire through so many trials; certainly it is this spirit which carried us successfully through the Great War. But, as it seems to me, warfare and stress are not the greatest trials to which either a cricket team or an Empire such as ours can be subjected. The mark of a good team is the manner in which it fights a steady uphill battle; the mark of a great Empire is the manner in which it can pull together with all its resources in order to make good.
>
> These post-war years are admittedly difficult. There are adjustments to be made in our Imperial team. Some of our players seem dissatisfied with their place in the team; there are whispers, although of the most irresponsible kind, of resignation. It is occasions such as this, far more than the stress of a crisis, which test both the skill in the captain and the loyalty of the team.
>
> Every cricketer knows how easy it is on certain occasions to allow himself to become discontented if he starts brooding over his own individual case. Every cricketer knows how strong is the temptation on occasion to criticise the policy of the captain; to blame him for not changing the bowling; and to criticise his placing of the field. Yet it is precisely this kind of temptation which cricket teaches us to avoid at all costs. How often have I wished that all the political leaders

in all the countries of the Empire were cricketers! For, if they had undergone the training and the discipline of the great game, I am sure they would find it easier than they appear to do at present to think first and last of the Team. I cannot help thinking that all of us in this great British Empire need more of the spirit which cricket inculcates.

For cricket is more than a game; it is really a matter of living. I am sure it is one of the greatest contributions which the British people have made to the cause of humanity. It is certainly among the most powerful of the links which keep our Empire together. So long as we can maintain in that Empire the spirit of sportsmanship which cricket inculcates, so long shall we be ready, as a team, to meet and defeat any adversity which the future may hold for us. In the crisis of the Great War, Britain captained the Imperial Team to a great victory. I am perfectly certain that, in the more difficult times of peace, we shall win by wisdom, patience, and generous good will.

The Princes of India, to whose Order I have the honour to belong, have been very old members of Great Britain's team; and both on easy and difficult wickets they have tried their best to play with a straight bat for the Empire. In times of peace, as in times of war, you will always find us ready. We are united to you and with you in the bonds of devoted loyalty to the King-Emperor. Throughout the period of adjustment of relations between Great Britain and India, upon which we are now entering, I am certain that the Indian Princes will do their best to play a part worthy of their best traditions. Like good cricketers, they endeavour to keep up their wickets even under the most difficult circumstances. You can rely upon us in the future, as you have relied upon us in the past, to play the game, and to give every support in our power to the harmony and to the success of the Imperial team.

The partisan British press lapped up this gratifying rhetoric from one of the Empire's most acclaimed citizens. The *Morning Post*, in a leading article, glowed:

We like the comparison between the English game of cricket and the British Empire, which was made by the Jam Sahib of Nawanagar in his speech. The immortal and beloved Ranji knows well—none better—

how to play the game both of cricket and of life; and he justly claims for his Order that they played the game when the British Empire—the great Eleven, as he calls it—was in danger. Like cricket, it is an affair of loyalty and co-operation. It is heartening when there is so much trouble in India to know that we have such good friends, and we know also that there are millions more like the Prince who would be prepared to play the game, if only they were allowed to play it. We could wish that our Government and the Government of India, who are so fond of listening to their enemies, would turn instead to their friends.

The *Cambridge Weekly News*, applauding 'Mr Ranjitsinhji on Imperial Federation', declared:

At the Old Higher Grade Cricket Club dinner last Tuesday Mr K.S. Ranjitsinhji contributed a few remarks which merit something more than a mere passing notice. The speaker struck a chord that will find a responsive echo wherever the English language is spoken.

Not often do Cambridge people have the opportunity of hearing one of the Queen's Indian subjects pleading eloquently for Indian Federation. That, if we mistake not, is the true inwardness of Mr Ranjitsinhji's remarks. The speaker may rest assured that in Cambridge at any rate he is not looked upon as a foreigner. He has developed qualities that appeal straight to the heart of the average Englishman. During his residence at the University of Cambridge he has unconsciously perhaps provided a powerful argument for Imperial Federation. Englishmen can appreciate and admire the qualities that have won for Mr Ranjitsinhji his Blue and although it is too much to expect that he is typical of his race it proves they have qualities dormant but which only need stimulating . . . .

Cricketer-writer Major C.H.B. Pridham was so bowled over by the Jam Saheb's discourse that he was inspired enough to name an Empire team with Britain as the obvious skipper. He, like many others, was only echoing an idea that was already in vogue for an 'Imperial Federation' to unite the Empire.

Its critics, like the Anglican missionary and Indian nationalist agitator,

Charles Freer Andrews, however, saw no reason why India should be part of this White Empire except on terms of 'actual and not merely theoretical racial equality'. Although the 'settlement colonies' were initially the preferred companions, the assertion of 'dominion status' by Canada in 1865, Australia in 1900 and South Africa in 1909 made Britain look for support to the non-white dependencies.

Pridham's batting order for 'The Empire Eleven' was as follows:

ENDLAND (Captain)
AUSTRALIA
SOUTH AFRICA
WEST INDIES
NEW ZEALAND
INDIA
CANADA (with Newfoundland)
EAST AND CENTRAL AFRICA
(Kenya, Uganda, Soudan, Nyasaland, Northern Rhodesia, Zanzibar, Somailand)
WEST AFRICA
(Nigeria, Gold Coast, Sierra Leone, Gambia)
MALAYA
CROWN COLONIES
(Ceylon, Fiji, Samoa, Tonga, Malta, Gibraltar, Bermuda, Mauritius, Aden, West Pacific and Other Islands)
TWELFTH MAN: Mandated Territories of Britain and her Dominions (Tanganyika etc.)

Britain's troubles on the Indian subcontinent forced Pridham to state that 'if India should finally decide to throw off her allegiance to the King-Emperor, then cricket will remain as almost the only tie between that great country and the British Commonwealth of Nations'. He reiterated that the Jam Sahib's fervent plea for 'more team work, more patience and more unselfishness' be extended to include also the political leaders of certain great nations—and of one in particular (India!).

BY the time the inaugural RTC opened at the Royal Gallery of the House of Lords on 12 November 1930, the Native Princes, surmounting last-minute hiccups, were ready to make their tryst with destiny. Some doubters had to be convinced though before consensus was reached. A natural conservative at heart, the Jam Saheb harboured genuine fears about the perils of Federation. He therefore had asked for a clarification on the key issues at an informal meeting held in Prime Minister Ramsay McDonald's room in the House of Commons between some members of the Indian States Delegation, the PM and the Secretary of State for India on 3 December 1930. While discussing the question of future relations of the Indian States with the Paramount Power and British India, the Jam Saheb insisted that only two points be clarified: the question of paramountcy and justiciable issues. The princes, he said, wanted a definition of paramountcy and some sort of court of arbitration for justiciable issues.

He had, in fact, been harping on these prickly issues and his position on this was clearly stated: ' . . . while asking for Federation we, also ask for "judicial" ascertainment of the rights of the States. The present position is that the Paramount Power can override the treaties is extremely unsatisfactory . . . I am making no secret about the feeling of uncertainty and insecurity in which the States have been plunged by the enunciation of a doctrine which empowers the Government of India to override all treaties, ... in the name of Paramountcy . . . '

However when D-Day arrived, the Jam Saheb, like his princely colleagues, decided to rise to the occasion. In response to a premeditated offer from the British Indian delegates, a galaxy of princes loftily announced that they were willing to come into an all-India Federation with their brethren from British India, albeit within the confines of the Empire. These rulers ranged from the Gaikwad of Baroda to Kashmir, Patiala and Alwar.[2]

The Jam Saheb also sang in unison with the princely chorus when

---

[2]Though he preferred the appellation 'United States of India' to Federation.

he came to the crease though he took a few potshots at paramountcy in the process:

> . . . Sir Tej Bahadur Sapru has asked us to federate with British India; we are prepared to federate so long as our internal autonomy is preserved and our present hardships are remedied. We the Ruling Princes are jealous of interference by others in our methods of Government. We therefore feel bound to refrain from making any suggestions about the exclusively domestic problems of British India . . . I see no reasons why a federation should not be effected as soon as the difficult matters which fall to be adjusted can be settled, and I feel sure that only by federation can those aspirations for the dignity and status of India which we all of us entertain in due time be achieved—namely the equality of status with the sister dominions within the Empire . . .
>
> So far as all those present at this Conference desire to remain within the British Empire as equal partners, in so far as we all are sincerely firm in our devotion to the King Emperor, what is the obstacle in the way of conceding India's demand? . . . One thing is certain—if those who have come to this Conference go back to India without the Parliament of Britain making it clear that the minimum constitutional demands of India will be conceded, not only will this Conference have been held in vain, but I am afraid that such a fiasco would strengthen beyond measure the extremist party in India. I therefore submit at my command that the recognition of India's status within the Empire and her right to be mistress of her own affairs as early as reasonably possible should not be left in any doubt.

Such lofty sentiments expressed at the RTC however made scant impression on the sullen masses back home. The Native Press ridiculed the farcical proceedings in London. They found His Majesty King George V's inaugural speech 'barren', 'insulting' and 'mere verbiage' and described Prime Minister Ramsay McDonald's as 'wretched, dishonest and foolish'. The Native Press further reaffirmed that the Congress leaders were right in refusing to take part in the ludicrous event. More so because of the RTC's abject failure to pronounce on 'Dominion Status'.

As the *Weekly Herald* wryly observed, 'instead of being called upon to recognize and accept the demand of the Indian delegates for Dominion Status at the outset, the Conference has been cleverly shunted off to the consideration of federation . . . ' As for the ennobling speeches of the Native Princes, the *Hindusthan and Praja Mitra* noted:

> The fact is that the newspapers and leaders have become pleased with the superficial speeches delivered by the Indian Princes who were crushing innocent people under the heels of despotism till yesterday really suggests the bankruptcy of the common sense on the part of those representatives of public opinion . . . The Indian Princes are making a show of sympathy towards the progress of India with a view to achieving the selfish purpose of retaining their autocratic powers through the Indian Representatives.

Reviewing the developments from the perspective of the Native States subjects, the *Lok Shakti* in fact argued (that):

> under the proposed Federal Constitution the same oppressive rule that is being exercised at present by the Native Princes on their subjects will continue, the very same Alwars will carry on massacres like that of Nimuchana, the very same Patialas will indulge in devilish activities, the very same Jamshahi will give birth to its unutterable tales of oppression . . .

The new-found ardour of the Native Princes for the political advance of British India however cooled down by the time they returned home. It suddenly dawned on them that they were flirting with the fires of democratic upsurge in British India. And it would be foolhardy to minimize or eliminate the role of the (British) fire-fighters and risk their own houses being burnt down. Accordingly, Patiala moved a resolution at a Chamber of Princes session in New Delhi in March 1931:

> It is my hope that this resolution expressing our bounden duty of loyalty and service to His Majesty may be read by two very diverse

parties; that it may be read firstly by those in England who profess to believe that the necessary constitutional changes in India as envisaged by the RTC must mean the loss of India to the British Empire and secondly, it may be read, too, by those in this country, who hold that India should cut herself adrift from any connection with the British Empire.

Our loyalties as Allies of the British Crown demands that we hold fast to that connection; our devotion to the person of His Majesty. Should any attempt be made by any one to translate into action the wild talk of severance from the Empire, then we ourselves will prove, true diehards ready to sacrifice everything for the defence of the Imperial connection . . .

I now move this Chamber resolves to tender its expressions of unfaltering loyalty to the person and throne of the King Emperor and to record its profound gratitude to His Majesty for opening in person the Indian RTC and for maintaining close interest in the proceedings throughout the sittings of that historic gathering in which the representatives of this Chamber willingly participated in a desire to draw England and India closer together for the collective benefit of the British Empire.

His Highness the Maharaja of Nawanagar promptly stood up and exclaimed: 'Your Excellency, Your Highnesses, I have the honour to second the resolution.'

IT must be mentioned here that the united front presented by the Native Princes while accepting the offer of Federation from British India representatives at the RTC would prove to be ephemeral. According to Ian Copland, many hostile princes were worked upon prior to the start of the RTC and 'a deal with the British Indian delegation was stitched up' (to support federation). Finally, on D–day, the major princely reps, one by one, 'in response to a carefully orchestrated 'invitation' from the 'British Indian delegation', got up and announced they were ready to join Federation.

The Chamber of Princes was always a house divided on this issue and none was opposed to it more stoutly than its Chancellor of the moment, Patiala. He was reputedly the leader of the reactionary faction in the organization and was engaged in a running battle with the progressives led by Bhopal[3] and Bikaner.

When the RTC process got off the ground, the Jam Saheb was very much in the liberal camp. And even though he thought that the inaugural event was 'even more a dismal failure than he had feared', he exuded optimism. 'I am a born optimist. Human nature is never satisfied, we must remember. It always longs for something different, something better, and that is India today,' he averred.

Even his letter to Arthur Somerset was tinged with hope: 'The RTC has its ups and downs from day to day, and I don't think it is going to be the success one would wish. But it is an effort worth trying, and let's hope that goodwill and the cooperation of all interests concerned will be genuine and increasing as we go on . . . '

When the Jam Saheb returned home, he invited regional rulers to Jamnagar so that he and Sir Prabha Shankar Pattani, the Bhavnagar state official, could give them the lowdown on the RTC. The Kathiawar states were already nervous as to what extent the ISD delegates representing them had signed away their rights by agreeing on their behalf to Federation. Several members of the Chamber of Princes from the Western India States Agency therefore turned up and listened intently to his account.

The Jam's commitment to Federation generally held till the second RTC when the other Princes had all but drifted away from it. In fact, Patiala had tried to lead a princely 'revolt' against Federation with his dissenting memorandum in June 1931. But the Jam Saheb tried to help the succeeding chancellor, Hamidullah Khan of Bhopal, defuse the crisis by campaigning in support of Federation in Kathiawar.

But there had come about a subtle shift in the Jam Saheb's approach.

---

[3]Although he would later gravitate towards the camp advocating furtherance of Muslim interests.

This was reflected in his efforts in England in June 1931 to present the case of the Princes to the Government and the Empire. He was still in favour of Federation but now also wanted 'safeguards' for the princes. In July, he aired his views to an all-party gathering of seventy-five MPs at the House of Commons. The audience included George Lansbury in the chair, Sir John Simon and two other members of the Royal Commission on India, several RTC delegates and Labour MPs of every shade of opinion:

> The Princes are in favour of Federation but they want safeguards for their States. They are absolutely opposed to the Extremist Party in the Congress and to all this talk of independence. They are determined to remain in the Empire, but at the same time they have no desire to stand in the way of India's ordered progress towards equality within the Empire.
>
> I suggest that one of the causes of the present difficult situation in India was the failure to send a delegation to India after the RTC, as was promised. I think the change has given Congress the chance of making a good deal of headway, but the boycott of British goods has been a great mistake, for it has alienated sympathy in this country, and injured the innocent in Lancashire.

The Jam Saheb however hoped that the princely differences over Federation would be smoothed out by the time they arrived in London for the second RTC and they would have an ordered scheme ready for bringing the conference to a successful conclusion. After the speech, an impressed Lansbury quipped, 'If we could handle our troubles in the same way that the Princes of India handle theirs, we would have no difficulty in running this country'.

Princely support of Federation however dwindled considerably after the second RTC as several inimical features had crept in into the scheme. The Lord Sankey Federal Structure Committee's interim report of early 1932, especially with its dangerous reference to 'fundamental federal rights' enjoyable by all subjects in a federating unit—a frightening proposition for autocratic rulers—rattled many princes.

But the Jam Saheb remained non-commital when he telegraphed his views on it: 'I neither oppose nor accept the Sankey scheme, but I am exploring the best method of Federation compatible with the safety of the States and the sound progress of India within the Empire'.

But slowly, the winds of change were blowing away the Jam's steely resolve. In truth, the Jam Saheb's views on Federation underwent a metamorphosis after a sustained campaign to seduce him by the Tory 'Diehards' began having its desired effects. Although the turnaround was partly prompted by the Jam Saheb's own fears about what the reforms entailed for the princes, his defection was ensured by a deep-rooted conspiracy hatched by the Diehard faction of the Conservative party comprising Sir Winston Churchill, Sir George Lloyd, a former Governor of Bombay, and others. They were upset by the Conservative endorsement of the Labour policy on the reforms, which they wanted to scuttle by all means. Getting the Jam Saheb on their side presented a great opportunity to further these prospects.

The Diehards wanted to hold on to the Empire at all costs and therefore could not countenance any concessions meant to loosen Britain's grip on the subcontinent. This looked a distinct possibility if the reforms were implemented. In this major aspect they differed from more mature imperialists like Lord Irwin and Sir Samuel Hoare, who took over as Secretary of State for India in August 1931 after the Conservative leader Stanley Baldwin's National Government assumed power.

Irwin was convinced that some initiatives were necessary as 'what is required is some facade that will leave the essential mechanism of power in our hands'. Hoare too supported the reforms as he believed that 'it is possible to give a semblance of responsible government and yet retain in our hand the realities and verities of British control'.

So the Diehards, as Ian Copland revealed, roped in Sir Leslie Scott and Rushbrook-Williams, the newly appointed foreign minister of Nawanagar who represented the state at the third RTC, into the conspiracy to derail Federation. They were aided in their machinations by the India correspondent of the *Morning Post*[4], N. Madhava Rao. Together they turned the heat on princes like Patiala and especially on the new chancellor of the Chamber of Princes, the Jam Saheb himself. He unfortunately fell into the Diehard trap and remained there till his untimely death brought the curtain down on his role in the Federation saga.

What also contributed to the Jam Saheb's disillusionment with Federation was the government's refusal to countenance his repeated petitions for arbitration and relief over the reimposition of the Viramgam customs line in 1927, which it had earlier abolished in 1917. This had cost Nawanagar a fortune in terms of lost revenues, about 1.5 million pounds from 1927–29.

The Jam Saheb had commissioned the Dwarka railway line extension and improved facilities at the Bedi port to generate those revenues. The reimposed customs tariffs nullified the competitive advantage of the Bedi port, which had helped the Nawanagar exchequer reap a windfall, vis-à-vis the other ports in western British India like Karachi and Bombay. It was only after the Jam Saheb's death that Lord Willingdon put the issue up for arbitration and the final decision announced a year later resulted in a compromise not inimical to Nawanagar's interests.

The government was, however, aware of the Jam Saheb's dithering on Federation even in early 1932. It had noted with concern how the Jam Saheb, who was then in the running for the chancellorship, was now advocating an alternative scheme formulated by Sir Prabhashankar Pattani, dubbed 'Confederation' or the 'Council of United India' (a milder sort of federal scheme), which also had the backing of some princely dissidents. This was because the alternative scheme would compromise the states' interests to a lesser extent than the official Sankey scheme.

Who provided the instigation for the Jam Saheb's turnabout on Federation however was apparent not only to the government but also to its nationalist rivals. A report in the *Kesari*, a Marathi bi-weekly

---

[4]The editor of *Morning Post*, H.T. Gwynne, was also part of the Diehard plot.

published from Poona, on the recent Conference of Princes in Kathiawar, hit the nail squarely on the head:

> If the scheme outlined by the Princes in Kathiawar is given full effect to, Indian *Swaraj* will receive a set-back and it is also doubtful whether the existing rights of the people will remain in force. It has to be said from the new move made by the Princes in Kathiawar under the leadership of His Highness the Jam Saheb and by members of the Princes Chamber that they are receiving inspiration from somewhere else. A consideration of even the outline of the resolutions passed by the Kathiawar Princes under the leadership of His Highness the Jam Saheb, or to speak more plainly, through the advice of his new minister Mr Rushbrook Williams, give support to this statement. Lord Sankey has, in his scheme for Federation, made provision for the Union of the Indian States and British India, though in the future and at a slow pace, but a scheme of the Kathiawar Princes is a mere mockery of even the moderate scheme of Lord Sankey and it need not be mentioned that it seals the doom of complete *Swaraj*. The conspiracy of the British statesmen and the Indian bureaucracy to sabotage constitutional advance is now progressing in this direction, and if they succeed in their game, they will get the best opportunity of absolving themselves by throwing on India the blame for the failure of the scheme of Federation. We therefore sound a note of warning that the people should closely follow the steps that the Princes and the British statesmen will take hereafter.

Ironically, the dithering Jam Saheb came to the forefront of the reforms process due to his surprise election as Chancellor following the 'Delhi Pact' of March 1932. To resolve the acrimonious tussle between Patiala and Bhopal for the coveted post, the Jam Saheb, who had played the role as 'peacemaker' in the dispute between the two factions, was himself thrust forward as a compromise candidate. Patiala announced that he was withdrawing from the race and asked that the Jam Saheb be elected as a 'non-party chancellor' who is likely to be acceptable to different shades of opinion. The Jam Saheb duly romped home, grabbing a comfortable forty-five votes to Alwar's thirty-seven, Bikaner's thirty-two and Dholpur's twenty-three in the polling for the top post.

Perceived as a 'safe candidate' who was expected to do the bidding of the Standing Committee, and especially the two men controlling it at that time, the redoubtable Patiala and the sagacious Bikaner, the seniors believed they had a malleable figurehead at the helm. Subsequent events however would show that the Jam was made of sterner stuff. Indeed, his chequered past had shown that he was never one to buckle down under any challenge or adversity.

The Jam Saheb had been party to the resolution at the same March 1932 Chamber of Princes session which gave a conditional okay to Federation provided certain *sine qua nons* were met and it was laced with adequate safeguards. But under the tutelage of the Scott-Rushbrook-Williams duo, he began undermining it no sooner had he begun steering the princely ship.

In one of his first dissenting moves in April 1932, he openly opposed the formation of the Centre Party[5] as well as the Standing Committee's decision to acquire *The Pioneer*. The latter move was opposed on financial grounds and also because it would not contribute much to the States' cause while giving a handle to British Indian politicians to poke their nose into princely affairs.

The new combative mood among the princes soon became apparent to all concerned, especially after they passed a resolution in Bombay in April 1932 that their treaty rights must remain inviolate, their sovereignty intact and the necessary safeguards be embodied in the new Constitution. 'The Princes feel, it seems,' said the *Mahratta* 'that they now have the whiphand and can dictate terms. It is true that with the active assistance of the Tory imperialists they have manoeuvred themselves in a position from which it is difficult to dislodge them'.

---

[5]By moderate British India politicians in association with the princes and other sectional interests.

Echoing the new combative mood, the Jam Saheb painted a gloomy scenario for the future. He observed, 'There is no ground for optimism as to their (the princes) entering a political adventure which most regard as dangerous. Their demands, it is expected, will be impossible of realisation, for there is no intention of surrender . . .'

However, after landing in England in the summer of 1932, on his eighteenth and last trip[6], the Jam Saheb did not reveal his hand and noted rather ambiguously about the mood in the princely camp, 'There remains many difficulties and some problems continue to present a threat to the general agreement of the Princes. It is, however, a great advance over the position in the early part of the year, when the Princes were apprehensive and alarmed'.

This unduly optimistic statement was perhaps misleading because Roland Wild has emphatically stated that 'long before he left these shores for the last time, he had set his face resolutely against any proposal that the Princes should throw in their lot with the Federation Scheme'. This was most likely true.

The Jam Saheb got down to the brass tacks of undermining Federation within a few months of landing in England. After confabulations with Scott and Rushbrook-Williams, he penned a circular on 5 July 1932, saying that the princes would not be willing to federate unless the 'doctrine of paramountcy' was replaced by the 'doctrine of sanctity of treaties'.

Alarmed by the developments and knowing who was manipulating the strings, Bikaner and Patiala begged the Chancellor not to fall prey to the machinations of the conservative Britishers. The Jam Saheb agreed to redraft the letter to read that the princes shared a 'definite assumption' that the paramountcy issue would be settled prior to the start of Federation. But the Standing Committee rejected this proposed amendment.

---

[6]There is contrasting evidence here. While Roland Wild says Ranji landed in England in May 1932, Ian Copland says he left for England in May.

In desperation, in late August, Bikaner and Bhopal then dispatched a jointly signed letter to the chancellor asking him to have 'no truck with Sir Leslie Scott'. A furious Jam Saheb hit back with another circular, again drafted by Rushbrook-Williams, reiterating his stand on paramountcy. This time he sent it to the members of the Chamber of Princes with copies to the Secretary of State and the Viceroy. Its receipt prompted Lord Willingdon to quip, 'The Jam Sahib, I am afraid, has got into the hands of that horrid little fellow Rushbrook-Williams.'

The anxious Standing Committee members back home were flabbergasted by the actions of the Jam Saheb who had now launched into an individual innings of his own, contrary to the order of the team management. They therefore took appropriate measures to rein him in. Bikaner, Bhopal and Patiala sent personal cables to Willingdon and Hoare repudiating the actions of the Jam Saheb.

K.M. Pannikar, the secretary of the Chamber of Princes, meanwhile put out a press release stating the official position of the organization on the various issues. He also conveyed a formal reprimand to the Jam Saheb. For this, the upwardly-mobile, Malayali scholar-statesman[7] had to endure a dressing down from its recipient for nearly an hour. This, despite the fact that he was only acting as a courier for the Standing Committee.

Roland Wild, who has camouflaged these sordid events well in the official biography, may be referring to this incident when he states that the Jam Saheb 'received a telegram that destroyed his faith in others and resulted in doubts conquering his mind'. A reluctant Jam Saheb however agreed to toe the official line and issue no more circulars without permission. But in a fit of pique he 'retired hurt' to the French town of Aix-les-Bains in September 1932.

Providing his own spin to these events, Pannikar would claim later in his autobiography that the Jam Saheb was prejudiced against him

---

[7]Pannikar actually enjoyed the best of both worlds, as pre-Independence princely official and post-Independence Indian diplomat.

following the publication of his book *Federal India* on the eve of the first RTC. The British authorities had apparently interpreted this book as an indication of the princes' positive attitude towards Federation. But the book and its interpretation had angered certain princes and their advisers who had come prepared to obstruct the claim for Indian independence at any cost, Pannikar alleged. Thus, their wrath was specially directed towards him. Foremost among these 'road blockers' was the Jam Saheb, who extracted his revenge on the Malayali two years later. When Pannikar's name was proposed as secretary at the Chamber of Princes session in February 1931, the Jam Saheb reportedly objected on the grounds that he was a radical who had on many occasions expressed views against the unlimited authority of the princes. Pannikar however, got the post only because he enjoyed the backing of Patiala.

The last factor which turned the Jam Saheb against Pannikar, so the latter claimed, was the appointment of the arch-conservative Rushbrook-Williams as foreign minister of Nawanagar and chief adviser to the Jam Saheb. 'The horrid little man' came to India as a professor of history and later served as the British intelligence chief in India and also conducted anti-Indian propaganda in America. He apparently poisoned the Jam Saheb's mind against Pannikar because he probably believed that the South Indian was a supporter of the independence movement and was trying to take the princes out of the British camp.

Pannikar alleged that when the Jam Saheb, under Rushbrook-Williams's tutelage, began doing various things 'prejudicial to the Indian independence movement', the working committee of the Chamber of Princes passed resolutions opposing these and sent him to London to put an end to the Jam Saheb's 'unauthorized activities'. Rushbrook-Williams then allegedly told the Jam Saheb that the Working Committee had repudiated his views at Pannikar's instance. This, and the fact that Pannikar had circulated a few notes to the Cabinet contradicting the Jam Saheb's views, would lead to another blazing showdown between the two within a few months of the first. One does not know how accurate Pannikar's testimony is, but he has certainly left behind his own take on those events.

Be that as it may, even as the Jam Saheb kept chipping away at the Federation edifice, the diehard Tory press had now joined in with their own tirade, especially on the issue of financial implications.[8] This was indeed a sticky wicket and even the conservative Maharaja Gulab Singh of Rewa felt that they were cloaked in 'dark shadows'.

Gwynne's *Morning Post* duly saw a warning for Lancashire with its textile mills in the proposal that the States should transfer their customs rights to the Federal Government and that the princes had no interest in British India's high protective system. Lord Rothermere's *Daily Mail* contended that the report shows 'the financial basis for a Federation does not exist'.

In early August 1932, the Jam Saheb too, airing his 'personal views' on the report of the Indian States Inquiry Committee, expressed his reservations on the financial implications of the report. While he acknowledged that the Davidson Committee had made an 'honest attempt' to make financial adjustments between the States and the Crown viable, he nevertheless averred that the report failed to satisfy the just claims of the States to relief from burdens, both direct and indirect. While stating that the findings of the committee were still claiming his detailed attention, the Jam Saheb however deemed that, from first impressions, the report failed to generate the confidence requisite for the voluntary assimilation of states in an all-India Federation.

Maintaining the attacking tempo, the Jam Saheb made an emotional plea for preserving the stability of the Native States and the solidity of the British connection while addressing a meeting at the Moot Club, an institution connected with the Law Society, in October 1932. Opening the innings was Sir Leslie Scott, who after tracing the history of the Indian Princes and their methods of Government, argued (that):

---

[8]John Davidson, MP, was appointed at the end of the second RTC to work out the provinces–states financial settlement.

... these factors lead many eminent people to the belief that this form of autocratic kingship is more suited to the Indian temperament and circumstances that the kind of Government prevailing in British India ... I consider that the guiding principle must be the duty of England to protect the position of the Princes and to prevent the insidious encroachment of the British-Indian point of view in the proposed federal legislation.

The Jam Saheb then took over the onslaught:

Why have the Native States remained until to-day? I submit that it is because they are essentially the right system for India ... I consider that the important feature of Indian kingship is the personal touch afforded by every man's right of access to his monarch, who is regarded rather as a senior citizen than as an overlord ...

The Nawanagar ruler then related an unusual tale of a Brahmin who was advocating the overthrow of the British and the setting up of an all-Indian Government. On being asked who was going to provide the military protection, he had replied:

Fancy you, a Rajput, asking me that! Why, you will fight while we rule! . . . I was brought up among the English and have a great affection for them ... but I am an Indian at heart, and would not hesitate to advocate the withdrawal of the English from India if I thought it wise. I do not think so, however, and I hope that the firm partnership between the King-Emperor and the Princes will continue indefinitely.

Things were however all quiet as the third and final RTC, which the Congress boycotted, got underway. Interviewed by Reuters, the Jam Saheb was at his statesman-like best. He said that the forthcoming RTC was small and business-like[9] and therefore offered the prospect of speedy progress. He maintained that the princes were not able to

---

[9] Only forty-six delegates attended.

make any definite pronouncement regarding their adherence to the Federation plan until they had seen the proposed federal constitution as a whole. But he hoped that they would be able to come to some workable agreement. He further stated that as Chancellor, he had received a definite mandate from the Chamber of Princes which he had instructed the representative of Nawanagar (Rushbrook-Williams) to adhere to strictly. Rushbrook-Williams himself reiterated that the Chancellor was bound by the mandate of the Chamber, but he added a plea for safeguarding the individuality of the States which entered Federation.

In actual reality, the Jam Saheb was headed on a confrontational course with his colleagues. Returning to England from France he used his position as chancellor to take charge of the Indian States' Delegation's policy meetings at the Metropole Hotel in London and tried to impose his own agenda on the others. Defying the Standing Committee's instructions not to have any official dealings with Scott, he invited him to attend the ISD's meetings as an observer and tried to force a decision on the paramountcy issue, albeit without success. The Jam Saheb's obstructive tactics forced many delegates to stop attending the meetings and they began deliberating separately.

The RTC turned out disappointingly for almost everybody concerned. A few days before it ended, the Jam Saheb hosted a private dinner at Hotel Metropole in honour of Hoare. The secretary of state, who outlined the British Government's policy towards the new Constitution, categorically said that 'in any scheme of federation that may be accepted, the rights and treaties of the Princes will be safeguarded in spirit and letter'.

'Paramountcy is outside the scope of Federation at all,' Hoare said. 'Paramountcy and all that it implies directs relations between the Crown and Princes themselves, as it always has done.' He urged the princes to enter Federation as it would give them 'a very great and very legitimate influence in the future Government of India'. Hoare also remarked (that):

. . . at this very important moment in the history of the relations between India and Great Britain two Princes, one a Hindu (the Jam Saheb) and the other a Muslim (the Aga Khan) as sportsmen in public life, are probably more popular than anyone else. As a Conservative, I regard that factor (the ability of Native State representatives) as vital in the many difficult problems we are now considering and I venture, with great deference, to say that the British Government want you to play your part—play the most important part—in the future Government of India. We want you to play the kind of part His Highness the Jam Saheb used to play in Test matches of this country . . .

Returning the compliment, the Jam Saheb said Hoare was one of the greatest Secretaries of State, not only for British India but also for the Native States. 'The Princes of India always stood by their treaty obligations and complete loyalty to the King Emperor,' he added. 'You may rely on us for this generation, and I hope those who succeed us will carry on these traditions'. But the *Bombay Chronicle* in an editorial on the '"Hoary" platitudes on paramountcy' dismissed the speeches of the duo as 'a glowing exhibition of the art of meaningless felicitations' between the members of the 'Mutual Admiration Society of India'.

Hoare's reassurances on paramountcy however would make no impression on the Jam Saheb whose determined opposition to Federation seemed irreversible. In another interview to Reuters on the results of the RTC in late December 1932, the Jam Saheb, after detailing the conditions for the princes' entry into Federation, said that as far as he could make out, nothing definite had been done to address these concerns in keeping with the policy laid down by the Chamber of Princes in March last year.

While lauding His Majesty's government for showing every desire to take India forward to a federal set-up by trying to achieve the greatest possible consensus among the invited representatives at London, the Jam Saheb nevertheless cautioned that there were issues on which agreement had not been reached. 'But in problems so unique and issues so momentous for one-fifth of the human race, it would be a mistake to rush matters without adequately and reasonably satisfying the views of the diverse interests concerned,' he pleaded.

But in a more sinister move he also cabled the Standing Committee asking to be released from his mandate to support the Delhi Pact. Overwhelmed by his long drawn efforts, the Jam Saheb admitted weariness, saying he was 'played out'. 'I am sorry that I have failed to do more for England, for my innings has not been very successful,' he confessed.

England actually saw two faces of the Jam Saheb during his last visit to the isles. One was totally at odds with British government on Federation. The other was the loyal foot soldier of Empire whose determined opposition to the boycott of British goods and the raging CDM was fetching.

Back home, nationalists were advocating a complete boycott of British goods. The *Saurashtra Mail* even exhorted Native States' citizens to show their solidarity with the people of British India and boycott foreign goods, which were being landed at Kathiawar ports and then disbursed all over India.

Indian nationalist leaders like Gandhiji and his Englishman comrade-in-arms, Charles Freer Andrews, took the battle of the boycott to British shores. 'Uncle Gandhi', who went to attend the second RTC and stayed in the poor quarters of London to express his solidarity with the working classes, got himself photographed with cheering Lancashire mill workers at a time when their jobs were threatened by the Indian boycott of British cotton goods. Andrews on his part made several tours of Lancashire and tried to explain India's viewpoint on the boycott to the textile industry there.

In contrast, the Jam Saheb made no bones that his sympathies lay with the Lancashire workers hit by the Indian boycott. He even boasted how he was performing a service for the Empire with his boycott-busting tactics and helping to defeat the machinations of Indian politicians—and making a killing in the bargain. In June 1932, in a speech at the 1924 Club of Liverpool, he took pains to refute the scurrilous propaganda that his newfound opposition to Federation was due to the financial setbacks he had suffered by the revival of the Viramgam Custom Line. This had depleted his takings from the Bedi port but through which he was now helping Britain beat the boycott:

> There could be no truth in that suggestion. The one matter was personal, the other bound up with the very future of the Empire. I don't wish Bombay ill but we felt that Bombay's stupidity was our opportunity.

Earlier, the Jam had linked up the problem of the Customs Line with the anti-British boycott in his own inimitable way:

> With the Port of Bedi prospering within the orbit of its rights as defined and guaranteed by the Treaty of 1917, Nawanagar would have found itself in a position to do some service—however slight—to the cause of the Empire by stimulating the inflow of British products . . .

At another meeting arranged by the Manchester Chamber of Commerce where the audience comprised hard-headed businessmen interested in trade with India, the Jam Saheb boasted how over the last two or three years his state had trebled, if not quadrupled, the sale of Manchester goods because of the Bombay port boycott:

> Could not the business men of England and India get together, undisturbed by politicians, to see whether a policy cannot be framed to mutual advantage? You want to trade with us. If Great Britain could enlist the sympathies of the industrial and commercial magnates of India, I believe a great fillip could be given to British trade . . . We must get rid of this terrible handicap of mistrust, for there is no hostility, and the Indian merchants don't want to mix politics with business. The British have always neglected the psychology of the Indian people. The mentality of these millions is worth studying for trade. I assure you that all the Princes are sound concerning the British connection, for we are, after all, one Empire. So we must make an effort, and I ask you to bestir yourselves, and come and help us. We on our side will help you, for if Bombay refuses to deal with you, we will . . . Your attention

in the past has been too taken up with Bombay, Calcutta, Madras and Karachi. Yet we have formed a company to do nothing but British trade, and in my State we have scrapped all American trade. There are others like us . . .

Quite ironically, the Jam Saheb once again earned some brownie points in the Indian press for his 'nationalism'. A report in the *Tribune* hailed him in early 1931 for taking a 'praiseworthy step', at the instance of a prominent Rajkot barrister, to encourage *swadeshi* by ordering that no foreign cloth should be sold in his territory for a period of three months and anybody selling foreign cloth would be punished. This move was made, said the report, after due consultations with his subjects and the merchants. Asked to confirm the development, the Durbar however issued a denial: 'There is absolutely no truth in the report of any authority in the State interfering in trade'.

Providing a rationale for the Jam Saheb's behaviour Alan Ross has argued that while Gandhiji advocated non-cooperation and boycott of British goods as a means of achieving *swaraj*, the Jam Saheb continued to believe in 'the enlightened exercise of autocracy under the Crown as being the method most suited for the betterment of the Indian people'. One does not know how much the Jam Saheb cared for the betterment of the Indian people. But he was certainly more interested in the continuation of the British connection for obvious reasons.[10]

The same dogged spirit that animated the Jam Saheb's ire against the boycott of British goods also marked his opposition to the CDM which inspired it. The Government of India sought the support of the Native Princes to combat the CDM as soon as it broke out. A call went out post haste to the rulers to prevent their territories from being used for 'rebellious preparations against the British Indian Government'. But the princes needed no second invitation to the party, being naturally

---

[10]And although he may have strongly disapproved of the movement to boycott British goods, the Jam Saheb would have secretly been pleased about the development at British Indian ports.

predisposed against insurrectionist activity in the first place. The Maharaja of Patiala had sounded the bugle in a speech to his constituents at the first instance:

> The position of the Indian Princes as guardians of law and order in their States would compel them to oppose with all their resources any movement which prepares to undermine authority and the foundation of social order. We cannot stand idle and look on while attempts are being made to drag out States down into a whirlpool. We are bound to offer our countenance and our cooperation to the Government of British India for the maintenance of peace in the country and for upholding the principles of ordered government.

The Native Princes came to the rescue of the government in their own ways. The Nizam, at the behest of Lord Irwin, issued a 'manifesto exhorting all Muslims to stand firmly aloof from (the) CDM'. The Nizam even offered about Rs 20 lakhs to the government to counter the CDM. But the offer was declined, the government reasoning that if this information leaked out it would inflame the people against the Native Princes and create one more front of trouble during this critical period. For another, it would make the paramount power beholden towards the obdurate Hyderabad monarch who could later ask for his pound of flesh in return.

In early 1932 the Government of India sent a letter to the States seeking their cooperation to defeat the Congress-inspired agitation. On 29 January 1932, Lord Willingdon was confident enough to publicly announce that nineteen princes had approved of the government's policies to tackle the situation and had offered to cooperate to the fullest extent possible. The Agent to the Governor-General of the Western India States Agency on his part informed his political bosses that 'offers have been received from practically every salute state (of Kathiawar) of cooperation with the Government in its attempt to put down the CDM'. A week later the official specified that 'offers of cooperation' had come in from Nawanagar, Morvi and Wankaner.

The Jam Saheb's personal response to the situation was no less commendable. In August 1930 he sent a cable to the AGG of WISA from England offering to return to India at once for a short time before the RTC and asking if he could be of any assistance in dealing with the CDM agitation in Kathiawar. The offer was declined. But Nawanagar's resolve to pursue 'a strong policy of suppression of Congress activities' along with states like Limbdi[11] and Morvi was much appreciated.

Being the homeland of the stalwarts of the freedom movement like Mahatma Gandhiji and Vallabhbhai Patel, Kathiawar was naturally engulfed by the CDM spirit. Local activists in fact took part in the boycott movement even against the advice of Patel. Congress activists hailing from Kathiawar but resident in British India, came back home to implant the seeds of the CDM in their territories. Such was the nationalist fervour generated in the region that the boycott of foreign cloth and government institutions even spread to the schools. Disciplinary measures had to be taken against both staff and students to maintain law and order. A number of ordinances promulgated in British India were also applied to the civil stations of Rajkot and Wadhwan and to Kathiawar in general to deal with 'the sinister activities of the Congress followers'.

As soon as the CDM broke out, the Kathiawar authorities were put on notice when a 'threatening letter' in Hindi signed by 'Muhammad the humble servant of God' was received by all the salute chiefs of WISA. It incited the Princes to raise armies, to arm their subjects and join the *satyagraha* movement in British India; to pay no taxes to the British, and to murder every Englishman in their state on 1 April. With the letter were enclosed two brass and wooden bangles to be worn by the prince if he proved himself a woman rather than a man by failing to join the movement! All salute chiefs in WISA admitted that they had received similar letters and bangles.

One does not know the Jam Saheb's private thoughts about this missive and what he did with the bangles. But Nawanagar's hardline

---

[11]Its repressive record was outlined in a 'Gujerati' booklet styled *Police Raj in Limbdi*.

public response in general assured the establishment no end. The Jamnagar regime immediately agreed to put clamps on subjects who had been visiting *thana* areas for agitational purposes.

The British had reason to be further pleased when their repeated pleas to the Kathiawar states to combine and agree on some joint policy to deal with Congress subversion was promptly acted upon by the Jam Saheb. At a fairly large gathering of chiefs in Rajkot during the Rajkot investiture and the Bhavnagar-Gondal wedding, he took the initiative to conference with the regional rulers on the subject. They met daily for three days and tried to devise a method to tackle the problem. But the Jam Saheb's efforts failed, leaving the authorities disappointed. Important states like Bhavnagar and Junagadh were unwilling to tie their hands in any way and preferred to be left free to act according to the dictates of their own situation.

The CDM, fuelled by Congress agitation in Kathiawar, had acquired a momentum of its own and by early 1931 the states were crumbling under the onslaught. Morvi was subded and Wankaner was under attack, after which the activists had threatened to invade Nawanagar, intelligence reports warned. The administration had, however, approvingly noted the Jam Saheb's intention to give 'short shrift' to the spreading Congress anti-British cloth campaign being spearheaded by activists like Manilal Kothari. Several durbars, including Nawanagar, had served prohibitory orders against this 'stormy petrel' of Kathiawar who was later arrested under the Emergency Powers Ordinance.

During the end of May 1931 there were rumblings in Jamnagar but it appeared to have nothing to do with the CDM. Rather, it took the form of rioting between Bohras on one side and other Muslims on the other. The State Lancers had to be called out to restore order though. On the CDM front however while states like Dhrol, Morvi and Wankaner were collapsing like dominoes before the *satyagrahis*, Nawanagar was stoutly holding out. In fact, the WISA agent could confidently report to his superiors:

The threatened attack on Nawanagar has not yet matured. I have no doubt the satyagrahists realised the warm reception awaiting them at the hands of the State troops and police, and discretion has once more proved the better part of valour!

But such optimism proved to be misplaced. Once Morvi was conquered, the Congress agitators then turned the heat on Nawanagar, unmindful of the 'warm reception' awaiting them. Their object was to obtain the release of three political prisoners who were convicted the previous year by the Nawanagar courts on charges of seditious activities against the Jam Saheb. An agitator, Abraram P. Bhatt, visited the prisoners but they asked him to withdraw the agitation as it was likely to prejudice their appeal to the Jam Saheb for clemency. Bhatt thereupon gave up his mission. But the leading agitators refused to accept defeat and began their campaign for the boycott of goods, especially sugar, which was being imported through the Nawanagar ports.

An increasingly perturbed Jam Saheb, who was watching this escalating threat from the safe confines of distant Britain, shot off an urgent telegram to the Viceroy requesting him for support to meet the threat:

One notorious agitator against Indian States, particularly those in Kathiawar by name Manilal Kothari is coming to Jamnagar today. It is reported that he will be followed by women picketers headed by Mrs Ambalal Sarabhai wife of Ahmedabad mill owner and some students of Gujarat College, Ahmedabad. In order to prevent disturbances to trade and peaceful business I will have to take strong action to exclude these British Indian agitators from repeating their well known methods in my state. If given a free hand they will ruin what little trade has remained with our merchants and any weakness on the part of my administration will mean delegation of my powers and authority to outsiders who have no concern with my state or its subjects. I have informed West India about this movement and I hope I will have full support of Your Excellency's Government in measures I may be compelled to adopt to keep them away. So far this poison has left us untouched. This is an insidious attempt to sow sedition in a state where they have no footing and where Congress authority does not exist.

The British response to his appeal was muted and careful. This only provoked the Jam Saheb into unleashing a flurry of petitions to top British officials in India imploring their assistance. He lamented about 'these outside agitators who are now trying to foment ill feelings in States for their own ends' and warned that his administration would be 'compelled to use force if necessary for they want to bend Jamnagar to their will as they have succeeded elsewhere in Kathiawar'.

What alarmed the Jam Saheb further was a cable from local sugar merchants that the 'whole Kathiawar has boycotted our goods' including sugar, silver, oils, petrol etc., imported through Bedi resulting in 'heavy losses'. They reported that one lakh bags were lying at Bedi and about the same quantity was lying unsold in Kathiawar and northern India where agitators were picketing very strongly.

The Jam Saheb's own state political secretary confirmed in another cable that 'the boycott is strengthening beyond anticipation' and that the collapse of business would prevent merchants from meeting their obligations to the state. The secretary suggested that to stop the agitation from gaining strength the three political prisoners could be released on bail, leaving the grant of full pardon on His Highness's arrival back home.

The Jam Saheb duly informed Lord Willingdon about the plight of his merchants and his port, and how he was compelled to give way and order the release of the prisoners on bail subject to a pledge of good behaviour. He stressed that this was necessary to enable him to meet his forced customs obligations to the Government of India even though his catipulation would encourage extremists to repeat such tactics whenever it suited them to bring his administration to an impasse:

I would respectfully urge Your Excellency to devise some means by which I and all others should be protected from such harassment in the future . . . These practices on the part of the agitators are becoming intolerable and unless an end is put to them no state can progress socially, politically and economically in these hard times of world depression.

Once again, the British refused to be taken in by his desperate pleas. They reasoned that the merchants had raised the bogey of the boycott as an excuse for failing to pay customs dues to the Jam Saheb. The ruler in turn had trotted the same excuse for failing to pay some heavy arrears on customs duties to the government. In any event, the British most likely did not have much sympathy for Nawanagar on this score. They were often saddled with reports that the Durbar was engaged in illicit import activities of goods like alcohol, cigarettes, matches etc. One tip off indicated that there was a conspiracy to purchase 15,000 gallons of whisky and seven million cigarettes and bring it in via the steamship *Jamnagar*. The whisky would profit by the thirty-five per cent rebate and on arrival was to be mainly sold in Ahmedabad.

On other counts too the British did not think on the same lines as the Jam Saheb. They felt that no case had been made in respect of the monarch's plea to take action against political agitators who threatened his commercial interests. They thought that the only concrete suggestion that the Jam Saheb had made was that the offence should be made extraditable. But it was unclear, they said, what offence the Jam Saheb was referring to. If it was that of persuading other people not to buy goods imported through Bedi port then this was not an offence under the existing law in British India unless it was accompanied by criminal force or intimidation. Hence the plea for extradition was untenable. Moreover, in a dampening conclusion they recorded:

> It is unfortunate that the Jam Saheb owing to heavy financial commitments upon his port should now be in so vulnerable a position but it is obviously impossible for the Government of India to force persons in other parts of Kathiawar or in British India to purchase goods from Nawanagar if they do not wish to do so. The previous history of the Bedi port is also such as to have made many enemies among other Kathiawar states who are only too ready to assist in damaging the prosperity of the port.

The Jam Saheb's pleas thus went in vain. All that the British were prepared to do was to send a 'soothing letter' suggesting that he was not the only ruler to suffer financially from the evils of political boycott for which no easy remedy could be found.

The Jam Saheb however on his own came up with an interesting remedy to tackle the problem of 'Congress propagandists' from British India who were rounded up in Jamnagar and had to be deported. He thought that putting them on a train and transporting them beyond his borders would be far from effective. Not only would the train journey cause them little discomfort but they could very well sneak back into Nawangar no sooner were they released. He therefore proposed to the authorities that since it was monsoon time it would be a good idea of putting them on board one of his steamers at Bedi port and sending them by sea to Bombay since the consequent discomfort of coursing through rough seas would inhibit them from going back, at least immediately. The British were consulted to see if this could lead to legal reprimand.

They thought that it would pass muster. But in the mean time the Jam Saheb had left for England and it was decided not to take any precipitate action during his absence.

By the time the Jam Saheb returned home from England for the last time in early 1933, Nawanagar had weathered the worst part of the CDM storm. But the turn of events in England still rankled and the threat of democracy still loomed on the horizon. The Jam Saheb knew beyond doubt that the future of Indian kingship was gravely imperilled. He voiced his fears and hopes in a way he had never done before at a farewell for the young Maharaja of Jaipur[12], his nephew by marriage, who was leaving for London:

We Princes whose generation is passing look to the generation of Your Highness to carry on those traditions of Indian Kingship which

---

[12]Sawai Man Singh II.

in the past has done so much for our people. Your State in itself provides a complete answer to those who say that Indian Kingship has not worthy achievements to its credit. The Princes of my time have striven to keep alive the torch passed into our hands by our great ancestors. We too have laboured for our people, we too have found in their welfare our own prosperity, in their contentment our greatest reward. Your difficulties may be greater than ours, for the wave of unthinking democratic sentiment, from which Europe has so long suffered, seems now to be bearing upon India at the very moment when it is discredited by the critics from which it drew its origin. Your rule will be tested by comparison with the rule of democracy in British India, and by the results of that test not only you but the very principles of Indian Kingship will be tried . . .

After attending to his various domestic obligations at home, with a heavy heart, the Jam Saheb then made his way to Delhi in March 1933 for the annual Chamber of Princes session. He was due to pass on the baton of chancellorship but he would use this final opportunity on the centre stage, to play one last defiant knock for the Empire.

VIII *The Final Countdown*

IT was a weary and washed out Jam Saheb who arrived in Delhi in March 1933 for the Chamber of Princes session where he would eventually make his last and most momentous stand for the Empire. His mind was made up on his course of action, even though he knew it would turn him into 'one of the most disliked—in the whole of India'. A foretaste of this was premiered two months earlier in January when forty Gujarat rulers voted 'to reject Federation—root and branch'.

Behind the glittering façade of banquets and Viceregal receptions for the galaxy of Native Princes assembled in the capital, the back-breaking work for the upcoming Chamber of Princes session was being quietly done. Conscious of the lurking threat to Federation and with the government's interests in mind, the *Times of India*, made an impassioned plea to the Princes to rally to Federation's cause:

> . . . We are, however, convinced that their (princes') true interests lie in a Federal constitution, and we hope that they will not at this juncture be influenced by petty local interests or by ingenious legal sophistries. The occasion calls for farsighted statesmanship which will balance consideration and interpret local interests in terms of national policy. The Princes of India played a vital part in making Federation possible. They may be trusted to resolve the jealousies and rivalries of the moment in order to lay the foundations of a progressive and self-governing India in which they will constitute a most important factor.

But the Jam Saheb had come primed with a script of his own. And he was determined to unveil it even at the cost of confrontation with his colleagues. A few days before the session, in a pre-emptive strike, the Nawanagar camp gave advance intimation of its destructive intent when Rushbrook-Williams launched a diatribe against Federation. The 'Jam Saheb stabs Federation in Back' and 'Dr Williams Threatens Hold-Up' screamed the *Bombay Chronicle* as it reported:

> Situation with regard to Princes attitude towards Federation is becoming more and more confused. There is no doubt that those like the Maharaja of Bikaner and the Nawab of Bhopal who pledged themselves to it stand solidly for it and that a majority of Princes still back the scheme
>
> But the fact remains that a minority is becoming daily more and more vocal and the hostile attitude of the Jam Saheb after his return from London has been causing some concern to those who wished Princes to act as a united body.
>
> A further proof of the breach occurred today (16 March 1933) when the Chief Adviser, Dr Rushbrook Williams, used the tactics of his political 'gurus', the Churchillian group, thumped the table, grew red and declared at one of the meetings that they would fight Federation coming into being . . .

The Jam Saheb then delivered another body blow—a 'bombshell' it was called—at an 'in camera' session of the Standing Committee of the Chamber of Princes on the eve of the publication of the White Paper. He apparently threatened that fourteen Kathiawar states would find it impossible to join the Federation under the present circumstances. It was by then known that the present scheme had failed to find the approval of the Gujarat rulers. However, neither Rushbrook-Williams's nor the Jam Saheb's threats were taken seriously by the leading princes. They hoped that after the publication of the White Paper and their deliberations on it, the states would be able to define their position more accurately.

On 14 March 1933, the Viceroy, Lord Willingdon, met the princes at an afternoon conference and outlined His Majesty's Government's policy towards the states as detailed in the White Paper containing the proposed reforms package. The discussion apparently 'left all imbued with a spirit of cooperation for the work ahead' according to the *Times of India* edition of 15 March 1933. The Standing Committee members also met to discuss the safeguards they wished to be incorporated in the proposals.

When the White Paper was eventually released on 17 March 1933, it fell short of everyone's expectations—the Indian nationalists and the British Diehards as well, who called it a sell-out. The princes too, on first reading of the document, were 'somewhat chilled' by its severely legal form and apprehensive of certain provisions.

But their hostility diminished considerably after a closer scrutiny. They realized that more concessions were being dished out for representatives of the upper house and the financial implications were an improvement on those proposed at the last RTC. The White Paper also promised the states protection from the Viceroy in case their interests were compromised. It also gave short shrift to the idea of 'fundamental rights' for Native States' subjects, a concession welcomed by the authoritarian rulers.

But an adamant Chancellor was not willing to be swayed. He promptly threw a spanner in the works by choosing to differ. He pointed out that eight of the seventeen *sine qua nons* outlined in Document 'A' that the princes had decided upon at Delhi in 1932 had not been conceded. These were 'important points discussed by the Princes at . . . the RTC and consequently pressed by them as essential.' Therefore, under the circumstances, he could 'not advise the Order to join an All-India Federation,' he argued.

Under pressure from Whitehall to manage a favourable outcome for the White Paper at the Chamber session, the Viceroy played his last card. He made an emotional appeal to the Chamber of Princes in his inaugural address on the opening day on 20 March to embrace Federation with open arms. He recalled that the princes themselves at the first RTC had made Federation a living ideal and a practical possibility, by expressing their determination to march along on the road towards responsible government. Emphasizing that His Majesty's Government was impartial, he stated:

I feel sure that you will take a statesmanlike view of the position and where mutual agreement may not prove possible, will accept the decisions of His Majesty's Government in the spirit in which they will be given.

I sympathise keenly with your doubts and difficulties, and as you gaze on a world where unrest and unsettlement are evident on all sides, where so much that has appeared unshakeable has crashed to ruin and where failings rather than virtues of all the existing forms of governments are under review, you may well wish to pause and consider deeply which way safety and happiness lie. It is for you to decide. Disadvantages and dangers lie in all the courses, but they may be countered with prudence, foresight and courage. It is my own personal conviction that for the Indian States, the balance of advantage weighs heavily towards accepting the Federation scheme and working wisely and prudently.

The Viceroy also assured the Princes that His Majesty's Government would welcome any reasonable amendments regarding the allocation of seats. They could also have their subsequent views regarding safeguards and other matters placed before the Joint Select Committee. In addition, there was nothing to prevent the states from pooling their seats together and forming an effective voting bloc in matters of common interest.

Luckily for the Viceroy, Sir Manubhai Mehta of Bikaner and Sir Liaquat Hyat Khan of Patiala, who were appointed by the Standing Committee to vet the White Paper, gave it their wholehearted approval. They in fact made a 'vigorous plea' for the acceptance of the Federal scheme in their report submitted to the Standing Committee. As members of the Committee of Ministers and delegates to the third RTC, they reviewed the assurances regarding the maintenance of the integrity of the States, their internal sovereignty, full autonomy and treaty rights, and opined that these points might now be treated as to have been accepted by the British government. They also argued (that):

Democracy and autocracy if brought together have equal chances of diluting each other. His Majesty's Government looks to us, Indian States, as an element of stability and moderation which would prevent the extremist section in British India from snapping the British connection and putting up the ideal of independence before the whole country. If conscience makes cowards of us all, the instinct of acquisitiveness and calculation ought to instill courage in States, leading them on to immediate accession to the Federal ideal. It is all the more necessary for the States to join at the outset, if they wanted to join at all rather than wait and haggle for better terms.

With Patiala, Bhopal and Bikaner straining every nerve to make Federation acceptable to the whole princely order by securing such safeguards as were considered essential, the Federation juggernaut was on a roll. An alternate scheme for allocation of seats inter se in the Federal Legislatures was also being worked out to placate the 13-gun salute states by giving Bhavnagar, Nawanagar and Junagadh individual representation.

The *Bombay Chronicle* Special Correspondent, who met several princes in the course of their informal talks with their ministers, confirmed the buoyant mood among the princes. He paraphrased their attitude as follows:

> Having encouraged the idea of federation at the first RTC we must play the game and stand by it. We cannot fool about the matter. At the same time there are many difficulties that have been unexpectedly caused by the British Government . . . We are as anxious as any British Indian politician for the progress of our Motherland, and we assure them that Federation will not be delayed on account of us . . .

The influential *Times of India*, eager to pitch in for the cause, made another emotional appeal to the princes, this time in the name of India herself, not to spurn this historic opportunity:

> . . . Federation, of course, implies that in the Federal subjects, States must part with some of their sovereign rights which they have hitherto enjoyed. This is part of the sacrifice which they are called upon to make in the interests of India as a whole, and it was implicit in the understanding they gave at the first RTC.

One day before the crucial debate on the White Paper, Willingdon met the princes at the Viceroy's House informally to elicit their views on it. The Chancellor apparently expressed disappointment over the absence of safeguards and the inadequacy of the seats allotted to the states in the Federal legislatures. Other princes too were upset by certain aspects of the White Paper. But they still assured the Viceroy that 'a requisite number among them were ready to join Federation to enable it to start early'. However, they desired that both in the matter of granting real responsibility to the Federal Government and the allocation of seats, their views should be heard and accommodated. The Viceroy reportedly agreed to communicate their views to London. The Princes on their part agreed to pass a resolution the next day generally supporting the idea of Federation and earnestly hoping to be able to accept the scheme after the final picture emerged.

As a result of this meeting a draft resolution was prepared for submission to the Chamber which reportedly indicated that the princes were prepared to negotiate further terms to make Federation acceptable to them. Accordingly, about two dozen terms were drawn up for communication to the Secretary of State.

It was under this cloud of anxious expectation that the Chamber went into session to pronounce on the key issues. Roland Wild has well prepared his readers for the denouement that took place on 25 March. The Jam Saheb, he wrote, had realized that there would be an open breach (in the princely order), a rift far wider than he had envisaged. But his speech, 'which ripped the temple veil of the Chamber of Princes', was a logical culmination of the views harboured by him over many years. Wild added a touch of mystery by mentioning that it was impossible to print the whole truth behind the speech since it was too close to the moment of the Jam Saheb's subsequent death[1] and therefore impossible to judge in its proper perspective.

Further, he induced sympathy for his hero by alleging that 'during

---

[1]Wild's biography was published in 1934.

Batting for the Empire: A Political Biography of Ranjitsinhji

a certain half-hour on March 25, the Jam Saheb sustained a blow to
his trust in human nature that hastened his death'. On that day, he
continued, 'there was implanted in the heart of the Jam Saheb a
bitterness and sorrow that had never been there before'. What exactly
happened was again left unsaid. Was Wild referring to the snub
administered by Willingdon or the open criticism of the Chancellor
by Bikaner and others? Or was there some unrecorded altercation
that took place before he rose in the Council House of the Chamber
of Princes to make his last stand? One can't say now.

The drama began with the Chancellor taking the floor, ostensibly
to present the report of the Indian States Delegation to the third RTC.
The Jam Saheb in fact began his exposition by making reference to
this task. But he had come prepared with his own agenda—to play his
last innings for his Order and the Empire. As the *Times of India* (dated
27 March 1903) reported:

> He unmasked a battery of heavy guns and poured an intense
> bombardment of high explosive, not only upon the White Paper scheme
> of Federation, but upon the whole principle of a constitutionally united
> India and upon the very idea of developing democratic institutions in
> India.

Providing a rationale for his actions, Wild intoned, 'He was looking
down the years, and with his renowned far-sightedness, was seeing
the end of kingship, the doom of monarchy, the beginning of anarchy
and nation-wide strife'. If he and his Order were to be bowled out
in due course, the Jam Saheb had decided to go down with all guns
blazing. In a speech the Jam Saheb made he said:

> I devoted the whole of my time during the summer, autumn and early
> winter of 1932 to a study of the problems of federation. No doubt,
> like the majority of Your Highnesses, I started on my work with a
> strong predisposition in favour of federation. The federal form of
> government seems at first sight well suited to India, providing as it
> does the means of establishing a joint administration of all-India matters,

while reserving to the States and Provinces the control of their local affairs. But it soon became plain to me that the form of federation which His Majesty's Government have in mind for India will differ from all modern federations in one important particular . . . In the case of India, His Majesty's Government are relying upon the Indian States, with their essentially monarchic politics, to contribute the necessary elements of stability and experience. For my own part I feel that it is very unfortunate that the realisation of British India's political ambitions should have been made contingent upon the acceptance of a particular type of federation by the Indian States. I do not see that there is any logical connection between the two matters. I have nothing but the friendliest and most brotherly sentiments for British India and I wish her leaders well. I hope that she will attain her aspirations, but I hope she will do this without involving the States in her own troubles.

We have to see whether the form of the Constitution is such as to protect the States in the enjoyment of their sovereignty and to secure for them the influence which is their due. (There was a need to consider) whether the tendencies to which the new Constitution will give rise are such as to preserve in effective form the ancient ideals and institutions of Indian monarchy, upon which the strength and stability of the States and their utility in the new Constitution will alike depend.

We, the States, have suffered from the application to ourselves of policies designed primarily in the interests of British India, and we have suffered economically and politically. What must we expect when the Crown parts with an effective portion of its powers in favour of British India? The experience of the world seems conclusive on this point . . .

The Chancellor said that three safeguards were necessary to preserve their states from the risk of being gradually swallowed up for, in the Federal Constitution, the centre tends to swallow the federating units. There was no provision in the Federal Constitution, he said, to effectively protect them from this kind of encroachment. Neither the Federal Court nor the Viceroy would be able to assist them when some crisis arises. The Upper House would not be effective if the policy of the Cabinet and Legislature conflicted with the rights of the states or with the effective sovereignty of the Crown in India, upon which the princes laid so much stress. And, if they entered the Federation as it was now proposed, they would, in the course of time, inevitably lose the effective exercise of those rights, which, according to the strict letter of the Constitution, they thought they were preserving.

To buttress his arguments, the Jam Saheb quoted arguments (mischievously, as Ian Copland claims) outlined in the *Manchester Guardian* by Dr Berriedale Keith, the eminent Constitutional theorist. This emphasized that 'the British Government still has the power by a wise constitution of the legislatures and by using the best elements of the States to create a form of responsible government, which, with advice and aid from the United Kingdom, may work. But the idea that it can operate safeguards, defying the Ministry and Parliament, is a chimera which will utterly disappoint in practice those unwise enough to accept at their face value the views of the Secretary of State'.

> These are strong words, and I confess that they cause me profound disquiet; for they coincide with certain apprehensions arising from my own small studies as to the difficulty of the Crown retaining in the future any effective sovereignty in India . . . If this assumption is threatened, then our *sine quo nons* and safeguards are valueless, and fall to the ground. How indeed can we seriously consider any scheme which is open to such grave objection? It seems to me that the tendencies likely to be set in motion by the proposed Constitution are such as to expose Indian kingship to severe and unfair attack. The ideals and institutions of our States must not be placed in a position in which they have no reasonable prospect of survival. It seems to me inevitable the principle of monarchy will from the first be prejudiced; its upholders will be placed at an unfair advantage and the centralising tendencies to which all Federations inevitably give rise will so operate so as to increase the power of the Centre, at the expense of the States, with their monarchial policy. For myself, I cannot help feeling that the constitution as it has emerged from the White Paper will inevitably so work as to destroy, at least in its effective form, the very principle of

Indian kingship and both economically and politically monarchial principles will suffer.

His blazing innings would have continued. There were several pages of the speech yet to be read. But an exasperated Willingdon, who was in the presidential chair and who knew that the Jam Saheb's rhetoric, came straight out of the pen of 'that . . . little scoundrel Rushbrook-Williams', interrupted:

It hardly seems to me to be a report of the Third Round Table Conference. It seems to me (I have allowed His Highness the Chancellor the widest possible latitude in this matter) a personal statement, a statement of views on the proposed Constitution. I do not wish to criticise, I do not wish to stop His Highness if he wishes to continue his remarks, but they are purely personal observations and in no sense a report on the Third RTC.

The Jam began to defend himself and there were a few verbal fisticuffs between the two. But the Viceroy finally exploded: 'If Your Highness is strongly of the opinion that you are keeping within the terms of the RTC report I have got nothing more to say. You can continue your speech.'

Stunned by the viceregal rebuke, the Jam Saheb mumbled, 'If Your Excellency thinks I am not doing the right thing, I will not proceed. I respect your ruling.' He then slumped down forlornly into his seat, his innings terminated prematurely by the umpire's ruling. It was the first time in the history of the Chamber of Princes that the Chancellor himself had been ruled out of order. The Viceroy explained:

I am sure we have listened with much interest to what we have heard. With regard to the remarks of His Highness the Chancellor I can only say that, while I have been extremely regretful to cause any inconvenience to His Highness, I do feel that he should have kept entirely within the terms of the report of the RTC. And what I have seen—I do not know what Your Highnesses feel—I think His Highness has been producing his own views, very gloomy views if I may say so, with regard to the future Indian federation, which I do honestly feel should not fall from the lips of the Chancellor of this Chamber which has for four years been endeavouring, supporting and assisting in introducing this all-India federation.

The Jam Saheb however had the last word: 'The Federation, Sir, which I had supported was the Federation suggested in the first RTC. Our representatives went away from that, and I parted company. That, really, Sir, is what I have to say on that point.'

Wild made much of the showdown and held forth on how the Jam Saheb 'mourned for the humanity of friends who had stabbed him in the back . . . his notorious belief in the goodness of humanity was torpedoed and wrecked. He felt himself the victim of treachery, and he could never understand that sometimes men are lacking in gratitude'.

Quite frankly, it was the other way round. It was the Jam Saheb who had betrayed the princely consensus on Federation and the White Paper[2] and who had conspired with the Diehards to derail it by his scare mongering speech penned by none other than Rushbrook-Williams.

As presiding officer the Viceroy was correct in insisting that the Jam Saheb stick to the agenda and give a report on the Indian States Delegation's performance at the RTC rather than ventilate his own futuristic views on Federation. Willingdon, a former president of the Marylebone Cricket Club, had initially come to India a year after the outbreak of World War I to take up residence as Governor of Bombay Presidency.

The Jam Saheb was present at the Apollo Bunder in Bombay to greet Willingdon when he docked. The incoming Governor singled him out at first glance and honoured him with a handshake. In his maiden speech soon after arrival, Willingdon described the Jam Saheb as his 'oldest friend' in the Bombay Presidency whose presence at Apollo Bunder 'provided me with the greatest encouragement in getting through the ordeal (of making a speech at 8 am)'. He also

---

[2]Wild conveniently makes no mention of this.

referred to Jamnagar, generally regarded as an uninhabitable place, as 'a veritable home of luxury'. In February 1916 the Governor visited Jamnagar in his official capacity and inaugurated the Willingdon Crescent, a public shopping complex.

Yet, such a long association did not prevent the Viceroy from discharging his duty to the Crown and pulling up the Jam Saheb when he stepped out of line. Ironically, there was a common intent uniting these old chums in the midst of this procedural wrangle—both wanted to save the Empire. The Jam Saheb thought that Federation would lead to an ultimate withering away of Empire, hence his intentions to wreck it; the Viceroy (whose commitment to the reforms was reportedly suspect), was only furthering Whitehall's plans to save Federation at all costs in order to prolong the imperial innings.

But that was not the end of the drama. With the Diehard agents lobbying intensely behind the scenes for the election of a panel which would be hostile to Federation the next day (26 March) of the Chamber session had more fireworks in store. A vengeful outgoing Chancellor, hell-bent on extracting revenge for his humiliation, seized the opportunity offered by the budget debate to launch a withering attack on his *bete noire*, the Chamber secretary, K.M. Pannikar. He accused the Southerner of all sorts of malfeasance and forced the working committee to terminate his services. Even Patiala, who was enamoured of Pannikar, was forced to go along.

Desperate to stem the tide of revolt which the Chancellor had succeeded in generating, a worried Standing Committee met over lunch. They drafted an amended resolution commending the general thrust of the White Paper but insisted on the essential safeguards being included in the Constitution before the States could consent to Federation. However, the Jam Saheb's camp followers also moved an amendment making accession to Federation conditional on 'an equitable and satisfactory settlement of the problem of paramountcy' by determining the justiciable issues by the judicial process. The Viceroy warned that this action would affect the personal ties between him and the princes if the resolution was passed. But both amendments were carried, with the Jam Saheb ruling from the chair in virtually his last act as Chancellor that they were not contradictory.

Supporting the resolution on the White Paper, Bikaner earlier made a stirring speech to the Chamber, asking them not to pass a premature judgement on Federation till all details were clear. 'What constitution was it that brought down the mighty Tsar of Russia? Are not democratic influences from British India already influencing the States?' he asked, suggesting that they could not avoid the onrush of democracy by keeping out of Federation.' The Jam chose not to reply to the jibe from his senior colleague.

In the elections that followed, Patiala wrested back the Chancellor's mantle whilst the anti-Federation acolytes of the Jam Saheb won a majority in the ten-member Standing Committee. The results had the Diehards dancing with delight. The wily Patiala, keen to project himself as a moderate, made the appropriate noises on taking over again:

> This is the time for deeds and not words. There are difficulties ahead but difficulties have to be and will be surmounted. There are differences of opinion but if we fail to reconcile the irreconcilable the fault will not be ours. We expect from His Majesty's Government and the representatives of British India the same hearty cooperation we have extended to them in bringing federation within the sphere of practical politics. We have played the game and will continue to play the game with credit to our order as patriots and with pride as citizens of the Empire.

The Jam Saheb's determined assault on Federation did not succeed in derailing it completely. The Chamber subsequently resolved to continue its dialogue with the government in order to evolve a framework for its acceptance. The near-fiasco also strengthened the British and Indian governments' resolve to go full steam ahead with the scheme. In fact the *Bombay Chronicle* mocked the futility of Rushbrook-Williams's efforts to sabotage Federation when the powers that be had decided to forge ahead with it:

The Jam Saheb's advisor will now realise that he must not rush in where angels fear to tread. Not for him to condemn Federation out of the Jam Saheb's mouth when Whitehall and Simla have already decided.

But the Jam Saheb's antics surely destroyed the unity of the princes. Disgusted by the ongoing developments, Bhopal, Jodhpur, Kashmir, Kolhapur, Udaipur and others, resigned from the Chamber one by one, some deciding to break away even before the session concluded. Thus, the man who had initially tried his best to unite his colleagues against the advancing tides of democracy, had now wrecked their unity precisely because they wanted to come to terms with it!

Among the reasons that influenced the Jam Saheb's animosity towards Federation was the question of representation in the Federal legislatures. The smaller states, which rallied behind the Jam Saheb, wanted a scheme that would give each of their members one or half a vote each in the proposed Lower or Upper Houses. This was not possible if the size of the house was to be kept down to a reasonable level. The fracas however forced the larger states, who were getting marginalized in the Chamber of Princes by the 13-gunners like Nawanagar, to go ahead with Federation on their own. This denouement partially saved the day for the government.

There was also a sting in the tail over the Pannikar issue for the Jam Saheb. As soon as he was elected Chancellor, Patiala, who ardently desired Pannikar's services for his state, confidentially told the latter that he would be back as Chamber secretary and the new executive would revoke the earlier resolution terminating his services.

That evening Pannikar went to the railway station to see off the Jam Saheb, who was returning home, even as the new executive committee was locked in meeting. According to his account, the Jam Saheb received him most cordially and said, 'Since we are both relinquishing our offices with the Chamber, there need be no disagreement between us hereafter.' Rushbrook-Williams, who was with the Jam Saheb, also extended his hand in compromise. But a triumphal Pannikar could not help rubbing it in: 'Your Highness is right, but while you are no longer the Chancellor, I have again been appointed secretary.' When Pannikar went back to the meeting, the princes who had only the previous day voted to terminate his services, began congratulating him on his reappointment!

WHEN the Jam Saheb returned to Jamnagar, his luggage was readied for yet another trip to England and Ireland. But with a sense of premonition he began preparing for another sort of journey—the final one—passing on last minute instructions to Digvijaysinhji, his nephew and chosen heir. When his English ADC remarked about how ill he looked, the Jam replied, alluding to his Delhi excursion, 'I have done my best. I can't do more. I have had other interests than Jamnagar which I thought to be greater. But in future I will look after my State. These other interests have come between me and my State for too long.' Was this an unintended acknowledgement of the shortcomings of his reign which was otherwise being trumpeted as an overwhelming success by his propagandists?

One night after struggling through dinner he went upstairs to bed, for the last time. He lay there for five days, his life ebbing away. His last intelligible words were apparently addressed to his nephew, Himmatsinhji, in Gujarati:

I have done what I could. Now you must do all you can.

At 3 a.m. on 2 April his heart began failing. Two hours later the Great Umpire in the Sky raised his index finger.

A complete voluntary *hartal* was observed throughout the city on the day of his death. The *Times of India* reported that the streets were crowded with mourners, which showed how deeply people felt the loss of the creator of modern Nawanagar, who ranked as second only to Jam Rawalji, the founder of the state, among the Jam Sahebs.

Pannikar had an interesting aside on his adversary's death. Having joined duty at Patiala, he was in the verandah of the palace talking with the Maharaja when a telegram arrived. It was from the new Jam

Saheb announcing the death of his predecessor. The deceased Jam Saheb had close ties with the Patiala clan, Bhupinder's father Rajinder, had backed Ranji's assault on the Nawanagar *gaddi*. After a brief silence, the Maharaja asked his secretary Radha Raman Das to bring him the confidential almanac, compiled by astrologer Lahori Ram at his instance and kept in close secrecy in his bedroom. In the almanac, the major events of the year were predicted. Patiala showed Pannikar a page where the main events of the month were listed as the death of two princes in South India and the Maharaja of Jamnagar.[3] Even the violent end of the Badshah of Afghanistan was listed for the month!

Though the Jam Saheb was physically silenced by the Viceroy during the Chamber session, his patrons were determined to have his censored speech published for public edification. It was splashed in full by the *Morning Post* on 28 June 1933, on the eve of the meeting of the Central Council of the Conservative Party. Keeping the heat on behalf of the Diehards, the rabble-rousing *Morning Post* rallied its English readers in a leading article headlined 'I cannot evade my duty'[4]:

> They were prohibited in India . . . no doubt in the interests of her constitutional liberties, but this, we hope, is still a free country. May we hope of Englishmen, who are also of a ruling race, that they will not evade their duty?

The speech was also printed in pamphlet form and used extensively by the India Defence League (as anti-reforms propaganda). The Jam Saheb had demanded 'distinct rights, distinct duties and distinct obligations' and had wanted the rights of the states to be founded 'upon something more solid than the shifting sands of political convenience':

> The cold logic of the situation has convinced me that the present scheme is dangerous alike to the States and to the British connection. At this juncture we have to think, not of ourselves, but of future generations

---

[3]Incidentally, the Jam's own astrologer had also predicted his death, according to Wild.
[4]These were words taken from the Jam's speech.

of Viceroys, of future generations of Princes, and perhaps, above all, of the future of the British connection.

Wishing British India well, he however emphasized that his only imperative was self-preservation and its problems were not his problems and no good would come of trying to confuse the two.

> We find that the safeguards upon which we have endeavoured to insist, pitiful as they are, have been denied to us; that our claims, alone among minority claims, have been subjected to ridicule. We have been told that we are over-expensive partners; that British India will never consent to become an appendage of the States. Your Excellency, I for one should be the last to thrust myself where I am not wanted, I prefer to remain as I am, and to take my chance either of surviving or of perishing honourably . . .
>
> If in these words I appear to have said anything contrary to the personal advice which you, Your Excellency, have given us, I am more than sorry. But I have no choice in the matter. My sense of duty urges me to place my apprehensions fully before you. I am not against Federation as Federation. I want Federation for the States only if they can join with safety, complete safety.
>
> I have made this statement with a full sense of my responsibility. My term of office expires within a few hours, and this frank estimate of the present crisis will be almost the last duty I shall be called upon as Chancellor to render to my Emperor, my country, and my Order. In this grave and decorous assemblage, where controversy rarely finds utterance, I should, had I been free to follow my own inclinations, have spoken merely smooth words. For I am of an age when my natural disposition in favour of peace has been powerfully reinforced by advancing years and impaired health. But I cannot evade my duty, even if I had to suffer the pain and grief of venturing to express a different opinion from His Excellency, whom I hold in high esteem and affection . . . I have spoken as my conscience and not my interests dictate. I earnestly pray that the Divine Wisdom will guide us all in the momentous choice which it is now the responsibility, as well as the right, of everyone here to exercise. May God so will it in his Divine Wisdom as to enable

us to decide to take the course which will bring prosperity to the people of my country, honour and glory to India and the Empire.

Writers like S.S. Careershar have interpreted the Jam Saheb's last stand as a refusal to become a tool in the imperial game by 'openly condemn(ing) those who wanted the Indian Princes to serve as mere pawns in thwarting the national demand.' A similar case was advanced by Scyld Berry who argued that 'although English in many ways and loyal to the Crown, Ranji wanted independence for India far sooner than the British planned.' This is preposterous. Even a cursory reading of the Jam Saheb's speech does not encourage any such view. Further, Alan Ross recounts that when a sinking Jam Saheb heard that Sir Robert Horne had glowingly referred to him in the House of Commons as 'one of the Empire's most loyal citizens', it brought a smile of pleasure to his face. Certainly not the reaction of a man who had just fought his last battle for advancing India's freedom.

Biographer Alan Ross himself harboured no doubts about where the Jam Saheb's true loyalties lay:

> It was inevitable, and in his heart of hearts, Ranji must have realised it, that the princely States and their rulers would be overtaken by events in British India. The surge towards democratic government was not going to be deflected by the interests of hereditary princes, however enlightened. Whatever fears Ranji entertained, many of his fellow rulers wanted to gamble on the future and join with the aspirations of the new India, if only to ensure a measure of survival. It was not Ranji's way. But, whatever delaying actions could have been mounted, in the long run history would always have been against a continually sub-divided India. For Ranji, the British connection, the independence of the States and their direct relationship with Whitehall, were precious possessions not lightly to be laid aside.

Quite coincidentally, the Jam Saheb died on the same day that Lord Chelmsford, Viceroy in India during the war years, passed away in England. Tributes to both flowed from all quarters. Much of the obituaries have gone down in posterity. But there were also some critical comments about the departed ruler in the Native Press that are not so well remembered:

'. . . . of his ability as a ruler there are no two opinions. He had a natural aptitude for administration that would have made him an ornament to any Civil Service. And he had statesmanlike capacities. But he was an autocrat of autocrats and while he introduced many improvements in the administration of his State and followed a far-seeing and effective policy in promoting its trade and prosperity, he was no believer in free political institutions and did nothing by way of reform to earn the gratitude of his people, but on the contrary, earned a great deal of opprobrium by his arbitrary, and, as many would say, his tyrannical methods of rule.

'. . . The latter day activities of the Jam Saheb were very much resented by politically minded people in India. After the boycott movement was started in India the Jam Saheb made common cause with the Manchester manufacturers for the export of cotton goods into the country. He, more than once, made public speeches in those manufacturing centres against the boycott movement and promised to cooperate with the merchants there in their export trade to India. He even promised them that he would throw open his own port for the purpose, to form a sort of base against the Indian *Swadeshi* movement, for he said the people in the States were hungering for foreign piece goods . . .'   —*Bombay Chronicle*

'. . . He was a faithful supporter of the Government and the people of India came into severe conflict with each other, for instance, in the matter of *Swadeshi*. We hope his successor will do his best to help *Swadeshi* in his State and outside and serve his subjects in a democratic spirit.'   —*The Mahratta*

'. . . The late Jam Saheb was a true Imperialist and it has been shown clearly in his utterances in England last year in connection with the imports of Lancashire goods in India. Besides this, his apparent apathy towards British Indian aspirations made him somewhat unpopular in British India, and perhaps it was due to this strong aversion towards democratic principles that Jamnagar has not witnessed any popular reforms as in Mysore, or Travancore, or Baroda . . .'

—*Gujarat Mitra* and *Gujarat Darpan*

'. . . Yet there are rumblings that he has not fulfilled the aspirations of his subjects and this is absolutely true. A couple of years ago handbills entitled 'State of Affairs in Nawanagar' criticising Ranji were published and distributed in Bombay. The *Bombay Chronicle* had flayed him severely on several issues and he even contemplated taking them to court. But the matter rested there. The Jam Saheb was in favour of monarchy. At that time he felt that developments in British India, where people blindly tried to follow democratic trends in the West, was improper. But there was no question of this kind of thinking becoming popular with the public. In 1932 when Ranji was elected as vice-Chancellor of the Chamber of Princess by a huge majority, people felt very threatened; it was quite natural for the people to feel insecure and in the end their fears came true because last week he presented a report in the Chamber of Princes and the Viceroy at that time, Lord Willingdon, strongly objected to his utterances . . .'

—*Gnyanprakash*

ONE year after his death the *Morning Post* canonized the Jam Saheb as a martyr to the Diehard cause with a flaming dispatch from its Special Correspondent in Delhi dated 19 July 1934. Headlined 'Tragedy of a Staunch Friend of England', the report described it as 'One of the most tragic stories in the history of our Indian Empire' and linked the untimely and tragic death of the Jam Saheb to the public rebuke administered by Willingdon at the Chamber of Princes session. This, it claimed, was proof of the British Government's determination to stiffle any opposition to their policy:

Ranjitsinhji, one of the best Princes India has ever known, one of the greatest cricketers and one of the best friends England has ever had, died of a broken heart . . . The full and terrible story of the last week of his life proves that his death was no coincidence, but a tragedy of slighted loyalty . . . As Chancellor of the Chamber of Princes and as a loyal friend of England, he had felt that he 'could not evade his duty' to deliver a warning against the danger of federation . . . . Feeling himself rebuked by the Power, he sought to save, from the moment he left the Chamber he lost all desire to live . . . So passed a great gentleman and one of the best friends that England possessed.

The story sparked off a spate of rejoinders from the Jam Saheb's acolytes—Naoroji Dumasia[5], his solicitor E.F. Hunt, Sir Leslie Scott and even Wild himself.[6] Ironically, the rejoinders were published in *The Times*, which naturally provoked adverse comment from the *Morning Post*.

On the Jam Saheb's death, his nephew Digvijaysinhji duly assumed the reins of office. But the fact that he was Rani's annointed successor was not known to all.[7] Ironically, Digvijaysinhji himself echoed Ranji's loyalist sentiments in his maiden Durbar speech when he assumed office. After describing His late Highness as 'a staunch admirer and supporter of our old Sanatan Dharma' who 'for its preservation' made 'a great improvement of state temples . . . at a heavy cost', Digvijysinhji evocatively declared:

> Just as, in Nawanagar, we are bound to each other by the ties of intimate affection and mutual esteem, so it the state of Nawanagar bound to the Empire by its unswerving loyalty to the British Crown. In this loyalty we have before us the example of our late Ruler. Only a few days before he was referred to in the British Parliament as one, than who the British Empire had no better citizen. With God's help, I hope to follow in this, as in all other respects, the example which he set before me.

Subsequent revelations however, put a question mark on Digvijaysinhji's pledge of loyalty to the British Crown, something that

---

[5]Dumasia glowingly referred to Willingdon as 'the man who has brought peace and quiet to India'.

[6]Quite surprisingly in this case, since his official biography itself lends credence to such a conclusion.

[7]The *Bombay Chronicle* even reported that Duleepsinhji would take over.

was unimaginable in relation to the departed monarch. According to the chronicles of Indian Political Service official, Charles Chenevis Trench, there arose 'an embarrassing obstacle to (British) victory' during World War II:

> This was none other than His Highness the Jam Saheb of Nawanagar, Chancellor of the Chamber of Princes . . . In 1940 Worth, the Secretary, was told by the Jam Saheb's step-brother, Revenue Minister of his state, that his loyalty to the British Crown made it impossible for him to remain in his step-brother's service; he was on his way to Delhi, where he hoped for some job connected with the war. He gave no further details, but shortly afterwards:
>
> The Bombay Salt Commissioner told us that cargoes of contraband goods were being shipped from Porbander (closely connected with Nawanagar) and Bedi (in Nawanagar) to Basra, eventually reaching Germany. It was hard to believe that the Jam Saheb could be a party to this trade, but a word was said and the trade stopped.

The British occupation of Iraq in 1941 probably was more effective in stopping this racket than the rap on the knuckles of the Kathiawar ruler. But according to Trench, if the Jam Saheb could not better himself by trading with the enemy, the introduction of rationing provided him (and other assorted chiefs), with more strings to his bow. This racket concerned the smuggling of ordinary white cotton cloth, worn by most Indians all the year round. During World War II this was rationed so that factories could turn out stout cloth for uniforms. The Jam Saheb, said Trench:

> . . . appropriated to himself the entire quota of his state and made millions by smuggling it to Arabia where it fetched an enormous price. A heavy-handed ruler, he simply ignored his subjects' complaints. These, however, came to the ears of the Resident and the customs authorities in Bombay. It was a very serious matter which, if proven, could and should result in his being deposed. But the Jam Saheb! The sainted Ranji's nephew! The Chancellor of the Chamber of Princes! The consequences in Britain and India, the discredit it would throw on the

whole princely order, would be horrific. Cotton, instructed to make a delicate investigation, found it was probably a true bill; but by then the war was over, and it was a bad time to disgrace one of the most articulate and influential princes. So the matter was dropped. But the Jam Saheb was mortified that in the Viceroy's Honours List His Majesty did not bestow on him any mark of royal approbation, not even promotion to Lieutenant-General, on which his heart was set. Although His Highness knew well what Cotton (the political secretary) was up to, and Cotton knew that he knew, the matter was never mentioned between them.

The new Jam Saheb, who himself was voted as Chancellor of the Chamber of Princes in 1938 following the decease of Patiala, would continue with the politicking over Federation. And when the time came for the accession of the princely states to the Indian Union in the countdown to independence, he would keep hedging his bets. He toyed with the idea of a union of Kathiawar states with the Maharaja of Dhrangadhra and also travelled to London to reactivate his predecessor's links with the Tory top brass. Trench even reported that during those hectic days of negotiations an important British official of the Gujarat states was casually informed that the Jam Saheb and some others proposed to take the Kathiawar states into Pakistan. Unless more light is thrown on this aspect by those who know better, one will never know what exactly transpired during those dark and turbulent days—whether this was perhaps meant to be a tongue-in-cheek ruse on Nawanagar's part or he was indeed trying to act as agent provocateur cannot be ascertained.

The new Maharaja of Bikaner, Sir Sardul Singh, put an end to all such princely pipe dreams by walking out of the States Negotiation Committee and appealing to the princes to opt for a united India. Fobbed off with promises of ambassadorship and governorship, most rulers fell in line. Ultimately, the Jam Saheb threw his lot in with India. His patriotic role in the accession process prompted V.P. Menon, the Malayali official involved in bringing the states into the Indian Union, to describe him as 'a tower of strength' in those days of hectic negotiations. The wheel had indeed turned full circle!

IX Crumbs for Indian Cricket

IF the formation of the Board of Control for Cricket in India in November 1927 announced the advent of Indian cricket, the conception of the national championship of cricket, the Ranji Trophy, signalled the 'great leap forward' for the game. The national championship was conceived by the proactive Anthony de Mello, founder-secretary of the BCCI and later its president, a sports organizer par excellence who was later associated with the inaugural Asian Games held at New Delhi in 1951.

The BCCI meeting, which sired the national cricket championship, was held in the summer of 1934 at Simla, 7,000 feet high among the foothills of the Himalayas. This was the summer capital of the Raj and also the happy hunting grounds of princes like the Maharaja of Patiala who was subsequently externed by the British from the hill station because of his amorous extra-curricular activities.

Sir Sikandar Hyat Khan, who was then the president of the BCCI and Governor of the Punjab, was in the chair. An impassioned de Mello put forward his detailed proposal for a national championship at the meet and also laid before the gathering an artist's illustration of the proposed trophy, a Grecian urn, two feet in height, with the handle of the lid representing Father Time.

Hardly had he finished his vivid description of the trophy when Patiala, representing the then Southern Punjab Cricket Association, impulsively leapt to his feet and claimed the honour and privilege of sponsoring the trophy in the name of the great Ranji, who had died only the year before. Patiala straightaway offered to present a gold cup of the design which de Mello had submitted, worth 500 pounds.[1]

---

[1] When the Brabourne Stadium at the Cricket Club of India in Bombay was

The thrust of his words caught the imagination of all those present. De Mello recounted in his semi-autobiographical *Portrait of Indian Sport*, that Patiala wanted the cup to be known as the Ranji Trophy, and the tournament to become the equivalent of England's County Cricket League, Australia's Sheffield Shield and South Africa's Currie Cup.[2] Further, the Maharaja also agreed to present, each year, a miniature cup, which would become the property of the winning association. The proposal was gratefully accepted.

But that was not the end of the matter. The clash of egos between Patiala and Vizzy[3], almost scuttled Patiala's proposal. Vizzy, the rising star of Indian cricket politics, wanted desperately to humour his mentor, Lord Willingdon, patron of the BCCI. The Viceroy was not enamoured of Patiala either.

Vizzy went ahead and got a trophy made in England of chiseled gold from a design provided by the Vicereine. At an emergency meeting of the BCCI on 26 October 1934, Vizzy vehemently argued that Ranji had done nothing for Indian cricket and that instead, the national championship should be played in the memory of Willingdon, who had assisted Indian cricket in several ways. The new proposal was accepted and the news about the 'Willingdon Trophy for the Cricket Championship of India' was leaked to loyalist media like the *Times of India* to prompt its favourable reception by the public.

This led to a farcical situation. By then, two matches of the Ranji Trophy had already been played and notwithstanding the lukewarm start to the national championship, there was an outcry about the 'insult' to Ranji. Vizzy's partisan designs were thus well and truly nipped in

---

inaugurated in 1937 Patiala also donated a cheque so that the stands could be named as the 'Ranji Memorial Stands'.

[2] The Santosh Trophy for the national championship of football, which kicked off in 1941–42, is also named after a princely figure, Manmathanath Roychowdhury, Raja of Santosh.

[3] The Maharajkumar of Vizianagram, Sir Gajapatairaj Vijaya Ananda, was popularly known as Vizzy.

the bud. Bombay won the championship in the inaugural year and the next edition as well. In the third year, the Nawanagar team, now promoted by Ranji's successor, Jam Saheb Digvijaysinhji alias 'Digooba', elected BCCI president in 1937, brought home the trophy under A.F. Wensley. Nawanagar finished runners-up to Hyderabad the next year. The Ranji Trophy has gone on to become the most sacred relic of Indian cricket, replete with its own heroes and records.

Vizzy's motives to erase the name of Ranji may have been suspect because of his burning desire to curry favour with Willingdon. But his allegations that Ranji did nothing for Indian cricket were not wide of the mark. They have been recorded for posterity in a poignant outburst by none other than de Mello himself. Incidentally, the portraits of Ranji and de Mello both adorn the walls of the Cricket Club of India in Bombay, envisaged as an oriental replica of Lord's by de Mello. Of this 'Great Dictator' of Indian cricket, respected cricket writer Berry Sarbadhikary fondly wrote in his memoirs, *My World of Cricket: A Centenary of Tests*:

> No one man has done more to put Indian cricket on the world map than he. From the historical point of view, we will always have reasons to be grateful to him for giving India cricket a 'christening', a shape and a status. He was the chief architect of 'modern' Indian cricket . . .

Although de Mello also powered the development of Indian sport in general by his enthusiasm and initiative, he was apparently to paraphrase Benny Green's description of Charles Burgess Fry, 'a dangerous duffer when it came to the politics of the twentieth century'. Fry became enamoured of Nazism, tried to organize paramilitary-style camps for youth and gave a clean chit to Hitler.

De Mello, on his part, regarded British rule as a '*ma-baap sarkar*'. He also lavished praise upon much-reviled characters like Willingdon and Patiala and called Fry 'a great friend of India' though as the Jam's private secretary, the former England cricket captain actually held a paid brief for princely India only.

De Mello also came forward to captain The Rest Team and expand the Quadrangular Tournament being played in Bombay into a Pentangular one even though nationalists had actively campaigned to put an end to this communal meet. Perhaps, de Mello, who was buried in MCC colours according to his wishes, was politically astute in his own way. His agenda was limited to promoting sport—hence his ability to win favour with the political establishment both sides of 1947. No matter that, this great builder of Indian sport, who longed for the day when 'an Indian team would boast of eleven Ranjis—not one', was constrained to record in agonizing detail this testimony about the Jam Saheb:

> Yet, and I tell it with deep regret, Ranjitsinhji was never at any stage prepared to combine his roles of sportsman and Indian Prince. The Ranjitsinhji who finally settled in Jamnagar (Kathiawar) after the First World War was an altogether different man from the great cricketer who delighted English crowds in earlier years. Ranji, in fact, did absolutely nothing for Indian sport and sportsmen.
>
> This perhaps, is the greatest enigma in our sporting story. It was natural, that, when Ranji returned home, we should look to him for guidance on the road to cricketing recognition . . . It was right—indeed inevitable—that then, and at many times in the future, those who controlled Indian cricket should turn to Ranji. It was right that we should crave, and expect, his help and advice, that he should lend the weight of his great name and reputation to helping us along the way.
>
> In later years, as his nephew Duleepsinhji showed signs of being a player of almost the same class, that we should again approach Ranji with the request that Duleep be encouraged to bring his cricket talents to the aid of India.
>
> To all our requests for aid, encouragement and advice, Ranji gave but one answer: 'Duleep and I are English cricketers.'
>
> He could not have been more blunt, nor could he have shocked and surprised us more, had he said that he didn't give a d—— for Indian cricket. For that was precisely what he meant. Even now, as I think of it, I find it hard to believe and harder to understand . . . .

It was not just that Ranji was too busy to help us, for he seemed intent on feigning a blindness which could not even perceive the existence of Indian cricket. Perhaps he maintained a contact with the game, playing a little and watching, within his own domestic circle, but otherwise he was never even seen at a game of cricket in India.

Yet each summer Ranji would go to England, to watch cricket, to mix with cricket people, perhaps to relive the days of his youth when his flashing bat and wondrously quick eye were the topic of everyone's conversation. In short, Ranji was a different man in England and India. That is not to say that he was disloyal; far from it—as his work in Nawanagar shows more vividly than could mere words.

But when work was done, and the time came for play and relaxation, Ranji's mind did not dwell amongst us in India. It was in England. And it is my understanding of this great and strange man that his heart was in England also. If, as I believe, this is true, then we approach as near as possible to solving the riddle . . .

There was talk, too, of an unhappy love affair . . .

(This last line may have been a reference to Ranji's reportedly unfulfilled love for Edith Borrisow, the red-haired daughter of his Cambridge guardian, the Rev. Louis Borrisow, who was the chaplain of Trinity College. It have never been quite clear why Ranji preferred to remain a bachelor all his life.

Apart from his assumed love affair with the Borissow girl, recent revelations also show that the young Ranji was infatuated with the Holmes sisters, Mary and Minnie, and carried on a lengthy and animated correspondence with them for years, apart from impressing them with precious gifts. But he could not somehow summon the courage to marry a white girl—this would in any case, have created succession problems for any issue from the 'mixed' marriage. Neither did he buckle down to the pressures that must have surely been exerted to settle for a token marriage or marriages with any of the eligible princesses whose hands must have been offered to him in alliance in the interests of siring an heir.

There has never been any taint of sexual scandal as far as Ranji was concerned. Far from there being any saucy revelations about his sexuality, the Jam Saheb is reputed to have always had a reverential and brotherly attitude towards women. As one of his chroniclers noted about this aspect of his character, 'He was religiously free from sex complex and greatly elevated the sex morals of Jamnagar people by dealing severely with any case of sex immorality'.)

De Mello continues:

Towards the end of his life Ranji gave the impression that he was disillusioned. Always, it seemed, he was waiting for something . . . waiting with the calm patience of the true Indian, for something which, deep within himself, he would never have. Not in his life, not ever . . .

Those of us who mourn the loss to Indian cricket of these two great players can take at any rate partial consolation as far as Ranji is concerned. Ranji, when he played for England, was not deserting the cricket of his own country, because India was not at that time established in world cricket.

With Duleep it was different. As he approached his best India had recently joined the Imperial Cricket Conference, and it was natural that we should look hopefully to Duleep to lend strength and class to our young, aspiring team. It was all the more disappointing then, to meet with Ranji's blank, uncompromising statements . . . 'Duleep and I are English cricketers.'

We felt, and I am sure we were right in this, that Duleep's cricket destiny was very much in his uncle's hands, to the extent that the younger man would have done whatever Ranji would have advised. Had Ranji said to Duleep, when his education was finished, 'I think you should now return and play your cricket for the benefit of India,' I believe Duleep would have done precisely that. But Ranji made no such suggestion; quite the opposite. It was Ranji, indeed, who was the keenest that Duleep should follow his own cricket career as closely as possible . . .

Let it not be thought that I begrudge Duleep his success in English cricket, or that I would wish to have deprived the English crowds of the joy of watching him bat. My point is that, when India needed Duleep, he should have recognised his duty. India needed him in 1932 and, though his health gave way late in that season, neither he nor we were to know this would happen . . .

One must criticise Ranji for Duleep's attitude to the cricket of his own country—an attitude that for the most part refused to recognise that there was any cricket in India. Duty had largely in the life of Ranji— I have explained how he remained sad and lonely to the end of his days—and Duleep, also, should have been prepared to give up the things he loved for the good of his native land . . . But it remains to me an enigma that Duleep, a great cricketer from a great Indian family, was unwilling to lift a finger to help the process.

Ranjitsinhji's prestige had, as I have admitted, been of value to us as we approached international status in cricket, but no such thing was true of Duleepsinhji. People merely noticed that here was an Indian who preferred to play for England; and, of course, their opinion of Indian cricket, reflected by Duleep's obvious view, became none the higher for it . . .

The numbing experience of Ranji's disdain, and, to an extent, Duleep's as well, must have rankled de Mello deeply for this indictment was made, not in the heat of the moment, but about twenty-five years after Ranji's demise when de Mello's memoirs were published. The reasons that de Mello has proffered for Ranji's disillusionment towards the end of his life—the romantic angle—may or may not be true. As a prince, Ranji would have surely risked antagonizing his traditional constituency by marrying a white woman. But it is more likely that Ranji's infatuation with the Diehard cause to scuttle any concessions to Indian nationalism during his last years might have consumed his being and made him distance himself from anything to do with British India.

But was de Mello overstating his case about Ranji? Perhaps not. De Mello's views were shared by others on the other side of the political divide—cricketer-writer E.H.D. Sewell, for example, who regularly enjoyed Ranji's hospitality. Sewell had his axe to grind with the BCCI because of the intrigues of its officials. He was also a man of inflated ego and perhaps felt frustration at not being accorded what he felt was his due in the emerging set-up. But what he recorded about Ranji and Duleep in *Cricket Under Fire*, tallied with de Mello's conclusions:

> Almost throughout its existence 'Ranji,' for one, had to all intents and purposes nothing to do with the Board. On the subject of which he could be, and often was, very terse and to the point. At a time when inspired nonsense was being sent to the Indian press from a sort of Goebbels centre at Delhi about Duleepsinhji being the next probable captain of the Indian eleven, there was actually just as much chance of Gandhiji being elected to that post. 'Ranji' would never have permitted Duleep to take the captaincy even had Duleep wanted to. Which he never did. I write from first-hand acquaintance with the facts.

On 10 September 1972, to commemorate the birth centenary of Ranji, a three-day match between the Board President's XI and a Ranji XI was held at Jamnagar. Top Indian cricketers, besides two Australian Test players and a few English county professionals, took part in the match. Goodwill messages on the occasion were received from the President of India, the Vice-President, Prime Minister and other luminaries. President of the BCCI, A.N. Bose, said that Ranjitsinhji, while 'immortalising himself in the world of cricket' also became the 'first Indian to bring name and fame to the country as a world-class cricketer'.

Ironically, later in the same decade, the BCCI would deliver a negative verdict on Ranji and Duleep. The then honorary secretary, Professor M.V. Chandgadkar, in an essay on the 'History of the Board' in the *Golden Jubilee Commemoration Volume, 1929-79* on the completion of a well-merited half-century, echoed his illustrious predecessor's charges:

> One would have hopefully looked at Prince Ranjitsinhji or for that matter his equally illustrious nephew, Prince Duleepsinhji, to have done something in the matter (to constitute a central controlling body). But that was not to be. It seems that although they made the cricketing world realise how good an Indian cricketer could be, they were more

keen to play for England and never encouraged the efforts being made by others in India and in England to create a national organisation which alone would accord India and Indian cricketers institutional status and recognition . . .

One does not know why other Indian cricketers or officials did not either support or contradict de Mello's views on Ranji or reveal their own experiences with Ranji. Perhaps the Indian cricket establishment was too much in awe of the titanic figure to commit such a heresy. To compound this inexplicable silence, Ranji's contribution to Indian cricket or his lack of it has also not been fully explored or investigated by Indian cricket writers of the past. But occasionally, Ranji's frosty indifference has come in for adverse short comment. As L.N. Mathur once observed:

> Duleep's name turned down by Ranji on plea that Duleep played all his cricket in England. What a funny argument the wise and bold Jam Saheb delivered. In the twenties and thirties, the atmosphere was charged with patriotism and it is indeed a wonder that in such a patriotic atmosphere Ranji could not rise to the occasion and ask his illustrious nephew to play for the motherland.

A few years ago, veteran cricket historian, Raju Mukerji, echoing de Mello's imagery mainly, penned this trenchant piece on 'The Other Side of Ranji' in *Sportstar*:

> The national championship of cricket in India is played in the memory of a genius who had no interest in Indian cricket. Ranjitsinhji, the doyen among cricketing artists, had no time for Indian cricket, no interest in Indian cricketers. He once bluntly observed that he and his talented nephew Duleepsinhji were English cricketers and that there was no worthwhile cricket in India. This was in response to the request to allow Duleep to play for India in the Tests in the 30s. Even when Amar Singh was reigning supreme in the 1932 English summer, Ranji remarked that he (Amar Singh) was no good . . .
> But ironically, on his infrequent visits to India he was an entirely

different persona. He would have no role to play: player, coach, administrator, promoter. A cricketing Jekyll and Hyde, if ever there was one. Unbelievable, indeed, to learn that this passionate prince of cricket had no time or desire to promote the game even in his own college or territory . . .

It is indeed remarkably sad that the batting genius would treat his fellow countrymen with such disdain. Never had a kind word for Indian cricket; never a kind gesture. Indian cricket and cricketers were anathema to him . . .

The Maharja of Patiala, a great lover of cricket, used means, fair and foul, to promote Ranji's political aspirations.

Ranji, it seemed had no inclination to see India gaining its independence. To be fair, it must be readily admitted, very few of the princely states were happy with the nationalist movement that was gaining ground in the country at the time.

Today as we look back we can only wonder what a remarkable enigma this genius must have been. So magnanimous, so cheerful, so popular in England; why did he choose to be so abrupt, so autocratic, so arrogant when he was among his own countrymen who literally worshipped him?

Details of Ranji's exploits in Indian cricket are at best sketchy. From the scattered references in local cricket literature here and there a fair list can be compiled of his engagements on the Indian maidans. As is well known, Ranji was initiated into the game at Rajkumar College, reputedly by a Parsee coach. He even told J.M. Framjee Patel that his first big score in India was just over 200 in a match for his school in 1887.

After blazing a trail of glory in England and Australia, Ranji returned home for the first time in late April 1898 to rally support for his political ambitions. Coming back with the MCC tourists after their disastrous tour Down Under, Ranji disembarked from the *Ormuz* at Colombo with Arthur Priestley, an MP from Grantham and amateur cricketer. The duo then hauled up at Madras.

This is the period when Ranji probably was the guest of the legendary Buchi Babu Nayudu, the 'father of Madras cricket', who founded the

Madras United Club in 1888[4] as a reaction to racial discrimination against Indians at the Madras Cricket Club. According to the account in Suri and Raja's *Buchi Babu (Father of Madras Cricket) and his Sporting Clan*, Ranji's first appearance on Indian soil as an adult was a disaster. He batted in the Madras United Club nets where Subbarayulu, a medium-fast bowler, bowled him a few times. Ranji may not have been accustomed to playing in Indian conditions, but Subbarayulu was nevertheless known to be a good pace bowler with an excellent record in local matches.

There was more humiliation in store for Ranji when he was requested to bat after being invited to Luz House, the home of Buchi Babu. He was bowled first ball by a syce named Madurai, who was trained to throw a cricket ball in practice and was fast and accurate. In fact Madurai embarrassed 'the prince' by castling him a few times. Commenting on Ranji's embarrassment, eminent cricket writer, R. Mohan, ascribed Ranji's discomfiture at Madras as a possible sign of Indian cricket nationalism expressing itself in mysterious ways! He noted that a certain 'nationalist feeling' must have prompted the BCCI to accept the offer of the Maharajkumar of Patiala for the Ranji Trophy for the national championship rather than the Willingdon Trophy offer of the Maharaja of Vizianagram. But he also added that 'it must still remain a riddle how the memory of a prince, who played for England and had very little to do with the development of cricket in India, should be perpetuated in the form of the Ranji Trophy'.

It was as an ADC to Rajinder Singh, Maharaja of Patiala and father of Bhupinder, that Ranji got his first taste of big-time cricket while playing in the Maharaja's colours (green and yellow) on his return to India. Rajinder had built a beautiful arena and had assembled a formidable team by securing the services of English professionals W. Brockwell (Surrey) and J.T. Hearne (Middlesex), the amateur Arthur Priestley, some top Parsee players and Ranji himself. Ranji played a

---

[4] It reputedly had Ranji and Vizzy among its patrons.

stellar role in a close victory over the British residents of Simla in a three-day fixture, top scoring in both innings with 40 and 74 and taking 7 wickets; he also caused a stir by resorting to what some regarded as a sharp practice when, while coming in to bowl, he ran-out a sergeant-major standing out of his ground at the non-striker's end. Moreover, Ranji starred in an entertaining partnership with His Highness—like his son Bhupinder, Rajinder was a swashbuckling bat in the princely tradition.

Ranji next cracked a 133 against Simla Volunteers and then dazzled with an unbeaten double century against a military team at Umballa (Ambala) when the Patiala XI posted a massive score of 633 for 4 declared. Brockwell and Colonel K.M. Mistry[5] had opened the innings and when Brockwell got out, Ranji came in at his customary position of one down and with Mistry posted a partnership of 376 for the third wicket, the Parsee finally getting out for 255. The Maharaja laid wagers with his staff that Ranji wouldn't make as many runs as the dashing left-hander. An ADC came up to him and whispered, 'For goodness' sake get more runs than Mistri, or we lose our bets!' Ranji replied that he would do his best. And he obliged by cracking a 257 not out. The feat was celebrated by a big dinner party and Rajinder marked his appreciation by presenting Ranji with a set of jewelled shirt studs. For the earlier century, the Maharaja gifted him with a pair of superb Purdey guns.

During that maiden trip Ranji also made his way home and played for the Kathiawar Cricket Club gymkhana, bowled in their nets and coached boys at the Rajkumar College where he was schooled. According to his host Charles Kincaid, fine all-round sportsman and future Ranji biographer, Ranji played only two innings for the KCC at home. Kincaid, who would skipper the KCC in 1902, said that although Ranji scored only 34 and 32, his driving was wonderful. 'The pace at which the ball covered the ground and the force with which it hit the boundary railings, had to be seen to be believed.'

---

[5]Ranji called him the 'Clem Hill of India'.

Playing for Rajkot against Wadhwan Ranji scored 54 and took 11 wickets for 94 runs but his side was routed due to a 'bad batting performance.' For the Rest of Kathiawar against Jhalawar (Zalawad) at Rajkot and made 31 and 39, the top score in both innings, and claimed 9 wickets. It was in this match, according to cricket historian, Ramachandra Guha, that the celebrated Dalit bowler, Palwankar Baloo, locked horns with the batting maestro but the left-arm spinner came up trumps by bagging Ranji's wicket.

He then left on a four-match tour of the Bombay, Poona and Ganeshkhind[6] with the KCC comprising players of mixed nationalities and a date with ignominy.

The occasion was the fixture against Poona Gymkhana on 30 August 1898. On a pitch soaked by heavy rain, Lieutenant Lionel Maury Ross Deas engraved his name in cricket lore by getting out the famed batsman for a duck in each innings off the third ball. Ranji c Grieg b Deas 0; Ranji c Bond b Deas 0, the scoreboard read, this being the only time in his career when Ranji bagged a pair of spectacles. The disappointed crowd sulked after his second dismissal but according to some accounts, Ranji was later allowed to play a third exhibition innings, an unheard-of occurrence, if true.

From Poona, the side travelled to Bombay, where Ranji was hosted by the Governor, Lord Sandhurst. He knocked 68 off the Governor's XI and then scored a superlative 78 and took 11 for 56 against the Bombay Gymkhana, which would later refuse him membership in the late 1920s. Framjee Patel reported after that match that everybody tried to imitate his leg glance—with the result that there were more lbws in one week than there had been in a couple of months. During this visit to Bombay, the Hindu Gymkhana organized an entertainment in his honour and presented him with an impressive memento. When he left the venue, he was escorted by a torchlight procession.

---

[6]The venue popularized by Lord Harris who had just relinquished his gubernatorial assignment at Bombay in 1985.

Ranji had good things to say about the master Bombay Presidency bat, Colonel John Glennie 'Jungly' Greig, a towering personality in Indian cricket in those days, who was later ordained a Catholic priest and ministered in Bombay. He considered him the best soldier-cricketer he had ever seen and superior to two other local heroes, Major Robert Montagu Poore and Major Edward G. Wynyard, who both became big cricketing names in England. Ranji even wrote out an introduction for Greig to Hampshire in which he stated, 'Greig is a better bat than I am, and is an excellent bowler as well'.

From there, Ranji again journeyed north and at Patiala he played against the mighty Parsees, who dismissed him cheaply in both innings. He had a poor run in succeeding matches and put his poor form down to being out of practice due to his pressing social commitments and the poor quality of the pitches.

There was speculation in England that Ranji would return with a team of native players in 1900; but that was not to be. When he returned to India again in 1901 he continued to play for Patiala but not many details exist about his exertions during this period. Ranji visited India one more time in December 1903, travelling back in the same P&O boat that bore Lord Lamington, Governor of Bombay. He graced the practice nets of the Parsee and Hindu Gymkhanas regularly where crowds applauded his every stroke and even watched some matches. He was also feted and dined by the Parsees at the Ripon Club and toasted by Sir Jamshetjee. Framjee Patel reported that the prince showed great interest in improving the standard of Indian cricket and gave free vent to his opinion; he deprecated the sending of a weak combination to England in 1904, particularly without Mistry, whom he regarded as the next-best left-hander to Clem Hill. He also strongly recommended importing professional coaches from England.

Ranji also played some cricket in Bengal, where he first toured with Patiala's team in 1898. It was in the 'City of Joy' over the New Year's Day of 1905 that Ranji cracked a memorable century. This was in a three-day fixture between I. Zingari, the travelling cricket road show, and the Calcutta Cricket Club. Archie MacLaren, his new personal secretary, and Lord Hawke (back in India on a shooting visit), also featured in the match.

The action was watched for some time by the Viceroy, Lord Curzon, a great cricket fan and Derbyshire supporter, who gained notoriety for the partition of Bengal. There was also one blazing knock of 132 at the Eden Gardens, which ended when he was brilliantly caught by Faguram, a *mali* of the Calcutta Cricket Club, fielding as a substitute. Fagu's palm reportedly cracked at the impact of the well-timed shot and Ranji shook hands with him in congratulation and offered a *bakshish* of two guineas. Ranji also played a fixture at Natore Park in Calcutta.

In 1907, Ranji began his new innings as the Jam Saheb of Nawanagar. Soon after taking on the reins of office he departed for England on an extended visit which lasted for over a year and also included some cricket for Sussex during the county season. On his return in early 1909, reported Roland Wild, 'history was being made in a small but very loyal corner of the Empire' by a man who was at his desk at 6.30 am, in the Council Chambers from noon to late afternoon and on the cricket pitch till seven.

Ranji threatened to unleash a cricket revolution, taking keen interest in the laying of a cricket pitch outside the palace grounds and the building of a new pavilion near the palace. He expressed determination to have all young men playing the game in his territory and prophesied that very soon he would be able to lead a team of Rajputs into the field that would rival even the Parsees. But despite this enthusiastic declaration of intent his team played only occasional matches and failed to equal in stature Patiala's team of yore. But thanks to his enthusiasm, cricket became a bazaar game, played by youngsters in the empty spaces of the city, the same kind of street-corner cricket they played in England at that time.

Of course, Ranji the ruler could not always spare time to impart cricket lessons or bat at length in the nets while his proteges bowled at him. So he contended himself with a brief visit to the ground, his favourite destination in the cool of the evening. Wild disclosed that the Jam played regularly in Jamnagar up to 1915. Herbert Evans, in *Looking Back on India*, has evoked memories of the Nawanagar Maharaja who played in gold-embroidered slippers and flowing robes and invariably celebrated his birthday with a match. He relates a memorable story of how the Jam Saheb once humbled a conceited bowler. Thinking it was time to make the trundler lose some self-esteem, the Jam sent for four stumps, three of which he put in the ground. 'Now bowl to me,' he commanded, and proceeded to cut and glide every ball with his single stump, until he felt the bowler had learnt his lesson.

In 1912 Ranji placed five of his nephews in public schools in England, four of them at Malvern, a famous cricket nursery and home to the Foster clan of seven brothers who represented Worcestershire and England. Ranji personally oversaw the career of Duleep, sending him to Clare College, Cambridge, and helping him qualify for Sussex and he could rightly take much credit for Duleep's success. Duleep further revealed that many other Jamnagar boys were financed by him in England and received the same allowances as the princes did, Jamnagar House at Staines being their home as well.

The grand legacy left behind by Ranji and Duleep and the lavish patronage extended by Digvijay saw the game flourish in Nawanagar and many a talented cricketer sallied forth to do the principality proud. The dynasty itself had reasons to be proud when its later-day scions, Kumar Shri Indrajitsinhji and Ajay Jadeja, made the international grade.

Indrajitsinhji (born 15 June 1937) may not have set alight the pages of Indian cricket history but he was an unobtrusive wicket keeper with no royal airs who represented India in four Tests between 1964 and 1969 plus an unofficial Test in 1964. He aggregated 51 runs for an average of 8.50 and a top score of 23, apart from scalping nine victims behind the sticks.[7] His international career might have flourished had he not come at the same time as the flamboyant Farokh Engineer and

---

[7]Six caught and three stumped.

the dependable Budhi Kunderan. The first batted like a Maharaja while the latter was a better keep. So Indrajitsinhji had to yield place. Yet, the princeling had his moment in the sun when he chipped in magnificently to help India record a historic Test win over Australia at Bombay in October 1964.

Ajay Daulatsinhji Jadeja (born 1 February 1971), on the other hand, who came into the game initially as an opener, was a charismatic cricketer whose accomplishments are well-documented. Although he enjoyed an indifferent Test career he more than proved his worth as a limited overs specialist and scripted many a match-winning feat with his effortless big hitting in the middle order. He even proved an inspirational captain when he took over the reins fleetingly at Sharjah in late 1998 when Mohammed Azharuddin got injured and next year at Nairobi. 'Jaddu' was blessed with the wristy strokes of his ancestors, had great hand-eye coordination and the ability to rotate the strike and take cheeky singles, of crucial importance in one-dayers. While his medium-pace bowling was utilitarian, he was athleticism personified on the field where he pulled off some amazing catches and effected some spectacular run-outs.

Altogether, Jadeja played fifteen Tests, aggregated 576 runs with an average of 26.18 and a best score of 96 versus the West Indies at Antigua in 1996-97. But his one-day record was excellent—196 matches, 179 innings, 36 not outs, 5,359 runs at an average of 37.47 with six centuries and 30 half-centuries and a highest of 119 versus Sri Lanka at Colombo in August 1997. Besides, he also claimed 20 wickets and pouched 59 catches. His one-day career would have continued fruitfully had he not been 'run out' by the match-fixing scandal in much the same way as his great granduncle was ruled out of order by the Viceroy in that fateful Chamber of Princes session. Jadeja appealed against the five-year ban on playing official cricket imposed on him by the BCCI for his alleged role in the scandal. In January 2003 an arbitrator of the Delhi High Court quashed the ban and cleared him to play at both domestic and international levels.

Apart from cricket, Ranji considered shooting and tennis ideal sports for young men. He never developed polo in the state because he believed that polo led to excessive drinking among young men, which he abhorred. He swore that he had seen enough of the effects of polo in British India to convince him that he was right. The strenuousness of the game in hot weather and the irresistible desire to hold an 'inquest' on the day's play, led to self-indulgence, which he was determined not to encourage.

Post-Jam Saheb, few records exist in local cricket literature of the matches that Ranji played in Kathiawar or elsewhere in India. There is mention of an undefeated partnership of 204 for the first wicket he shared with a Bromwell in 1909 and a 233 he cracked for Nawanagar versus Rajkot the same year. In July and August 1910, according to Durbar records, the Jam Saheb took his cricket team to Rajkot, Wadhwan and Bhavnagar for a ten-day tour while Bombay and Poona were visited in September. But details of the Jam's performances on these excursions are not mentioned.

A few years later, in 1914, a Lt. Col. H.G. Tranchell reported that he had the honour of playing for the Bombay Gymkhana against a Kathiawar team which had Ranji in its ranks. In the first innings, H.L. Simms, a fine all-rounder who represented Sussex in 1912 and had come out to Bombay to join a business firm, bowled Ranji for 1 with a beautiful off-break. In the second innings, Ranji made about 48. 'I had the honour of bowling at him; he was very kind and did not knock me all over the place, but mine was not the class of bowling to get past the bat,' Tranchell modestly admitted. Ironically, in the official biography by Roland Wild, there is no mention of any match Ranji played in India during his entire life. A perplexing oversight no doubt!

But there were occasional sightings of the royal visage at a handful of matches in the Native States. In 1919 Ranji witnessed a young Maharaja of Porbander[8] make 67 for Rajkumar College against a strong

---

[8]He was appointed India captain for the 1932 tour of England but sportingly stood

Jamnagar side in the capital. He was also present when the Maharawal Lakshman Singhji of Dungarpur clouted a rapid-fire 72 with four sixes for the Maharaja's team in the final of the Alwar silver jubilee tournament. Ranji praised the innings lavishly, remarks that Dungarpur cherished like a rare treasure.

No account of Ranji's interactions with Indian cricket, limited though they were, can be considered complete without reference to his encounter, probably apocryphal, with the old Maharaja of Kashmir. At Mayo College, the famous public school for royalty, Ranji was involved in a celebrated exchange with the Kashmir ruler. Whenever the Ajmer college played the Kashmir XI, in true princely tradition, strict orders were given that when the Maharaja came to bat, the bowler had to bowl away from the stumps and reduce his speed—if slow much slower, if fast, as slow as possible; the Maharaja could touch the ball with bat and the fielders, instead of fielding it, would kick it to each other and it would result in a couple of runs; similarly if the ball passed the fielder, he would kick it to the boundary.

When the Maharaja returned to the pavilion for tea, he queried of Ranji in Hindi: '*Apne kabhi anda banaya* (Have you ever scored a duck)?' to which Ranji modestly replied, '*Bahut dafa* (Many times).' The Maharaja instantly retorted, '*Maine to kabhi nahi banaya* (I have never scored one).' The whole table applauded and the gratified Maharaja gave the principal a h*ukum*: 'Give the boys another day's *chhutti*.'

Alan Ross, quoting Fry however, has a slightly different tale to tell. He says that in the early days, Ranji visited Kashmir as a guest of the old Maharaja. A match was played and Ranji was out first ball. When he returned to the pavilion the Maharaja chided him: 'But, Ranjitsinhji, you have made duck; surely, I never make duck.' When the Maharaja's turn to bat came he was soon bowled. He just picked up the bails and continued batting!

---

down from India's first ever Test at Lord's because of his obvious limitations in favour of the immortal C.K. Nayudu.

This apart, it appears that Ranji began to distance himself from (British) Indian cricket even before he became Jam Saheb. In 1906 he turned down an invitation to lead the Hindus in their first-ever match against the Europeans in Bombay. Later, Ranji also spurned the opportunity to become the first captain of 'India' when he rejected an offer to lead an 'All India' team to England in 1911, a honour that eventually went to Maharaja Bhupinder Singh of Patiala. He also refused to contribute anything towards the expenses of the tour. Framjee Patel, who had a few years before thought Ranji extremely keen to do something for Indian cricket, was a selector for that 1911 squad. He rued being left in the lurch at the time of the team's departure:

> . . . Only one great name is missing from the list of those selected—it is that of His Highness the Jam Saheb Ranjitsinhji. All I can say is that I have left no stone unturned to secure the greatest cricketing asset of the country for our team, but unfortunately without success . . .

An anonymous letter published in the *Times of India* dated 5 May 1911, mourned the fact that India and England would equally share the regret of the Jam Saheb's omission from the team, but nevertheless explained that 'state reasons' prevented Ranji from undertaking the trip. This may have been true since his year-plus sojourn in England from mid-1907 to early 1909 immediately after taking over as Jam Saheb was not viewed kindly by the British and he was reportedly asked to stay put at home for some time. He visited England next only three years later in 1912. But it is also possible that Ranji, who considered himself an England cricketer, may have been least interested in accompanying the 'All India' team, even as captain.

Ranji betrayed his apathy for Indian cricket two decades later. Despite his disassociation with BCCI affairs, he accepted several decorative posts, lending his name to the BCCI masthead probably because since Willingdon was chief patron and friends like Sir Stanley Jackson, Sir Leslie Wilson, General Charles Harrington and the Maharaja of Patiala were vice-patrons. As a vice-patron of the BCCI and titular chairman of the selection committee for the 1932 tour, he declared in a terse goodwill message, 16 dated June 1932, in the official souvenir for the *Indian Cricket Tour to England, 1932*:

> . . . I have not had the pleasure of seeing anything of Indian cricket. It will therefore be a mere presumption on my part to offer any opinion about *their* cricket. However, as one interested in the game of cricket and being an Indian myself, I can only wish the Team going out a very successful tour . . . .

Incidentally, this startling admission, which confirms de Mello's observation that he 'was never seen at a game of cricket in India', came after Ranji had spent thirty-five years in India[9] from 1898-1933, and inclusive of twenty-six years as Jam Saheb!

On the other hand, Ranji continued to immerse himself in English cricket. The thirty-nine-year-old, who in 1911 had just refused the 'All India' captaincy despite the earnest entreaties of his countrymen, slipped on his whites soon after reaching England on his second visit as Jam Saheb. The day after his arrival in England in the spring of 1912, informed Wild, he was at Lord's, practising in the nets. He played the county circuit for the season.

Again, in 1920, though he declared on arrival in England that cricket was far behind and that he had lost touch, his first visit was to the Oval to see Sussex play, then to Lord's to see Hampshire and Middlesex.

By August he was ready to don the pads, at the ripe old age of forty-eight. This was despite, or perhaps because of the loss of one eye in a shooting accident on the Yorkshire moors in September 1915. The aftermath of that tragedy added to Ranji's towering personal reputation in England. He steadfastly refused to name the man who had wielded the gun. This may have been a politically canny thing to do since the list of suspects included several influential peers of the realm and the British establishment had reason to be grateful for the Jamsaheb's refusal to go public with the details.

---

[9]Interspersed with numerous visits abroad.

It was said he wanted to write a book on how to play cricket with one eye. Another motive may have been to oblige his sovereign and liege. As he confessed: 'I am practising cricket. The King is so keen I should play again, why I don't know. It is rather a severe strain, but I have been successful in the attempt. I think I shall make a few runs after all unless I am unlucky . . . '

Reported Wild: 'So, after twelve full years, the spell of cricket once more held him. The smell of English field, the glint of sunlight, pale against the brilliance that he knew in Kathiawar summers, stirred in him, the desire to stand again at the wicket, to hear again the sleepy sounds of the English game to which he had brought his own electrifying magic.'

But interpreting His Majesty's whimsical wish as his royal command proved disastrous and ill-advised. Ranji did make a few runs, just a few in fact[10], and he bowed out of the game with a whimper.

But a decade later Ranji again showed that the spirit was willing though the flesh was weak. On being elected president of Sussex in 1930, he stated in a telegram, 'Have unabated interest in cricket and would play now if selected, if it were not for my eye and Anno Domini'.

Ranji played forty first-class matches in England over three seasons in 1908, 1912 and 1920, an amazing number for a player whose track record in India was practically nonexistent after his ascent to the Nawanagar *gaddi* in 1907. His love for English cricket was also expressed in other ways. In the summer of 1912 he donated dressing-room armchairs to the Sussex club[11] and in 1930, as president of Sussex, he announced a contribution of £1,000. During this period of financial crisis he also bore the summer salaries of four professionals and then invited them to India for the winter. In addition he contributed fifty pounds to the benefit of the medium-pace legend Maurice Tate.

---

[10]39 in four innings and three matches at an average of 9.75, his highest score being 16.

[11]Though they were not paid for until many years later, according to Simon Wilde.

His complete identification with the English way of life was seen in his support for the benefit cricket match to help the Gilling parish church restore its bell-tower and install a clock, which prompted the famously fatuous remark by a female parishioner. 'Fancy! A Christian clock started by a heathen.' He partook of several other parish activities besides at Gilling as also in community activities at Ballynahinch in Ireland. But for all his munificence towards Sussex, the small scoreboard near the secretary's office at Hove which was rebuilt in his memory, is all the remembrance he got as compared to the magnificent honour India accorded him after his death.

In the case of Duleep, there are just two recorded instances of participation in Indian cricket of any significant level. In his first ever match in the Bombay Quadrangular at the Oval maidan from 1–3 December 1928, he scored 84 and 38 for Hindus versus the Parsees. From 12–14 February 1932, he turned out for the Viceroy's XI against the Roshanara Club at Delhi and returned scores of 6 and 173, putting on 189 for the fifth wicket in the second innings with the Nawab of Pataudi Sr in the drawn match.

Ross claims that Ranji himself took time off from his work with the Chamber of Princes in Delhi to see the innings. Duleep was too much indebted to his uncle to disobey his diktat not to play for India in 1932 though he himself may have not wanted to play since he was still in the running for an England cap. But to his credit he got involved with Indian cricket on his return home in December 1934 after his playing career was prematurely terminated at the age of twenty-eight due to illness.

Duleep became secretary of the Cricket Club of India, conducted camps for cricket coaches at the Brabourne Stadium, took part in developmental activities in Jamnagar[12], was a national selector and continued to assist Indian cricket in many ways. In 1936, Duleep married Princess Jayrajkumari of Rajpipla. After Independence, he continued

---

[12]The legendary all-rounder, Vinoo Mankad, was one of his proteges.

to be prominent in public life. He served as India's High Commissioner to Australia from 1950 to 1953, was the Chairman of the Public Services Commission of Saurashtra in 1954 and until his death in December 1959 remained Chairman of the All-India Council of Sports. After his death, the BCCI immediately decided to inaugurate an inter-zonal competition, the Duleep Trophy, in his memory.

Ranji took great pride in his nephew's accomplishments and always goaded Duleep to try and excel himself. When one media report insinuated that he had promised Duleep an incentive for every run over a century that he scored in first-class cricket, Ranji retorted that it was 'unfair to a family that has done all that lies in its power to sustain the best tradition of British sportsmanship'. The nephew however, made an astonishing revelation in his autobiography, *Duleep: The Man and his Game*, about a bit of advice that his illustrious uncle had once proffered:

> God has given you the gift He gives to few. If you want to play cricket
> I will give you every help you need but you will have to remember
> that every time you are playing you are not playing for yourself but
> for your country. Thousands of English people will be watching you
> play and millions reading the papers. To them you will be representing
> India . . . I don't want you to do anything you will be ashamed of later
> and do harm to your country. Remember that God has given you a
> gift which you can use for the benefit of India.

Stirring words indeed! But if Ranji had actually told Duleep that he was representing India every time he played cricket in front of Englishmen, why did he reportedly oppose Duleep from going all the way and representing India?

It has been argued that Ranji's duties to his small and impoverished state cut short his playing career and prevented him from playing as much as he would have liked to, or contributing otherwise to Indian cricket. For example, the Australian writer, Richard Cashman, has claimed in *Patrons, Players and the Crowd: The Phenomenon of Indian Cricket*, that de

Mello's criticism was unduly harsh since Ranji became the head of a relatively backward state and 'chose to channel the limited resources of that kingdom into providing improved communications, health and sanitation and to the encouragement of trade and commerce, rather than to sporting patronage'.

Cashman further contended that Ranji did promote cricket in India by his 'example'. He shared cricket coaches with other states and also 'assisted Indian cricket in small and often unnoticed ways'.[13] Cashman related an anecdote, told by Indian cricket great Vijay Merchant, that showed Ranji as being a shrewd judge of cricket potential and a well-wisher of Indian cricket when he spotted Amarsingh in the 1932 cricket trials. When the bowler took six wickets he suggested cautiously that 'he bowled well; can make a good bowler', but a few days later when the same bowler took no wickets for more than eighty runs, Ranji declared with confidence that 'there you have a great bowler in the making'. But Raju Mukerji has contended that even when Amar Singh was reigning supreme in the English summer of 1932, Ranji dismissed him as no good!

But there is no doubt that Ranji's influence on Indian cricket was phenomenal and awe-inspiring. Ranji was a towering hero of Indian cricket in the bygone days and his successes inspired an entire generation of Indians to seek excellence in the willowy game and in life itself. N.S. Ramaswami, who trailed Indian cricket in *From Porbander to Wadekar*, gushed that 'Ranji was the genius of India liberating himself through the cricket bat'.

The doughty Lord Harris, no fan of Ranji as an English cricketer, opined in *A Few Short Runs* that Ranji's success in England fired India's imagination and gave a spurt to the game. 'I have no doubt that the prowess of Kumar Shri Ranjitsinhji, now the Jam of Nawanagar, did a good deal to encourage Indians to take up the game, and, as is well known, several have since distinguished themselves on Indian cricket

---

[13]So small that they went unnoticed as compared to his munificence in England.

fields.' Others, like Arbi, went so far as to endow Ranji with the halo of a political and social liberationist:

> Prince Ranji, appearing as if from the pages of a book of legends, like a prince on a white charger, cast a spell on the Indian mind to lure it to adventure in the strange land of cricket.
>
> Far back in the nineteenth century, when the racial superiority of the English people was an accepted fact beyond question, Ranji smashed the English claim to superiority in the most English of all things . . . The theory of intrinsic racial superiority and the complexes that had long plagued mankind received its first blow from Ranji's achievements . . .
>
> Ranji's contribution to Indian life was mainly through cricket no doubt. But the influence was not confined to the realm of cricket alone. In an age when Indians were considered an inferior race, incapable of achieving great things—long before Tagore or Gandhiji or Raman was heard of beyond India—Ranji demonstrated to the race of our rulers and to the world at large, the merit of the Indian stock in matters of modern life. Success in cricket, the most English of games, by an Indian proved for the first time that Indians were capable of beating England in her own game. Meritorious performances in other fields which followed were admitted by our ruling people as a possibility because of Ranji's cricket.

Another service that Ranji indirectly rendered to Indian cricket was to inspire the princes to get associated with the game and therefrom reap success on the political pitch as he had done. Even though Patiala Sr. was already into cricket before Ranji could return home[14], the Native Princes deduced that Ranji's ascension to the Nawanagar *gaddi* was helped by his association with, and excellence in the game. They were thereby encouraged to take to cricket in a big way themselves. This infusion of patronage, though not without its drawbacks, gave Indian cricket a shot in the arm and took it to a higher level. That said, with

---

[14]Patiala Sr. had employed Ranji on his staff way back in 1898.

their public school education, often in England, the princes would have taken to cricket anyway to imitate the English way of life.

As an aside it can be argued that while India should be immensely grateful to Ranji for his towering inspiration to her cricket, Ranji also owes a debt to India, which like his many monetary debts, he conveniently neglected to repay. Remember how Ranji got his break into big-time cricket in England? According to Ranji legend, Sir Stanley Jackson (then the Cambridge captain) was initially unimpressed by the alien's ability when he chanced upon Ranji playing in a local fixture in England. It was only after Jackson toured India in 1892-93 with Lord Hawke's team that he began to appreciate native proficiency in the game and decided to give Ranji the 'nod' when he got back home. Thus, it was India's emerging status as a cricketing power that was responsible for one of her sons getting a deserving break into big-time cricket a few thousand miles away. There was some merit in Jackson's appraisal of India's latent talent as the 'Heathen Parsees' had humbled three successive teams from 'Old Blighty'—George F. Vernon's in 1889-90, Lord Hawke's in 1892-93[15] and K.J. Key's Oxford University Authentics in 1902-03.

It is also a moot point as to who India's first cricket superstar is. In Dr Mehallasha Edulji Pavri, India had by contemporary accounts, a titan in the making. In 1888, the same year that Ranji landed in England as a callow teenager, Pavri was scattering timber there during the second Parsee tour of England, bagging an astounding 170 wickets at an average of 11.66 runs, albeit against modest opposition. In one match he turned certain defeat into victory, by skittling out the Gentlemen of Eastbourne, chasing a target of 123, for a paltry 56 with a six-wicket haul. One of his express deliveries sent the bails flying a distance of almost fifty yards while another delivery uprooted the leg stump, which after doing a somersault, pitched itself again nine yards away.

Wisden noted that 'one of the most notable features of the tour was the wonderfully successful bowling of Mr Pavri.' The *Lillywhite*

---

[15]Though they lost a return match by seven runs.

Annual too had good things to say about the Parsee player. 'Some of the bowling was quite up to the average. Mr Pavri's figures in particular were above the ordinary. He bowled fast round-arm, of a good length and towards the tour developed a very good style, varying his pace and pitch well, besides making the ball do a great deal at times. He delivered, as will be seen, over 5,000 balls, at a cost of just under 2,000 runs, and took in all 170 wickets for an average of less than 12 runs— really good figures . . .'

Pavri returned to England later to study medicine and played for Forest Hill and Surrey Club and Ground, his skills earning him a place with Middlesex as an amateur for one match (13–15 June 1895). Ironically, the match was against Sussex, at Hove, and the two English counties had an Indian playing for rival teams and against each other, a historic occurrence for the nineteenth century! Pavri batted at No. 9 and had figures of 12–4–26–0 and 13–2–53–1 in the match in which Ranji had scores of 22 and 64 and a bowling analysis of 4–0–21–0.

Due to the pressure of studies and his medical practice, Pavri did not pursue his cricket career in England actively and played on subsequent visits for Eastbourne Club where he performed a double—1028 runs (average 34.8) and 168 wickets (average 13.61). The *Sussex Daily News*, reviewing the cricket season of 1900 at Eastbourne, described him as 'the most consistent bat and undoubtedly the best all-round player . . .' On his return to India, this superb all-round sportsman immersed himself in Parsee cricket and is widely considered the first homegrown superstar of Indian cricket.

But all and done, Ranji remains a hero to an entire generation of Indians and a magnanimous de Mello was willing to forgive Ranji his trespasses when he observed:

> India is a country of hero-worship. We love a man to whom we can look as an example and a paragon. It is better by far that Ranji should be remembered in this way rather than for his faults of omission, if I may so describe his lack of interest in Indian cricket. Even at the time he was held in too much respect for us to criticise his attitude openly.

We felt, of course, that it was sad that we could not have the benefit of his assistance, that his name could not be lent in our aid as we struggled for cricket recognition. We felt also that it was a pity that he could not have persuaded Duleep to play for his own country.

Yet, even then, there were consolations. We could be happy in the knowledge that Ranji and Duleep, by their successes on the cricket fields of England, were indirectly bringing respect and admiration to the name of Indian sport. Although I hope we did not seek only reflected glory, I am sure that, when we came to apply for admission to the Imperial Cricket Conference in 1929, the knowledge that our country could produce great cricketers was of the utmost assistance to us. In this indirect way Ranji was of help and it is in this way that I like to remember him.

Presenting his own later-day take on Ranji's fractured relationship with Indian cricket, Mihir Bose has pointed out in *A Maidan View: The Magic of Indian Cricket*, that de Mello's indictment was rather harsh and the latter was 'not a disinterested witness' whereas Ranji's loyalties were to his state, Nawanagar, to his people in Nawanagar and to the King Emperor:

So if Ranji did not do much for Indian cricket it is because he did not think of India as a cricketing nation. He did not think of India as a cricketing nation because he could not conceive of India as a political nation. India as a political nation was born fourteen years after Ranji died and, had he lived, as his successors' actions show, he would have undoubtedly opposed it. He advised Duleep to play for England rather than India and he did so because to him an Indian team meant nothing. Had Nawanagar managed to get together a Test team then, I am sure, Ranji would have advised Duleep to play for Nawanagar. For inasmuch as a king is ever a nationalist, Ranji was a Nawanagar nationalist. He was, perhaps, a Rajput nationalist, if that term can have any meaning. He was not an Indian nationalist and to accuse him, as de Mello does, and other Indians do, of not doing much for Indian cricket is to miss the point.

Two English writers, who have produced differing volumes on Ranji, have made a point which is not dissimilar though laced with sympathy. Alan Ross, discussing the de Mello diatribe, has reasoned (that):

> Ranji never attempted to fuse the English cricketer and the Indian prince (as) England was his glorious past, not India, which represented a present and future fraught with problems and frustrations.

Simon Wilde, also inclined to take a sympathetic view of Ranji's actions, said that he was doing no more than tenaciously fighting his own corner and using all the clout his status entitled him to to keep his princely wicket intact:

> The fact was that Ranji could only conceive of Indians as British subjects, and failed to understand how they could wish to set up a national cricket team as a separate and rival entity to an English one— nor indeed, as we shall see, establish their country as an individual political unit.

'Nobody is forgotten sooner than a famous cricketer,' Ranji once observed sardonically to Fry. In his glorious and eventful life he may have got a lot of things right. But how wrong he was on this one! Five decades after India shook off the colonial yoke, he is still fondly remembered by his countrymen and the national championship continues to be played in his name.

Indian cricket writers of the past have tended to romance Ranji's 'idealism' for the game by approvingly quoting his memorable words: 'When I have finished, I hope I may be remembered not only for the success it has brought me but rather as one who tried his best to popularize the game for the game's sake.' It may however not be impertinent to ask whether this applied to Indian cricket.

Appendix

RANJI'S CAREER STATISTICS

First-class Cricket

Season	Innings	Not out	Runs	Average	Highest Score
1893	19	2	439	25.82	58
1894	16	4	387	32.25	94
1895	39	3	1,775	49.30	150
1896	55	7	2,780	57.91	171★
1897	48	5	1,940	45.11	260
1897–98	22	3	1,157	60.89	189
(in Australia)					
1899	58	8	3,159	63.18	197
1899	2	0	125	62.50	68
(in America)					
1900	40	5	3,065	87.56	275
1901	40	5	2,468	70.51	285★
1902	26	2	1,106	46.25	234★
1903	41	7	1,924	56.58	204
1904	34	6	2,077	74.17	207★
1908	28	3	1,138	45.52	200
1912	28	2	1,113	42.80	176
1920	4	0	39	9.75	16
Total	500	62	24,692	56.37	285★

Test Cricket (England vs Australia)

Season	Innings	Not out	Runs	Average	Highest Score
1896	4	1	235	78.33	154★
1897–98	10	1	457	50.78	175

(Table cont.)

★Not out.

(Table continued)

Season	Innings	Not out	Runs	Average	Highest Score
(in Australia)					
1899	8	2	278	46.33	93 ★
1902	4	–	19	4.75	13
Total	26	4	989	44.96	175

SOME CAREER HIGHLIGHTS

- a record century in each innings (100 and 125 not out) of the same match *on the same day* (22–08–1896) for Sussex versus Yorkshire at Brighton
- topped the county batting averages in 1896, 1900 and 1904 (57.91, 87.56 and 74.17 respectively), was second in 1903, third in 1899, 1901 and 1902, fourth in 1895 and fifth in 1897
- topped the combined England and Australian batting averages in the 1996 Test series in England with 78.33 and an aggregate of 235 runs
- the first batsman to score 3,000 runs in a season, a feat he registered in 1899 (3,159 runs) and repeated in 1900 (3,065 runs)
- a record five double centuries in a season (1900) when the previous record was three
- the first batsman to score 1,000 runs in a month twice in the same year—1,037 runs in June and 1,011 runs in August of 1899
- a century (150) on debut for county, Sussex, versus the MCC at Lord's in 1895 (it was also his maiden first-class century)
- a Test century on debut—154 not out for England versus Australia at Manchester in 1896
- the first batsman to score 100 runs in a single session of a Test match (for England versus Australia at Manchester in 1896)
- Ranji's highest first-class score was a 285 not out for Sussex versus

---

★Not out.

Somerset at Taunton in 1901 (of which 200 came in boundaries which included 46 fours, 2 fives and a six), his highest Test score was 175 for England versus Australia at Sydney in 1897-98, his best first-class bowling performance was 6–53 for London County versus Cambridge at Crystal Palace in 1901

- *Wisden* 'Cricketer of the Year' in 1897
- overall career record: Tests: two centuries, 989 runs (average 44.96). First-class: 72 centuries, including 14 double hundreds, six double century partnerships (including two with C.B. Fry with whom he recorded 25 century partnerships), 24,692 runs (average 56.37), 62 times not out, 133 wickets (average 34.59) and 233 catches
- his best partnership of 344 with W. Newham for the seventh wicket for Sussex versus Essex at Layton in 1902 was a world record for the seventh wicket till it was broken. It still stands as the best seventh wicket partnership in England.

FIRST-CLASS CENTURIES

The following are Ranjitsinhji's seventy-two centuries in first-class cricket:

Season

1895	150	Sussex vs MCC at Lord's
	137★	Sussex vs Oxford University at Hove
	110	Sussex vs Middlesex at Lord's
	100	Sussex vs Nottinghamshire at Hove
1896	171★	Sussex vs Oxford University at Hove
	165	Sussex vs Lancashire at Hove
	146	MCC vs Cambridge University at Cambridge
	138 ⎤ 100 ⎦	Sussex vs Yorkshire at Bradford
	125★	Sussex vs Yorkshire at Hove
	114★	Sussex vs Gloucestershire at Hove

★Not out.

	107	Sussex vs Somerset at Hove
	100★	Sussex vs Nottinghamshire at Hove
1897	260	Sussex vs MCC at Lord's
	170	Sussex vs Essex at Hove
	157	MCC vs Lancashire at Lord's
	149	Sussex vs Hampshire at Hove
	129★	Sussex vs Middlesex at Eastbourne
1897–1898 (in Australia)	189	A. E. Stoddart's XI vs South Australia at Adelaide
	112★	A. E. Stoddart's XI vs New South Wales at Sydney
1899	197	Sussex vs Surrey at the Oval
	178	Sussex vs Nottinghamshire at Hove
	174	Sussex vs Surrey at Hove
	161	Sussex vs Essex at Hove
	154	Sussex vs Gloucestershire at Bristol
	120	Sussex vs Middlesex at Lord's
	107	Sussex vs Cambridge University at Eastbourne
	102	Sussex vs Lancashire at Hove
1900	275	Sussex vs Leicestershire at Leicester
	222	Sussex vs Somerset at Hove
	220	Sussex vs Kent at Hove
	215★	Sussex vs Cambridge University at Cambridge
	202	Sussex vs Middlesex at Hove
	192★	Sussex vs Kent at Tonbridge
	158	Sussex vs Nottinghamshire at Nottingham
	192★	Sussex vs Kent at Tonbridge
	158	Sussex vs Nottinghamshire at Nottingham
	158	A. J. Webbe's XI vs Cambridge University at Cambridge
	127	Sussex vs Gloucestershire at Hove
	109	Sussex vs Gloucestershire at Bristol
	103	Sussex vs Surrey at Hove

1901	285★	Sussex vs Somerset at Taunton
	219	Sussex vs Essex at Hove
	204	Sussex vs Lancashire at Hove
	170★	Sussex vs Lancashire at Manchester
	139	Sussex vs Worcestershire at Worcester
	133	Sussex vs Somerset at Hove
	115	England vs Yorkshire at Hastings
	100★	Sussex vs Surrey at Hove
1902	234★	Sussex vs Surrey at Hastings
	130	Sussex vs Essex at Leyton
	135	Sussex vs Surrey at the Oval
1903	204	Sussex vs Surrey at the Oval
	162★	Sussex vs Gloucestershire at Hove
	144★	Sussex vs Lancashire at Hove
	132	London County vs MCC at Crystal Palace
	105	Sussex vs Lancashire at Hove
1904	207★	Sussex vs Lancashire at Hove
	178★	Sussex vs South Africans at Hove
	166★	MCC vs Cambridge University at Lord's
	152	Sussex vs Surrey at Hove
	148	Sussex vs Yorkshire at Sheffield
	142	MCC vs Oxford University at Lord's
	135	Sussex vs Kent at Tunbridge Wells
	121	Gentlemen vs Players at Lord's
1908	200	Sussex vs Surrey at the Oval
	153★	Sussex vs Middlesex at Lord's
	101	England vs MCC Australian Team at Scarborough
1912	176	Sussex vs Lancashire at Hove
	128	Sussex vs Kent at Hove
	125	Sussex vs Australians at Hove
	101	MCC vs Cambridge University at Lord's

THE MAJOR RAJPUT KINGDOMS OF GUJARAT

Jadejas

Dhrol
Gondal
Morvi
Nawanagar
Rajkot

Jhalas

Dhrangadhra

Limbdi
Wankaner

Gohels

Bhavnagar
Palitana

Jethwas

Porbander

THE NAWANAGAR DYNASTY[1]

Jam Rawalji (1540–1562)

Jam Vibhaji (1562–1569)

Jam Satarsal (Sataji) (1569–1608)

Jam Jasaji (1608–1624)

Jam Lakhaji (1624–1645)

Jam Vibhaji (1645–1661)

Jam Ranmalji (1661)

Jam Raisinhji (1661–1663)

Jam Tamachi (1663–1690)

Jam Lakhaji (1690–1708)

Jam Raisinhji II (1708–1718)

Jam Hardholji (1718–1727)

Jam Tamachi II (1727–1743)

Jam Lakhaji (1743–1768)

Jam Jasaji II (1768–1814)

Jam Sataji II (1814–1820)

Jam Ranmalji II (1820–1852)

Jam Vibhaji III (1852–1895)

Jam Jasaji III (1895–1907)

Jam Ranjitsinhji (1907–1933)

Jam Digvijaysinhji (1933–1966)

Jam Satrusalyasinhji (1966–)

---

[1]This genealogy has been compiled after sifting through a few sources which do not tally with each other in all respects. According to one source, there was no Jam Saheb ruling on the throne for the period 1664–1673 when Raisinhji (1661–1663) was defeated in battle after which Jam Lakhaji came to the capital and established himself.

THE CHAMBER OF PRINCES[2]

Salute of 21 guns

The Maharaja (Gaikwad) of Baroda
The Maharaja (Scindia) of Gwalior
The Nizam of Hyderabad ★
The Maharaja of Jammu & Kashmir
The Maharaja of Mysore

Salute of 19 guns

The Nawab of Bhopal
The Maharaja (Holkar) of Indore
The Maharaja of Kolhapur
The Maharaja of Travancore
The Maharana of Udaipur (Mewar)

Salute of 17 guns

The Nawab of Bahawalpur
The Maharaja of Bharatpur
The Maharaja of Bikaner
The Maharao Raja of Bundi
The Maharaja of Cochin
The Maharao of Kutch
The Maharaja of Jaipur
The Maharaja of Jodhpur (Marwar)
The Maharaja of Karauh
The Maharao of Kotah
The Maharaja of Patiala
The Maharaja of Rewa
The Nawab of Tonk

Salute of 15 guns

The Maharaja of Alwar
The Maharwal of Banswara
The Maharaja of Datia
The Maharaja of Dewas (Senior Branch)
The Maharaja of Dewas (Junior Branch)
The Maharaja of Dhar
The Maharaj-Rana of Dholpur
The Maharwal of Dungarpur
The Maharaja of Idar
The Maharwal of Jaisalmer
The Mir of Khairpur
The Maharaja of Kishengarh
The Maharaja of Orchha
The Maharawat of Partabgarh
The Nawab of Rampur
The Maharaja of Sikkim
The Maharao of Sirohi

---

[2]This fairly representative gathering of the Chamber of Princes was present at a session in 1932. The Secretary to the Chancellor, Chamber of Princes, was also considered a member.

★ The Nizam was a most recalcitrant member of the august body.

Salute of 13 guns

The Maharaja of Benares
The Maharaja of Bhavnagar
The Maharaja of Cooch-Behar
The Maharaja of Dhrangadhra
The Nawab of Jaora
The Maharaj-Rana of Jhalawar
The Maharaja of Jind
The Nawab of Junagadh
The Maharaja of Kapurthala
The Maharaja of Nabha ★★
The Maharaja of Nawanagar
The Nawab of Palanpur
The Maharaja of Porbandar
The Maharaja of Rajpipla
The Maharaja of Ratlam
The Maharaja of Tripura

The Nawab of Janjira
The Raja of Jhabua
The Nawab of Maler Kotla
The Raja of Mandi
The Maharaja of Manipur
The Maharaja of Morvi
The Raja of Narsingarh
The Maharaja of Panna
The Raja of Pudukkottai
The Nawab of Radhanpur
The Raja of Rajgarh
The Raja of Sailana
The Raja of Samthar
The Maharaja of Sirmur (Nahan)
The Raja of Sitamau
The Raja of Suket
The Raja of Tehri (Garhwal)

Salute of 11 guns

The Maharaja of Ajaigarh
The Raja of Alirajpur
The Nawab of Baoni
The Rana of Barwani
The Maharaja of Bijawar
The Raja of Bilaspur (Kablur)
The Nawab of Cambay
The Raja of Chamba
The Maharaja of Charkhari
The Maharaja of Chhatarpur
The Raja of Faridkot
The Maharaja of Gondal

Salute of 9 guns

The Nawab (Babi) of Balasinor
The Nawab of Baganapalle
The Raja of Bansda
The Raja of Bariya
The Raja of Chhota Udepur (Mohan)
The Maharana of Danta
The Raja of Dharampur
The Thakur Saheb of Dhrol
The Raja of Jawhar
The Raja of Khilchipur
The Thakur Saheb of Limbdi

★★The Maharaja of Nabha was dispossessed of his kingdom by the British in 1923.

The Nawab of Loharu
The Raja of Lunawada
The Raja of Maihar
The Maharaja of Mayurbhanj
The Raja of Mudhol
The Thakur Saheb of Palitana
The Thakur Saheb of Rajkot
The Nawab of Sachin
The Chief of Sangli
The Sar Desai of Savantwadi
The Raja of Sant
The Raja Saheb of Vankaner (or
Wankaner)
The Thakur Saheb of Wadhwan

Representative Members

The Raja of Baghat
The Raja of Baud
The Thakore of Bhadarwa
The Chief of Jamkhandi
Durbar Shri Vala Mulu Surag,
C.I.E., shareholder of Jetpur
The Raja of Kalahandi
The Raja of Kalsia
The Raja of Korea
The Chief of Phaltan
The Raja of Surguja
The Raja of Sarila
The Raja of Talcher

Bibliography

RANJI BOOKS

Ranjitsinhji, Prince. *The Jubilee Book of Cricket*. William Blackwood and Sons Ltd, 1897.

Standing, Percy Cross. *Ranjitsinhji, Prince of Cricket*. Arrowsmith, 1903.

Dumasia, Naoroji. *Jamnagar: A Sketch of its Ruler and Its Administration*. Times Press, 1927.

All India States' Peoples' Conference. *Indian Princes As Their People See Them: An Inside View of the Administration of the State of Nawanagar of 'Prince Ranji'* (1927).

Dumasia, Naoroji. *Nawanagar and Its Critics*. Times Press, 1929.

Kincaid, Charles A. *The Land of 'Ranji' and 'Duleep'*. William Blackwood and Sons Ltd, 1931.

Wild, Roland. *The Biography of Colonel His Highness Sir Shri Ranjitsinhji Vibhaji, Maharaja Jam Saheb of Nawanagar*. Rich and Cowan Ltd, 1934.

Shah, Manecklal H. *Sketches of Life and Administration of the late Jam Saheb of Nawanagar*. Gujarat Times Press, 1934.

Raiji, Vasant. *Ranji: The Legend and the Man* (1963).

Raiji, Vasant, ed. *Ranji: A Centenary Album*. Seven Star Publications, 1972.

Ross, Alan. *Ranji: Prince of Cricketers.* William Collins and Sons Co. Ltd, 1983.

Wilde, Simon. *Ranji: A Genius Rich and Strange.* The Knightwood Press, 1990.

CRICKET BOOKS

Altham, H.S. *A History of Cricket.* George Allen and Unwin, 1926.

Guha, Ramachandra and Vaidyanathan, T.G., ed. *An Indian Cricket Omnibus.* Oxford University Press, 1994.

Arbi (Bhattacharya, Rakhal). *Indian Cricket Cavalcade.* Eastlight Book House, 1957.

Berry, Scyld. *Cricket Wallah: With England in India 1981-2* (1982).

BCCI Golden Jubilee Commemoration Volume, 1929-79.

Bose, Mihir. *A Maidan View: The Magic of Indian Cricket.* George Allen and Unwin, 1986.

Suri and Raja, ed. *Buchi Babu (Father of Madras Cricket) and his Sporting Clan* (1993).

Cashman, Richard. *Patrons, Players and the Crowd: The Phenomenon of Indian Cricket.* Orient Longman Ltd, 1980.

de Mello, Anthony. *Portrait of Indian Sport.* P.R.Macmillan Ltd, 1959.

Extra Cover: The Indian Cricketers' Tour of 1911. D.B. Taraporevala, Sons and Co., 1911.

Patel, J.M. Framjee. *Stray Thoughts of Indian Cricket.* Times Press, 1905.

Fry, C.B. *Life Worth Living: Some Phases of an Englishman* (1939).

Harris, Lord. *A Few Short Runs.* John Murray, 1921.

Gordon, Sir Home. *Background of Cricket.* Arthur Blake Ltd, 1939.

Green, Benny. *A History of Cricket.* Barrie and Jenkins Ltd, 1989.

Guha, Ramachandra. *A Corner of a Foreign Field: The Indian History of a British Game.* Picador, 2002.

Warner, Sir Pelham. *Imperial Cricket.* The London and Counties Press Avenue Ltd, 1912.

BCCI. *Indian Cricket Tour to England, 1932* (souvenir).

Mathur, L.N. *Indian Skippers* (1993).

Morawala, Mahiyar Dara. *Cricket Cavalcade* (1966).

Pavri, Dr M. *Parsee Cricket.* J.B. Marziban and Co., 1901.

Plumptre, George. *The Golden Age of Cricket.* Macdonald and Co. Ltd, 1990.

Pridham, Major C.H.B. *The Charm of Cricket Past and Present* (1949).

Raiji, Vasant. *India's Hambledon Men.* Tyeby Press, 1986.

Rajasthan Cricket Association: Golden Jubilee Commemoration Volume, 1933–1983.

Ramaswami, N.S. *From Porbander to Wadekar.* Abhinav Publications, 1975.

Ramaswami, N.S. *Indian Willow: A Short History of Indian Cricket.* Uma Books, 1971.

Sarbadhikary, Berry. *My World of Cricket: A Centenary of Tests.* Cricket Library, 1964.

Sewell, E.H.D. *An Outdoor Wallah*. Stanley Paul and Co., 1945.

Sewell, E.H.D. *Cricket under Fire*. Stanley Paul and Co. Ltd, 1945.

Sissons, Ric and Stoddart, Brian. *Cricket and Empire: The 1932-33 Bodyline Tour of Australia*. George Allen and Unwin, 1984.

Ross, Alan, ed. *The Cricketer's Companion* (1979).

Maqsood, Syed M.H., ed. *Who's Who in Indian Cricket* (1943).

NON–CRICKET BOOKS

Allen, Charles and Dwivedi, Sharada. *Lives of the Indian Princes*. Century Publishing House Ltd, 1984.

Bence-Jones, Mark. *The Viceroys of India*. Constable and Co. Ltd, 1982.

Caveeshar, S.S. *The Non-Cooperation Movement in Indian Politics* (1998).

Chand, Tara. *History of the Freedom Movement in India*. Vol. IV. Publications Division, Ministry of Information and Broadcasting, Government of India, 1972.

Chudgar, Popatlal. *Indian Princes Under British Protection: A Study of Their Personal Rule, Their Constitutional Position and their Future*. Williams and Norgate, 1929.

Copland, Ian. *The British Raj and the Indian Princes: Paramountcy in Western India 1857-1930*. Orient Longman, 1982.

Copland, Ian. *The Princes of India in the Endgame of Empire: 1917-1947*. Cambridge University Press, 1999.

Crewe, Quentin. *The Last Maharaja: A Biography of Sawai Man Singh II Maharaja of Jaipur*. Michael Joseph Ltd, 1985.

Deo, N.G. *The Princes of India* (1921).

Dumasia, Naoroji. *A Brief History of the Aga Khan.* Times Press, 1903.

Edwardes, Michael. *The Last Years of British India.* Cassell and Co. Ltd, 1963.

Evans, Hubert. *Looking Back on India.* Frank Cass and Co. Ltd, 1988.

India's Struggle for Independence (Visuals and Documents). NCERT, 1986.

Handa, R.L. *History of Freedom Struggle in Princely States.* Central News Agency, 1968.

Kaul, Ranjana. *Constitutional Development in Indian Princely States.* Vikas Publishing House, 1998.

Kincaid, Charles A. *Forty-four Years A Public Servant.* William Blackwood and Sons, 1934.

Kulkarni, V.B. *British Dominion in India and After.* Bharatiya Vidya Bhavan, 1964.

Low, D.A. *Britain and Indian Nationalism: The Imprint of Ambiguity 1929-1942.* Cambridge University Press, 1997.

Low, D.A. *Eclipse of Empire.* Cambridge University Press, 1991.

Masani, P.R. *Dadabhai Naoroji.* Publications Division, Ministry of Information and Broadcasting, Government of India, 1960.

Menon, V.P. *The Story of the Integration of the Indian States.* Orient Longman, 1956.

Minto, Mary, Countess of. *India, Minto and Morley, 1905-1910.* Macmillan and Co. Ltd, 1934.

Montagu, Edwin S. *An Indian Diary*. William Heinemann Ltd, 1930.

Morrow, Ann. *Highness: The Maharajas of India*. Graffon Books, 1986.

Nanda, B.R. *Gokhale: The Indian Moderates and the British Raj*. Oxford University Press, 1977.

Nehru, Jawaharlal. *An Autobiography* (1953).

The New Encyclopaedia Britannica (1993).

Pannikar, K.M. *An Autobiography* (translation). Oxford University Press, 1977.

Jeffrey, Robin, ed. *People, Princes and Paramount Power: Society and Politics in the Indian Princely States*. Oxford University Press, 1978.

Phadnis, Urmila. *Towards the Integration of Indian States, 1919-1947*. Asia Publishing House, 1968.

Rajyogar, S.B. *History of Gujarat*. S. Chand and Co. Ltd, 1982.

Ramusack, Barbara N. *The Princes of India in the Twilight of Empire: Dissolution of a Patron-Client System, 1914-1939*. Ohio State University Press, 1978.

Reynolds, Reginald. *White Sahibs in India*. The Socialist Book Centre Ltd, 1946.

Rizvi, Gowher. *Linlithgow and India: A Study of British Policy and the Political Impasse in India, 1936-43*. Londres, 1978.

Robinson, Andrew. *Maharaja*. Sumio Uchiyama, 1988.

Singh, Maharaj Kumar Raghubir. *Indian States and the New Regime*. D.B. Taraporewala and Sons and Co., 1938.

The Round Table Conference: India's Demand for Dominion Status (Speeches). G.A. Natesan and Co., 1931.

Thorat, Dr N. M. *Formation of Maha Gujarat: Memorandum Submitted to the States Reorganisation Commission, Government of India by Maha Gujarat Parishad* (1954).

Tinker, Hugh. *The Ordeal of Love: C.F. Andrews and India*. Oxford University Press, 1979.

Trench, Charles Chenevis. *Viceroy's Agent* (1987).

Lee-Warner, Sir William. *The Native States of India*. McMillan and Co. Ltd., 1910.

Wilberforce-Bell, Captain H. *The History of Kathiawad from the Earliest Times*. William Heinemann, 1916.

Wolpert, Stanley A. *Morley and India, 1906-1910*. University of California Press, 1967.

NEWSPAPERS AND MAGAZINES

Akbar-e-Islam, Akhbar-e-Soudagar, Ajmal, Amrit Bazar Patrika, Arjun, Baroda Gazette, Bhala, Bharat Jyoti, Bharat Seva, Bombay Chronicle, Bombay Samachar, The Briton, Cambridge Review, Cambridge Weekly News, Daily Telegraph, Daily Mail, Daily News, Dainik Bartaman, Dainik Vritta, Dhyanprakash, Gujarati, Gujarat Mitra and Gujarat Darpan, Gujarati Punch, Gujarat Vartaman, Gnyanprakash, Hind Swaraj, Hindusthan, Hindustan and Advocate of India, Hindustan and Praja Mitra, Hindustan Times, Indian Cricket, Indian National Herald, Indian Spectator, Indu Prakash, Jain, Jam-e-Jamshed, John Bull, Kaiser-i-Hind, Kathiawar News, Kathiawar Opinion, Kathiawar Samachar, Kathiawar Times, Kesari, Leader, Lok Shakti, Lokmanya, Manchester Guardian, Mahi Kantha Gazette, Mahratta, Morning Post, Nava

Kal, New Republic, New Times, Parsi, Patriot, Phulchab (75th Anniversary
Special), *Political Bhomiya, Praja Bandhu, Praja Mitra and Parsi, Punch,
Rajasthan Kesari, Rashtramat, Roznama-e-Khilafat, Salar, Sanj Vartaman,
Saurashtra, Saurashtra Mail, Sayamkal Samachar, Servant of India, The
Sportstar, South Australian Advertiser, Surya Prakash, Sussex Daily News, The
Swaraj, Taqat, The Times, Times of India, Tribune, Weekly Herald, West Coast
Observer, Westminster Gazette, Wisden, Young India*

ARCHIVAL MATERIAL

Political Department, Political Department Compilations, Political
Department Reforms Office, File Nos. Vol. III, 79 of 1907, 99 of 1907,
P 3353/12 of 1916, Vol. XIII of 1917, 752 of 1918, 1188 of 1918, 267
of 1919, 339 of 1921, 647 of 1921, 1857 of 1921, 1876 of 1921, 2194
of 1921, 18 of 1922, 994 of 1922, 43 of 1931, 159 of 1932, 341/28 of
1932, 197 of 1933

Foreign and Political Department, File Nos. 88-9 of 1928, 209–P of
1928, 254–P of 1928, 102–P of 1929, 113–P of 1929, 237–P of 1929,
263–P of 1929, 345–P of 1929, 405–P of 1929, 464–P of 1929, 11(7) R
of 1930, 20–Special of 1930, 115–P (Secret) of 1930, 147–P of 1930,
240–P of 1930, 354–P of 1930, 368–P of 1930, 9–Special of 1931, 18–
G of 1931, 40–P (Secret) of 1931, 1(28)–R/31 of 1931, 256–P (Secret)
of 1931, 20–P (Secret) of 1932, 260–P of 1932,

Political and Services Department, File Nos. 1040 of 1922, 1054 of
1923, 3700–III of 1931

Home Political Department Political File Nos. 141 of 1929, 364 of
1930, 5/4 of 1932, 20–P (S)/32 of 1932

Confidential Reports of Agent to the Governor General in WISA (HDP
Files): For the months of March, August, September 1930, January,

February, March, May, June, July, August, October 1931, January, March, May, August 1932

Files from the Oriental and India Office Collections, London:
1–P (Secret) of 1929, R/2/621/88 of 1925, R/2/623/109 of 1926, R/2/Box 635/286 A of 1933, C/107 of 1927, L/PandS/10/157 of August 1912, L/PandS/13/557 of 1930, L/PandS/11/197 of 1929, L/PandS/11/545 of 1930-31, L/PandS/13/287 of 1933,

Administrative Reports of Nawanagar State:
1907-08, 1908-09, 1910-11, 1912-13, 1913-14, 1914-15, 1915-16, 1916-17, 1917-18, 1918-19, 1920-21, 1921-22, 1922-23, 1923-24.

Memorandum of the Indian States Peoples Conference presented to the Indian States Committee (1928).

Gazetteer of the Bombay Presidency, Bombay Gazetteer. Vol. VIII. Kathiawar, 1880.

The Imperial Gazetteer of India. Vol. XV. Oxford, 1908.

The Imperial Gazetteer of India. Vol. II. Provincial Series, Bombay Presidency, 1909.

Report of the Indian States Committee 1928-29.

Index